启航
SAILING
—2013 中国—新西兰职业教育论坛文集
—2013 SINO-NEW ZEALAND VOCATIONAL EDUCATION FORUM PAPERS

主编：覃 川　马克·华　戴裕崴
顾问：刘育锋
编委：于水善　马喜峰　王文中　石 磊　冯 瑛　朱海燕　孙国栋
　　　李 震　陈旭仁　李占军　李 娜　张驷宇　郑萍萍　岳 华
　　　明国英　武 文　赵心宁　赵 静　逄 强　高玉飞　温黎明
　　　谢金领　樊晓光（按中文笔画顺序）

EDITORS IN CHIEF: QIN CHUAN　MARK FLOWERS　DAI YUWEI
COUNSELOR: LIU YUFENG
EDITORIAL BOARD MEMBERS: YU SHUISHAN　MA XIFENG　WANG WENZHONG
　　SHI LEI　FENG YING　ZHU HAIYAN　SUN GUODONG　LI ZHEN
　　CHEN XUREN　LI ZHANJUN　LI NA　ZHANG SIYU　ZHENG PINGPING
　　YUE HUA　MING GUOYING　WU WEN　ZHAO XINNING　ZHAO JING
　　PANG QIANG　GAO YUFEI　WEN LIMING　XIE JINLING　FAN XIAOGUANG
（According to the Chinese Stroke Order）

图书在版编目(CIP)数据

启航:2013中国—新西兰职业教育论坛文集/覃川,(新西兰)华,戴裕崴主编. —青岛:中国海洋大学出版社,2016.4
ISBN 978-7-5670-1155-7

Ⅰ.①启… Ⅱ.①覃…②华…③戴… Ⅲ.①高等职业教育－对比研究－中国、新西兰－文集 Ⅳ.①G718.5-53

中国版本图书馆CIP数据核字(2016)第088936号

出版发行	中国海洋大学出版社		
社　　址	青岛市香港东路23号	邮政编码	266071
出 版 人	杨立敏		
网　　址	http://www.ouc-press.com		
电子信箱	wuxinxin0532@126.com		
订购电话	0532—82032573(传真)		
责任编辑	吴欣欣	电　　话	0532—85901092
排版设计	张洪振		
印　　制	日照报业印刷有限公司		
版　　次	2016年4月第1版		
印　　次	2016年4月第1次印刷		
成品尺寸	170 mm×230 mm		
印　　张	22.5		
字　　数	420千		
定　　价	35.00元		

前　言（一）

高等职业教育是高等教育的重要组成部分。中国高职教育经过十多年的发展，在规模和内涵方面，都取得了令人瞩目的成就；而新西兰的高等职业教育的竞争力在世界上更是名列前茅。当今，国际合作与交流已成为世界职业教育发展的鲜明特征，这一点明显体现在中国和新西兰两国职业教育的合作与交流之中。

2013年4月，中国政府与新西兰政府在北京签署建立职业教育合作伙伴关系协议，青岛职业技术学院与新西兰怀卡托理工学院、天津轻工职业技术学院共同签署合作协议，开启中新两国间的职业教育合作与交流。同年9月，青岛职业技术学院在青岛成功承办第一届"中国—新西兰职业教育论坛"，打开了双方多方位、多领域、多层次交流合作的通道，为中国和新西兰开展更加深入的教育合作与交流提供了范例。2013年11月，新西兰高等教育、技能与就业部长史蒂文·乔伊斯和中国教育部副部长杜占元共同为"中国—新西兰职业教育发展研究中心"揭牌，标志着两国之间技术和职业教育与培训方面的交流进一步加强。

作为"中新职业教育发展研究中心（青岛）基地"，青岛职业技术学院在中新高职教育研究和合作办学等方面进行了积极探索。"中国—新西兰职业教育论坛"以"高职教育优秀教学法研究"为主题，既有关于中·新高职教育的高端理论阐述，也有来自高职教育教学实践的鲜活经验，还有来自两国的现场课堂观摩点评。作为论坛的后续成果，这一本中英文对照的纪实性文集收录了开幕致辞5篇、主旨演讲4篇、优秀教学法研讨16篇、教学现场3篇、教学点评5篇，生动再现了论坛过程，记录了思想火花。对高职教育的探索与研究，不再是一些抽象的教条，那些充盈着生命活力的发言和精致设计的课堂细节，相信会带给所有教育工作者深深的感动。

本书的出版，不仅是对中新职教研究成果的一次展示和推广，为中新职业教育的进一步研究提供借鉴和参考，并为全球职业教育发展提供鲜活的研究案例；也是青岛职业技术学院课程改革的阶段性成果，新西兰职业教育的先进经验将为学院课程改革融入国际化元素，让中新职教合作成果实现本土转化，促进人才培

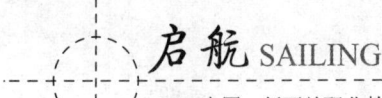

养质量的提升。

随着经济全球化的发展,文化和教育交流越来越频繁。培养具有国际竞争力的高素质技术技能人才,已经成为各国职业教育发展的共同目标。中新职教合作具有广阔前景:专业课程共建、教师互访交流、学生互换游学、研究项目合作……未来,青岛职业技术学院将与新西兰高校共同努力,推进中新合作与交流项目的开展,为双方职业教育的发展做出积极贡献。

合作之舟已经扬帆,我们怀抱信念和热情,在青岛开启中新职业教育新的航程。

覃川

2015年4月

Preface I

China's higher vocational education, over the past decade, has obtained remarkable achievement both in terms of scale and in terms of quality. While in New Zealand, the technical and vocational education and training (TVET), a main part of its higher education, is well known to the world for its competitiveness. Nowadays, international cooperation and exchanges has become a distinct feature of the global vocational education, as reflected in the ones between China and New Zealand.

In April 2013, China and New Zealand signed in Beijing an agreement to build up a partnership for vocational education development, based on which Qingdao Technical College (QTC), Waikato Institute of Technology (Wintec) and Tianjin Light Industry Vocational Technical College signed a joint agreement, embarking on a new stage of cooperation and exchanges for vocational education between these two countries. In September of the year, QTC successfully held 2013 Sino-New Zealand Vocational Education Forum in Qingdao, commencing a new communicative channel for the two countries' TVET and also providing a model for its further development. In November 2013, Steven Joyce, Minister for Tertiary Education, Skills and Employment, New Zealand, and Du Zhanyuan, Vice Minister of Ministry of Education, China, jointly unveiled the nameplate for China-New Zealand Research and Development Center for TVET, marking further enhancement of the two countries' TVET communication.

As China-New Zealand Research and Development Center (Qingdao) for TVET, QTC has been enthusiastically conducting research in vocational education and joint programs between the two countries. The forum, themed Excellence in Vocational Teaching, involves a series of comprehensive educational activities both in terms of high-end theories and fresh experience, and in terms of open class and comments. As follow-up work of the forum, this Chinese-English book is a collection of all the speeches, teaching experience and live reviews at the forum, including 5 opening addresses, 4 keynote speeches, 16 excellent vocational teaching, 3 transcripts of the open class and 5 of the class comments, which vividly reproduce the forum and record all the ideas. Instead of the abstract theories on higher vocational education, the transcripts of energetic speeches and delicate design for class teaching activities will surely bring new thought-provoking ideas to all the educators.

The publishing of this book not only showcases the research achievements of China and New Zealand vocational education, but also provides references and case studies for the two nation's further research as well as the world's vocational education. In addition, it is also viewed as the QTC's preliminary achievement of curricula reform. The international cooperation has brought an international feature to its curricula reform, and will upgrade its education quality by applying the new cooperative achievements to its own teaching.

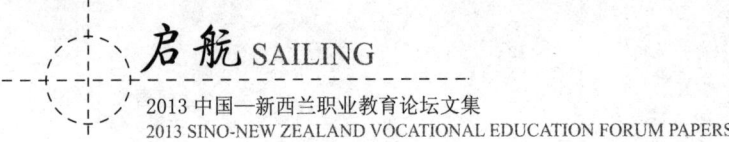

With the globalization of the world's economy, there will be more and more cultural and educational exchanges. It has become a common target for all the nations' vocational education to educate high quality skilled talents with international competitiveness. The vocational education cooperation between China and New Zealand has a broad prospect—joint curricula development, teachers exchange and mutual visits, students exchange and study tour, joint research programs, and the like. Next, QTC will work together with New Zealand institutes to promote the joint projects and contribute to the development of vocational education of both countries.

The ship of cooperation has been set sail. With faith and passion, we have opened a new voyage for China-New Zealand vocational education in Qingdao.

Qin Chuan
April 2015

前 言（二）

2013年，中国与新西兰两国共同签署协议，以加强双方职业教育的合作。协议中强调了职业教育在经济发展中发挥的重要作用。通过举办年度的论坛活动分享教与学的实践案例是协议的一个重要条款。

青岛职业技术学院是第一届中新职教论坛的承办单位，24名中新职教专家参与了此次活动，论坛的主题是"高职教育优秀教学法研究"。2013年9月，论坛正式举行。本书收集了论坛中的发言与演说，深度阐述和分享了中新两国在职业教育领域的知识与经验。

论坛举办得非常成功，大家围绕着教与学的策略和方法进行了热烈的讨论与辩论。中新两国的教师们展示了他们在职业教育领域的教学方法以及为了提高教学能力而持续做出的努力，同时提出了与当今教学实践相关的众多研究和批判性思考。

本书可为中新两国的教育研究者、政策制定者和职业教育从业人员提供借鉴。

马克·华

2015年2月

Preface II

In 2013, The People's Republic of China and New Zealand signed an agreement to collaborate and strengthen their vocational education systems. The agreement also highlighted the important part vocational education plays in growing our economies. An important aspect was to share examples of best practice in teaching and learning through a series of annual forums.

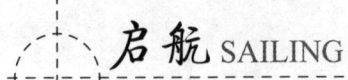

Qingdao Technical College were selected as the host of the first forum and 24 speakers were invited from around New Zealand and China to present at the forum. The theme was industry engagement and teacher development. In September 2013, the forum was hosted and this book is a collection of the various presentations and speeches. The presenters demonstrated the depth of knowledge and experience within the vocational sectors in China and New Zealand.

The forum was a great success with stimulating discussions and debate on teaching and learning strategies. It shows that vocational teachers in China and New Zealand are reflecting on how they teach and constantly seeking to improve their teaching practice. It provides an insight into current teaching practice informed by many hours of research and critical thinking.

The book should be read by educational researchers, policy makers and those involved in vocational education in China and New Zealand.

Mark Flowers
February 2015

目录

会议掠影 ·· 1

一、开幕致辞
青岛市委高校工委副书记王金生致辞 ··· 3
中国教育部国际合作与交流司政策规划处处长陈跃致辞 ················· 7
新西兰教育部中国地区主任 Alexandra Grace 致辞 ······················ 11
中国教育部职业教育研究所副所长高瑛致辞 ······························· 15
中国教育国际交流协会秘书长邵巍致辞 ····································· 19

二、主旨演讲
建设现代职业教育，中国的路径选择 ······················· 刘育锋 /27
学教做合一，让每位学生成为最好的自己 ················· 覃　川 /39
职业教育与培训的全球化——互相学习 ··················· 马克·华 /49
行业指导、校企合作是高职人才培养的有效途径 ········ 戴裕崴 /61

三、优秀教学法研讨
学徒制教学法 ··· Selena Chan /73
逆向教学强化知识应用　考核改革提升自我认知 ······· 张　毅 /83
英语教学要适应时代发展 ·· Jo Thomas /95
多种教学法在物流管理专业课程中的应用 ················· 邵宁平 /109
通过体验式教学激发学生的学习动力和学习热情 ······ Kelly Pender /125
化工单元操作及设备维护课程教学创新 ···················· 陈晓峰 /131
挑战性受教者的教学过程参与 ································· Julia Bruce /143
团队合作 ·· Malcolm Doidge /155
让大专工程专业一年级学生参与教学过程的两种教学方法：
翻转课堂式教学法和基于项目教学法 ······················· Aidan Bigham /169
在高职学生顶岗实习中开展桥接教学的思考
——基于顶岗实习教学指导的反思 ··························· 谭子安 /175

强烈的欲望——以学生为中心的学习……………………Peter Bilous/187

模拟学习体验及在情境化学习中解决问题………………Sam Honey/209

行业中基于工作过程的教学，通向成功的体系、策略和实践
………………………………………………………Karen Vaughan/217

乐学引起兴趣，好学达成目标——寓教于乐互动式教学方法探讨…郑志丽/229

由"是的，厨师长"到"为什么，厨师长"的教学策略转换
…………………………………………………Adrian Woodhouse/241

在沙特阿拉伯朱拜勒工业学院建立的优质教育发展中心…John Clayton/253

四、教学现场

观摩课：传感器与过程控制……………………………………杜晓妮/263

观摩课：卖场陈列技巧……………………………………………李 琴/283

观摩课：挑战性受教者的教学过程参与……………………Julia Bruce/307

五、教学点评

课堂点评………………………………………………………John Clayton/319

课堂点评………………………………………………Malcolm Doidge/323

课堂点评……………………………………………………………崔秀光/327

课堂点评……………………………………………………………刘育锋/331

课堂点评……………………………………………………………覃 川/337

CONTENTS

A Glimpse of the Forum ··1
1. Opening Address
    Speech by Deputy Secretary Wang Jinsheng, Municipal Party Higher Institutions Committee of Qingdao ··4
    Speech by Director Chen Yue, Division of Policy Planning, Department of International Cooperation and Exchanges, MOE, China ··8
    Speech by Alexandra Grace, ENZ's Regional Director in China ···············12
    Speech by Deputy Director Gao Ying, CIVTE, P.R. China ·······················16
    Speech by Secretary-General Shao Wei, CEAIE, P.R. China ···················20

2. Keynote Speeches
    The Construction of Modern Vocational Education, the Path Choice of China
    ··Liu Yufeng/30
    Teaching and Doing in One, and Let Every Student Be the Best of Him/Herself
    ··Qin Chuan/42
    Internationalisation of Vocational Education and Training—Learning From Each Other
    ··Mark Flowers/53
    Industry Guidance and School-Enterprise Cooperation is the Effective Way of the Vocational Education ··Dai Yuwei/64

3. Symposium: Excellent Vocational Teaching
    Learning a Trade Through Apprenticeship ···············Selena Chan/77
    Strengthening Knowledge Application by Inverted-Teaching; Improving Cognitive Outcome-Based Inverted Education and Comprehensive Assessing System
    ··Zhang Yi/88
    English Language Teaching for a Changing World ···············Jo Thomas/100
    The Applications of Various Teaching Methods on Logistics Management Courses
    ··Shao Ningping/116
    Empowerment and Compassion Enhanced Through Experiential Learning
    ··Kelly Pender/127

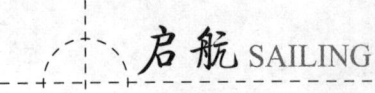

The Teaching Innovation of "the Chemical Engineering Unit Operation and Maintenance" ················Chen Xiaofeng/135

Engaging Challenging Learners················Julia Bruce/147

Mahi Tahi (Work Together)················Malcolm Doidge/159

Two Scenarios of Engaging First Year Engineering Students: The Inverted Classroom and Project Based Learning················Aidan Bigham/171

Study on the Bridging Teaching Practice in the Post Internship of Higher Vocational College Students—Reflection on Teaching Guidance About Post Internship ················Tan Zi'an/179

Burning Desire—Students Centered Learning················Peter Bilous/195

Simulated Learning Experiences and Using Problem Solving in Contextualised Learning················Sam Honey/212

Learning On-the-job for Industry: Systems, Strategies and Practices for Success ················Karen Vaughan/222

Interest Aroused in Enjoyment, Teaching Objectives Achieved in Curiousness —Discussion on the Interactive Teaching Method of Edutainment···Zheng Zhili/233

Learning Strategies for Transforming From a "Yes Chef" to a "Why Chef" Learning Environment················Adrian Woodhouse/246

The Establishment of a Quality Education Development Centre in Jubail Technical Institute: Kingdom of Saudi Arabia················John Clayton/256

4. Open Class

Transducer and Process Control················Du Xiaoni/270

Skills for Setting Shopping Mall················Li Qin/293

Engaging Challenging Learners················Julia Bruce/310

5. Class Comments

The Class Comments················John Clayton/320

The Class Comments················Malcolm Doidge/324

The Class Comments················Cui Xiuguan/328

The Class Comments················Liu Yufeng/333

The Class Comments················Qin Chuan/339

会议掠影
A Glimpse of the Forum

"2013 中国—新西兰职业教育论坛"会场
2013 Sino-New Zealand Vocational Education Forum

青岛职业技术学院海尔学院杜晓妮老师在传感器与过程控制观摩课中
Open Class: Transducer and Process Control by QTC, taught by Teacher Du Xiaoni

内蒙古电子信息职业技术学院党委书记雷德荣主持文科类专业教学研讨会
Symposium: Excellent Vocational Teaching (Arts), Chaired by Lei Derong, President of Inner Mongolia Technical College

学生在讲解程序
Student making presentation

青岛市委高校工委副书记王金生致辞
Speech by Deputy Secretary Wang Jinsheng, Municipal Party Higher Institutions Committee of Qingdao

铜仁职业技术学院院长侯长林主持优秀教学法研讨(理工类)
Symposium: Excellent Vocational Teaching (Science), Chaired by Hou Changlin, President of Tongren University

中国教育部国际交流与合作司政策规划处处长陈跃致辞
Speech by Director Chen Yue, Division of Policy Planning, Department of International Cooperation and Exchanges, MOE, China

青岛职业技术学院商学院李琴老师在卖场陈列技巧观摩课中
Open Class: Skills for Setting Shopping Mall by QTC, taught by Li Qin

新西兰教育部中国地区主任 Alexandra Grace 致辞
Speech by Alexandra Grace, ENZ's Regional Director in China

中国教育部职业教育研究所副所长高瑛致辞
Speech by Deputy Director Gao Ying, CIVTE, P.R. China

中国教育国际交流协会秘书长邵巍致辞
Speech by Secretary-General Shao Wei, CIVTE, P.R. China

两位新西兰学者讨论观摩感受
Two New Zealand Tutors Discussing Open Class

会议掠影
A GLIMPSE OF THE FORUM

新西兰怀卡托理工学院 Julia Bruce 在挑战性受教者的教学过程参与观摩课中
Open Class: Engaging Challenging Learners by Julia Bruce, Waikato Institute of Technology

第一组讨论
Group Discussion

新西兰怀卡托理工学院 Shirley Huang 女士主持主旨演讲环节
Keynote Speeches, Chaired by Shirley Huang, Wintec, New Zealand

中国教育部职业教育中心研究所比较教育研究室主任刘育峰发表演讲
Speech by Liu Yufeng, Director of Comparative Education Research, CIVTE

全体参会人员合影
All the Participants

一、开幕致辞
Opening Address

开幕致辞
OPENING ADDRESS

青岛市委高校工委副书记王金生致辞

尊敬的艾利克斯女士，

尊敬的邵巍秘书长、高瑛副所长、徐曙光总督学，

各位领导、各位专家，女士们、先生们：

上午好！

金秋时节，美丽的青岛迎来了职业教育的盛会"中国—新西兰职业教育论坛"。在此，我代表青岛市委高校工委对论坛的召开表示热烈祝贺，向出席论坛的各位嘉宾表示热烈欢迎，向为论坛召开给予支持的中新两国教育部、新西兰驻华大使馆表示衷心感谢，向论坛的承办方青岛职业技术学院表示亲切慰问。

青岛是一座美丽的海滨城市，红瓦绿树，碧海蓝天。青岛同时又是一座经济发展迅速、充满生机活力的开放城市，目前已与世界200多个国家和地区有着经贸往来，孕育了青岛啤酒、海尔、海信、双星、澳柯玛、青岛港等一批知名企业和知名品牌，现代工业和服务业产业体系正逐步完善。经济的迅速发展对高素质技术技能人才提出了更高要求，多年来青岛市政府高度重视职业教育的发展，持续推进职业教育改革试点，鼓励引进国内外职业教育资源，为职业教育的发展积极创造了良好的政策环境，提升了职业教育的发展水平。

青岛职业技术学院是中国首批示范性高职院校，在全国高职教育发展中走在前列，为青岛市的经济社会发展培养了大批高素质技术技能人才，做出了重要贡献。学院一直坚持国际化办学道路，与29个国家和地区的148所院校建立了友好交流与合作关系；同时积极以自身力量通过组建高校联盟，影响和带动中西部高职院校等共享职教资源，共同发展进步。

今天，由教育部职业技术教育中心研究所、新西兰怀卡托理工学院、青岛职业技术学院和天津轻工职业技术学院共同主办的中新高职教育论坛的胜利召开，我相信，必将为世界高职教育的发展奉献一场智慧与思想的交流盛宴，为中新两国高职教育的研究和探索产生积极的影响。

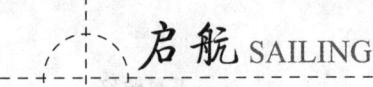

最后，衷心祝愿"中国—新西兰职业教育论坛"获得圆满成功，祝各位来宾身体健康，在青岛生活愉快。谢谢！

Speech by Deputy Secretary Wang Jinsheng, Municipal Party Higher Institutions Committee of Qingdao

Dear Mrs. Alex,

Respected Secretary-General Shao Wei,

Deputy Director Gao Ying,

Chief Inspector Xu Shuguang,

Distinguished leaders, experts, ladies and gentlemen,

Good morning!

In golden autumn Octomber this year, the vocational educational gathering Sino-New Zealand Vocational Education Forum is held in Qingdao. Here, on behalf of the Qingdao Municipal Party Committee in University, I would like to express my warm congratulations on the opening of this forum, to extend warm welcome to the distinguished guests who attend the forum, to express sincere thanks to the support of the Ministry of Education of China and New Zealand, as well as the New Zealand Embassy in Beijing, to extend greetings to the organizer of the forum—Qingdao Technical College.

Qingdao is a beautiful seaside city, with red tiles, green trees, blue sea and azure sky. Qingdao is also an open city with rapid economic development, full of vitality. At present, Qingdao keeps economic and trade exchanges with more than 200 countries and regions around the world.

It breeds Qingdao Beer, Haier, Hisense, Double Star, Aucma, Qingdao Port and a number of other well-known enterprises and famous brands. Modern industrial and service industry system is in the gradual process of improvement. The rapid development of the economy puts forward higher requirements on high-skilled applied talents. Qingdao municipal government attaches great importance to the development of vocational education, to promote vocational education reform, which will create good policy environment for the development of vocational education. It encourages the introduction of domestic and foreign vocational education resources, and enhances the development of vocational education.

Qingdao Technical College is one of the first demonstrated vocational colleges in China. It sets pace at the forefront in higher vocational education development in the country. QTC has trained a large number of highly skilled talents for the economic and social development of Qingdao, making an important contribution to society. Qingdao Technical College has always insisted on the internationalization of education, and it has set up friendly relationship of cooperation and exchanges with 148 schools in 29 countries and regions. QTC has shed its influence and leadership on the sharing vocational resources of Midwest higher vocational colleges through forming the higher education alliance.

Today, with the opening of the Sino-New Zealand Vocational Education Forum hosted by the vocational and technical education research institute center of Ministry of Education, Waikato Institute of Technology in New Zealand, Qingdao Technical College, and Tianjin Light Industry Professional Technology Institute, I believe that this opening will bring a feast of the exchanges of wisdom and ideas to the development of higher vocational education in the world, and extend a positive impact on the research and exploration of the higher vocational education between the two countries.

Finally, I wish "Sino-New Zealand Vocational Education Forum" a complete success. I wish you all healthy and happy in Qingdao. Thank you.

中国教育部国际合作与交流司政策规划处处长陈跃致辞

尊敬的 Alexandra Grace 主任,
中国教育部职业教育研究所副所长高瑛女士,
青岛职业技术学院院长覃川先生,
女士们、先生们:

大家上午好!

很高兴来到"红瓦绿树,碧海蓝天"的海滨城市青岛,与各位共同出席2013年中国—新西兰职业教育论坛。首先,我谨代表中国教育部国际交流与合作司向论坛的召开表示衷心祝贺!

"中国—新西兰职业教育论坛"作为中新两国职业教育合作的重大成果,由来已久。2010年10月,新西兰高等教育部长史蒂夫·乔伊斯先生在拜会我部郝平副部长时,达成了关于进一步扩大中新两国职业教育合作的共识。为进一步推进中新职业教育合作,我司与新西兰驻华使馆专程赴青岛职业技术学院和天津轻工业职业技术学院进行了调研。在征求地方教育部门及相关学校意见后,支持教育部职业教育中心研究所与新西兰国际教育推广局成立了政府层面的中新职业教育研究中心,定期举办座谈会、研究会、论坛等活动,并设立以青岛职业技术学院及天津轻工业职业技术学院为试点院校,以怀卡托理工学院为牵头院校的中新职业教育合作项目,共同开发课程,与国际标准接轨。2013年4月,新西兰总理约翰·基访华期间,我部与新西兰教育部签署了《关于确认和指导战略性教育伙伴关系的安排》,双方同意启动"中国—新西兰职业教育与培训合作示范项目"。今天的论坛便是示范项目的重要内容。

中国政府高度重视职业教育。新世纪以来,我国已两次召开全国职业教育工作会议,出台了一系列加快职业教育发展的政策措施。教育规划纲要明确要求职业教育展现创新人才培养模式,开发、整合、共享优质教育教学资源,建设现代职业教育体系。在此,我衷心希望大家能够在中新职教论坛互相学习优秀经验,不断拓展

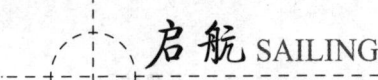

国际视野，在与新西兰各理工学院的合作交流中化整为零、提高层次，设置一系列领先课程与国际通用行业标准接轨，进一步提高教师和学生国际化交流的数量和质量。同时，继续关注中新职业教育事业的发展，发挥双方优势，深入开展研究，共同破解如何使职业教育更好地服务于经济发展的时代命题。

预祝论坛取得圆满成功！

谢谢大家！

Speech by Director Chen Yue, Division of Policy Planning, Department of International Cooperation and Exchanges, MOE, China

Repected Counselor Alexandra Grace,
Deputy Director of CIVTE, Ms. Gao Ying,
President of Qingdao Technical College, Mr. Qin Chuan,
Ladies and Gentlemen:

Good morning!

It is my great pleasure to attend the 2013 Sino-New Zealand Vocational Education Forum with you in this coastal city of Qingdao, which is well known for its red tiles, green trees, clear ocean and blue sky. First of all, on behalf of the Department of International Cooperation and Exchanges, MOE, China, I extend our sincere congratulations on the opening of this forum.

Sino-New Zealand Vocational Education Forum is the great achievement of TVET cooperation between China and New Zealand over the years. In October, 2010, an agreement was reached on enlarging Sino-NZ TVET cooperation when Steve Joyce, Minister of New Zealand Higher Education made an official visit to Hao Ping, Deputy Minister of MOE, China. In order to carry forward Sino-NZ TVET cooperation, our department and New Zealand embassy made a special trip to Qingdao Technical College and Tianjin Light Industry Vocational Technical College for investigation. After asking for opinions from local educational departments and relative colleges, we supported CIVTE and ENZ to establish a Sino-NZ Vocational Research Center on the government level to hold symposiums, seminars and forums at regular intervals. Taking QTC and Tianjin Light Industry Vocational Technical College as pilot colleges, led by Wintec, Sino-NZ TVET cooperation program has been set up to develop curriculum together and to integrate with international standards. In April, 2013, during Prime Minister of New Zealand John Key's visit to China, Arrangement of Confirming and Guiding Strategic Education Partnership was signed by and between MOE, China and Education New Zealand to launch the Pilot Project of Sino-NZ TVET Cooperation. This forum is the significant content of the project.

Chinese government pays high attention to TVET. Since the turn of the century, two national vocational education working meetings have been held and a series of policies and measures on accelerating the TVET development have been made. It is required in the Educational Planning Outline that TVET should set up modern vocational education system by innovating its talent cultivation model, developing, integrating and sharing high-quality educational resources. I, hereby, wish all of us could learn excellent experiences from each other at this forum and constantly enlarge international vision. Cooperating and communicating with colleges from New Zealand, we could break up the whole into parts, get improvement, develop series of advanced curriculums to integrate with international professional standard and to improve teachers' and students' quality and internationalization. At the same time, we will keep a watchful eye on the development of Sino-NZ vocational education, give full play of advantages of both sides, carry out deep research and get together to address the modern issue of how to make TVET better serve the economic development.

I wish the forum a complete success.

Thank you all!

新西兰教育部中国地区主任 Alexandra Grace 致辞

尊敬的各位校长，来自教育部、职业技术教育中心研究所的同事们以及来自新西兰和中国职业培训的专家们，尊敬的各位来宾、朋友：

首先，请允许我代表新西兰政府，对这次会议的主办方和组织者表示真诚的感谢。这次会议是一个很好的机遇，凸显了中新两国在政府层面及制度层面对职业技术教育的重视。

职业技术教育在为国家培养训练有素和有创新性的劳动力方面发挥了基础性作用。2012年6月，作为新西兰驻中国的政府教育代表，我与中国教育部的同仁们有幸陪同怀卡托理工学院院长率领的代表团，参观访问了青岛职业技术学院和天津轻工职业技术学院。正是这次访问，建立了两国在职业技术教育方面的良好的合作关系，促成了今天我们在这里的相聚。今年4月，我有幸目睹中国的教育部长和新西兰高等教育部长在人民大会堂签署两国教育战略伙伴关系协议，随着这一协议的签署，"新西兰—中国职业教育和培训模式计划"正式启动，本次会议也正是基于这项计划而召开。如此快速的进展非常鼓舞人心，这再次证明了建立良好关系对两国职业技术教育合作的重要性以及促进作用。

我的新西兰的同事们都是职业技术教育的专家，他们稍后将谈一谈新西兰在这一领域发展的优势。我远谈不上是专家，但我可以作为代表，简单谈一谈中新两国政治交流与教育合作关系的"大背景"。目前，两国的双边关系发展势头良好，高层互访频繁，正如中国领导人所言，"新西兰和中国的关系正处于历史最好时期"，李克强总理指出，"新西兰和中国在贸易、旅游和教育这三个领域为世界其他国家的发展做出了贡献。"正如教育部长袁贵仁之前提到的，4月签署的协议明确肯定了两国的教育关系是"战略性的教育伙伴关系"，这是一个不小的成就，为新西兰—中国职业教育和培训模式计划的开展以及推向更高水平，提供了一个优秀的平台。

我相信，无论是在政府层面还是机构层面，大家团结起来就是教育业未来的希望。彼此间不断增进理解，相互学习专业知识和经验，会让我们更好地为学生的未来做

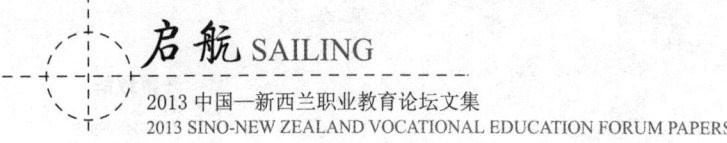

准备，这不仅是为了他们的利益，也是为了我们国家的发展。

预祝本次会议取得圆满成功！

谢谢。

Speech by Alexandra Grace, ENZ's Regional Director in China

Presidents; colleagues from the Ministry of Education and the Central Institute for Vocational and Technical Education; New Zealand and Chinese vocational training experts; distinguished guests; friends:

On behalf of the New Zealand government, I'd like to express sincere thanks to our hosts and conference organisers. This conference is an excellent initiative and underlines the importance that is placed by both our sides on technical and vocational education and training, at the government level as well as at the institution to institution level.

With its prime role in creating a well-trained and innovative workforce, TVET is of major importance to both of our countries. As the New Zealand government education representative in China, in June 2012, with Chinese Ministry of Education colleagues, I had the pleasure of accompanying a delegation led by the President of Wintec to both Qingdao Technical College and Tianjin Light Industry Vocational Technical College. That visit began the relationships which have led to us all being here today. In April of this year, I also had the pleasure of witnessing China's Education Minister and New Zealand's Tertiary Education Minister sign a Strategic Education Partnership Arrangement at Great Hall of the People. This Arrangement officially "launched" the New Zealand-China Vocational Education and Training Model Programme, under which this Conference sits. It has been inspiring to see such quick progress, and this is again testament to the good relationships on all sides and the importance placed on TVET collaboration.

My New Zealand colleagues are the TVET experts, and will talk about New Zealand's strengths in this area. As I am far from a technical expert, I thought my contribution today could be to talk about the "bigger" context, as represented by the political relationship between our two countries, China and New Zealand. It is the political relationship at the highest levels which sets the tone for every other strand of bilateral engagement, including in tourism, trade, and of course—education. And the political relationship is in great shape, evidenced by frequent high-level visits, and by comments by Chinese leadership such as "the relationship between New Zealand and China is at its best ever in history". Premier Li Keqiang has noted that in the three areas of trade, tourism, and education— "New Zealand and China set the pace for the rest of the world". Education Minister Yuan Guiren has described the education relationship as "model and strategic". As earlier mentioned, the Arrangement signed in April explicitly affirmed the bilateral education relationship as being a "Strategic Education Partnership". This is no small achievement, and again serves to emphasise the excellent platform in place for taking this New Zealand-China Vocational Education and Training Model Programme to even greater heights.

People work in education, whether at the government level or institution level, for different reasons, but I suspect that one thing which unites us all is the hope for the future which education represents. Increasing mutual understanding and learning from each other's expertise and experiences will better equip us all to better prepare our students for the future, for their own benefit and the benefit of our countries.

All the best for a very successful conference.

Thank you!

中国教育部职业教育研究所副所长高瑛致辞

尊敬的新西兰教育部中国地区主任 Alexandra Grace，
尊敬的各位专家、各位来宾：

大家上午好！

很高兴在收获的季节来到美丽的青岛，出席"中国—新西兰职业教育论坛"开幕式。首先，请允许我代表教育部职业技术教育中心研究所，对"中国—新西兰职业教育论坛"的顺利开幕表示热烈的祝贺，对中新两国教育部、新西兰驻华大使馆以及各位新闻界朋友的支持表示由衷的感谢，对各位专家、各位学者参加此次论坛表示热烈的欢迎！

职业教育是与经济联系最为紧密的一种教育类型，它对于促进经济发展、增进社会公平以及完善教育体系，都有重要意义。多年来，我国政府将职业教育摆在了更为突出的位置，采取了大力发展职业教育的政策。职业教育与继续教育战线围绕建设现代职业教育体系和终身教育体系，大力推动职业教育改革创新，深化继续教育综合改革，取得了重要进展。2012年，全国共有职业院校近1.4万所，年招生1 076万人，在校生近3 100万人，非学历教育注册学生5 076万人。中等职业学校毕业生就业率连续多年保持在95%以上，高等职业院校毕业生半年后就业率达到90%以上，成为高素质技术技能人才的重要来源，为构建合理教育结构、推动经济发展方式转变、缓解就业结构性矛盾提供了有力支撑。

在看到成绩的同时，我们也清醒地看到我国职业教育改革发展依然面临若干问题与挑战。对于职业院校而言，需要解决的一个基础性问题是如何选择并利用适合学生背景与教学目标的教学方法，培养学生学习兴趣，提高学生综合能力，为提高职业教育总体水平奠定坚实的基础。中外情况有所不同，但职业教育具有相同的属性。为此，需要与包括新西兰在内的国际社会一道，共同探讨解决问题、迎接挑战的方法。

此次"中国—新西兰职业教育论坛"以"高职教育优秀教学法研究"为主题，反映了职业教育发展基于实践的理论诉求。在全球化背景下，如何使教学方法改革

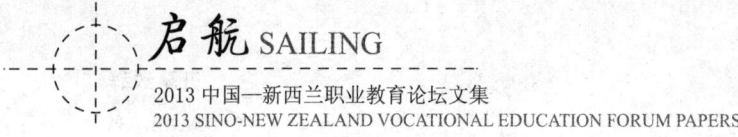

跟上现代职业教育发展的步伐,为提升职业院校学生的核心竞争力服务;如何依据不同的教学内容选择教学方法等问题,都需要开展交流与探讨。新西兰职业教育在发展过程中形成了许多典型经验与做法。我们相信,此次论坛,通过经验交流与问题探讨,一定能够使中新双方代表得到有益启示,同时增进对中新双方职业教育的理解,为深化中新两国职业教育合作做出积极贡献。

预祝"中国—新西兰职业教育论坛"圆满成功,祝大家身体健康、阖家幸福!

谢谢。

Speech by Deputy Director Gao Ying, CIVTE, P.R. China

Respected Alexandra Grace, New Zealand's Education Regional Director in China,

Ladies and gentlemen,

Good morning!

It is my great pleasure to be here, in the beautiful city of Qingdao, to attend the opening ceremony of 2013 Sino-New Zealand Vocational Education Forum in the harvest season. First of all, permit me, on behalf of Central Institute for Vocational and Technical Education, to express our warmest congratulations on the successful opening of Sino-New Zealand Vocational Education Forum, and our sincere thanks to both the Ministry of Education in China and in New Zealand, New Zealand Embassy in China and our media friends for your support and to extend our warm welcome to the experts and scholars.

Vocational education, as a type of education, is closely related to economy. It is significant for promoting economic development and social justice as well as for perfecting education system. For many years, our government has put vocational education in a more outstanding position and adopted the policy of vigorously developing vocational education. Important progress has been made on TVET by establishing modern vocational education system and life-long education system, greatly promoting vocational education reform and innovation and deepening comprehensive reform of continuing education. By the end of 2012, there were 14 thousands vocational colleges in China, and 10.76 million students were enrolled. The total number of students nearly reached 31 million and the number of students registered in non-degree education reached 50.76 million. The employment rate for secondary vocational school students remains above 95 percent for years and that for higher vocational college students, six months after their graduation, hits over 90 percent. These students have become the important resource of high-quality talents with technical skills. They are a strong support in forming reasonable education system, promoting the transformation of economic development mode and releasing structural contradictions of employment.

Acknowledging the successes, we are also aware of the issues and challenges to face in the vocational education reform and development. For vocational colleges, to increase the overall level and to settle solid foundation of vocational education, the very basic issues to deal with are how to choose and adopt suitable teaching methods to fit students' background and teaching objectives, how to develop students' learning interests, and how to improve students' comprehensive abilities. Vocational education has the same property, though situations are different at home and abroad. Therefore, we need to discuss with international community including New Zealand, the methods to deal with the issues and to meet the challenges.

With "Excellence in Vocational Teaching" as its theme, 2013 Sino-

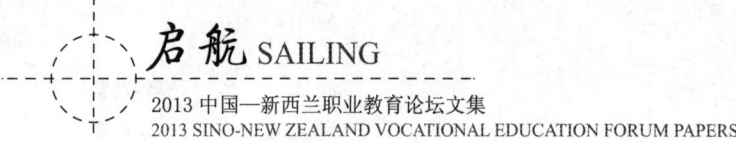

New Zealand Vocational Education Forum 2013, based on practice, reflects the theoretical demands of TVET development. Under the background of globalization, many issues need to be discussed and explored, such as how to keep the teaching method reform in line with modern TVET development, how to choose teaching method according to different teaching contents in order to improve core competence of vocational college students. Many typical experiences and practice have been formed in the development of TVET in New Zealand. I believe, during this forum, through experience sharing and issues discussing, delegations from both China and New Zealand will obtain beneficial inspiration. And also, this forum will make positive contribution in promoting the understanding of TVET for both sides and deepening Sino-NZ TVET cooperation.

    In conclusion, I wish the Forum a complete success. I wish you all good health and a happy family!

    Thank you.

开幕致辞
OPENING ADDRESS

中国教育国际交流协会秘书长邵巍致辞

尊敬的葛佑兰参赞、玛丽董事长、华马克校长，

尊敬的陈跃先生、高瑛女士、王金生先生、徐曙光先生，

尊敬的覃川院长、戴裕崴院长，

各位来宾，女士们、先生们、朋友们：

大家好！

很高兴应邀来到美丽的黄岛，参加本次中国—新西兰职业教育论坛。我谨代表中国教育国际交流协会，对论坛的举行表示热烈的祝贺！

青岛职业技术学院是交流协会的会员单位，在众多的中国高职院校中独具办学特色，在协会开展的"高职院校领导海外培训项目"和其他国际合作项目中发挥了骨干和带头作用。今年4月，青岛职业技术学院、天津轻工职业技术学院、教育部职教所和新西兰怀卡托理工学院签署合作协议，促成了本次会议的举行。对于三校一所的这种合作进取精神，我们表示赞赏，对会议主办方向我们发出的邀请表示衷心感谢！

中国、新西兰建交40多年来，两国人民建立了深厚的友谊，在政治、经济、文化、教育等领域的交流与合作取得了丰硕的成果。我了解到，在中新两国政府支持下，相关机构正酝酿在中国建立"中国—新西兰职业教育研究中心"，这无疑将是推动两国职业教育领域合作与发展的一项重要举措。借助这个有效的平台，中新两国的职业院校和教育工作者将一起研究学术，交流经验，取长补短，互通有无，增进理解，深化友谊，提高办学质量和效益；通过合作培养人才，推动双边教育、文化和经贸合作，促进两国社会经济发展。

本次论坛以教学法为主题，很有意义。职业教育究竟培养什么类型的人才？如何培养？通过这种培养，对学生未来的职业生涯将产生何种作用和影响？这是学生、家长、学校和社会共同关心的问题。解决这个问题的关键就在于教育理念和教学方法的不断革新。一方面，社会发展的变化、经济增长模式的变化对技能型人才的需

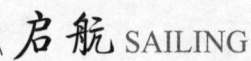

求带来了影响；另一方面，信息技术的发展对传统的教学理念、模式和方法也带来了挑战。同时，随着信息社会的发展，人们的认知和学习能力也发生了巨大的变化。这些都对我们如何去更新教育理念和教学方法提出了新的课题。中国有句俗语"授人以鱼，不如授人以渔"。意思是说，给人鱼吃，不如交给他钓鱼的方法。给一条鱼管一时，会钓鱼则管一生。我认为，这次会议的实质，就是研究用什么样的方法，更有效地教会学生如何钓鱼。

中国教育国际交流协会是中国教育界开展民间对外合作的全国性组织。近年来，我们一直不断探索和拓展职业教育领域的国际合作交流：2010年上海世博会期间，在中新两国政府的支持下，交流协会与新西兰理工大学联盟合作举办了"中新职业教育研讨会"。今年11月初，在交流协会主办的"2013年中国国际教育年会"中，"职业教育国际论坛"也将作为一个重要版块。明年10月下旬，交流协会将接受"世界职教联盟"委托，与"中国国际教育年会"同期举办"2014世界职教联盟大会"。为更好地推动中国职业教育的国际化进程，交流协会将在近期成立职业技术教育国际交流分会，明天下午将借助本次论坛的契机召开职教分会筹备工作会议。此外，交流协会还承担了国家专项设立的"高职院校领导海外培训项目"的组织实施工作，目前已圆满完成第一期5年培训计划，取得了阶段性成果。根据鲁昕副部长的指示，我们将于10月中旬召开推广项目成果的全国视频会议，在此，也欢迎大家届时参加。

最后，预祝本次论坛圆满成功！祝愿中新职教合作不断取得新的成果！

谢谢大家！

Speech by Secretary-General Shao Wei, CEAIE, P.R. China

Respected New Zealand Education Counselor Ms. Alexandra Grace, Mm. Mary, President Flowers,
Respected Mr. Chen Yue, Mm. Gao Ying, Mr. Wang Jinsheng, Mr. Xu Shuguang,
President Qin Chuan, President Dai Yuwei,

Distinguished guests, ladies and gentlemen,

　　Good morning!

　　It's a great pleasure to be here in Huangdao, a beautiful place, to attend today's event. On behalf of my organization, China Education Association for International Exchange (CEAIE), I would like to extend warmest congratulations on the opening of the 2013 Sino-New Zealand Vocational Education Forum.

　　Qingdao Technical College is a higher vocational institution with distinct characteristics. It is a member institute of CEAIE and plays a leading role in our TVET programs such as Vocational Education Leadership Program. In April 2013, QTC, Tianjin Light Industry Vocational Technical College, Central Institute for Vocational and Technical Education and Wintech signed an agreement which makes today's forum possible. We appreciate this spirit of going forward through partnership, and the kind invitation to us to take part in this forum.

　　Ever since the establishment of diplomatic relations between our two countries, friendship among the two peoples has been fostered; political, economic, cultural and educational collaboration has been promoted and great outcomes have been achieved. I've learned that with government support, a Sino-NZ Vocational Education Research Centre is going to be set up. There's no doubt that this centre will serve as an important platform to push forward bilateral cooperation in TVET sector. Through this platform, vocational education institutions of the two countries have the opportunity to share perspectives and learn from each other's best practice, so as to build up mutual understanding and friendship, enhance quality and effectiveness of educational programs, promote bilateral cooperation in education, culture and trade, and benefit social and economic development of both countries.

　　The theme of this forum is excellence in teaching, which is very

important. What type of graduates shall vocational and technical education cultivate? How to achieve that? And how our education and training impact our students' future career life? These are common concerns of students, their parents, educational institutions and the society as a whole. The key to address these issues is to keep reforming our teaching theories and methods. Because, on the one hand, social and economic developments bring new demands for skilled workforce; on the other hand, the advancement of information technology brings challenges to the traditional teaching ideas, modes and methodology. In the meantime, in this information society, students' cognition and learning ability has changed too. All these produce new topics for us to think about. There's a Chinese saying "Teach a man how to fish is better than feeding him with fish", which means "Give a man a fish and he can eat it for just a meal; but if you teach him how to fish, he'll have enough to eat for a lifetime". Today's forum, in my view, is to explore ways to better teach students how to fish.

CEAIE is a nation-wide organization in China conducting international exchanges and cooperation for education. Over the past years, we've been committed to expand programs and activities in the TVET sector. In 2010, with support from the two governments, we hosted a Sino-NZ Vocational Education Symposium during the Shanghai Expo. In the upcoming early November, we're going to host a series of seminar to compose the Int'l Forum on Vocational and Technical Education, which will be an important part of CEAIE's 2013 Annual Conference. In late October of 2014, during our Annual Conference in Beijing, we will host the World Congress of World Federation of Colleges and Polytechnics. Besides, in order to further promote the internationalisation of the TVET sector in China, CEAIE is planning to set up a commission on vocational and technical education in the near future. Tomorrow afternoon, we're going to have a working group

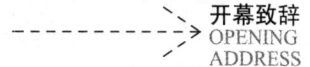

meeting for this. In addition, we've been implementing the Vocational Education Leadership Overseas Training Program over the past five years. This is a fully government-funded program and we've just completed its first five-year plan. The Ministry of Education of China has asked us to organise a nation-wide video conference to promote the outcomes of this program in mid next month. Colleges present today are welcome to attend.

I wish a full success of this forum, and more and greater achievements of China-NZ TVET collaboration in the future!

Thank you.

二、主旨演讲
Keynote Speeches

建设现代职业教育，中国的路径选择

中国教育部职业教育研究所比较教育研究室主任　刘育锋

尊敬的邵巍秘书长，尊敬的覃川院长，女士们、先生们：

大家上午好！很高兴有机会参加中新职业教育论坛。这次论坛的题目选得非常好，因为对于职业院校来说，一切要从基础做起。这是第一次中新职教论坛，利用这个机会，我将中国职业教育的一些发展思路、战略性的选择给大家做一下介绍。

今天，我发言的题目是"建设现代职业教育，中国的路径选择"。发言内容主要涉及三个方面——一是背景，二是路径选择，三是对中新职教合作未来的期待。

中国自改革开放以来，经济发展非常快速。1978年以来中国的GDP总量和人均GDP增长快速，从1978年人均GDP几百元到2012年的将近4万多元人民币。在这期间，中国实现了两大飞跃。根据世界银行有关统计，经济发展分为四个阶段：人均GDP在975美元及以下属于低收入水平国家阶段，976~3 855美元属于中等偏下收入国家阶段，3 856~11 905美元属于中等偏上收入国家阶段，高收入国家阶段在11 906美元以上。2001年，中国人均GDP实现第一次跨越，人均GDP突破1 000美元，已经走出低收入国家阶段。2010年实现第二次跨越。我们很高兴地看到，中国目前GDP总量在全球GDP总量排名中名列第二。我们也很高兴地看到，中国的国家竞争力排名也得到了提升，总排名为全球第29位。但在看到这个成绩的同时，我们也要清醒地看到，中国其实并不是一个发达国家，为什么这么说呢？我们还是要看人均GDP。从国际有关报告中，我们知道，我国人均GDP在140多个国家中排名第80位。根据全球竞争力指标划分，现在的中国经济发展属于项目驱动经济阶段，也就是瑞士国家发展报告中提到的第二阶段，与发达国家相比，还有较大差距，很多发达国家，包括新西兰，经济发展属于第三阶段。所以我们应该看到，一方面中国经济得到快速发展，另一方面，我们的发展尚未令人满意，而且我们为这种发展付出了惨重代价，比如环境污染问题、能耗问题。这些问题，都需要我们去解决。

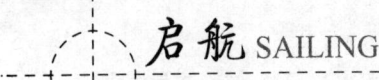

面对这些问题,中国的发展方向是怎样的?《国民经济和社会发展十二五规划纲要》(以下简称《规划纲要》)中明确提出了发展目标及发展要求。这些目标包括经济平稳较快发展、结构调整取得重大进展、科技水平明显提升、资源节约和环境保护成效显著、人民生活持续改善、社会建设明显加强、改革开放不断深化等,每一个目标里面都有很多具体数字。《规划纲要》里面还包括经济结构战略性调整、科学技术进步创新、保障和改善民生等。中国政府看到了发展职业教育对实现这些目标的促进作用,所以提出要大力发展职业教育。

发展职业教育,方向是什么?十八大明确指出是现代职业教育。现代职业教育到底是什么样的教育呢?我个人认为,现代职业教育既是时间概念,又是性质概念。从时间概念上来讲,现代职业教育是能够满足当下社会的主体需求的教育;作为性质概念来说,现代职业教育是现代社会中的职业教育,它反映现代社会中相关各方对职业教育提出的主体需求,所以现代社会中满足各方主体需求所体现出来的属性就是现代职业教育属性。

现代职业教育属性包括三个方面:一是社会发展的适应性;二是经济的适应性,三是学习者要求的适应性。关于社会发展的适应性,我们现代社会的发展强调公平、绿色、环保和持续发展等,都是职业教育发展需要考虑的要素;关于经济适应性,职业教育与经济联系较为紧密,因而如何使职业教育与我们的产业发展需求相匹配,是衡量现代职业教育的属性是否具有经济适应性的主要指标;学习者要求的适应性,则强调体系的衔接,它需要灵活、开放和满足不同学习者的不同时间段的要求。去年,中国政府所提出的现代职业教育建设内容及其属性的概述,与联合国教科文组织第三次世界职教大会提出用"三个透镜"来评价职业教育的思路十分契合。我们强调经济的适应性,教科文组织强调经济透镜;我们强调办令人民满意的教育,教科文组织强调公平透镜;我们强调经济要适应社会的发展,职业教育要适应社会的发展,教科文组织强调改革透镜。

中国该如何选择自己建设现代职业教育的路径呢?我个人认为主要是选择三个路径:一是中高等职业教育衔接的路径;二是校企合作的路径;三是社会公平的路径。中国政府为了实现每个路径,颁布了一系列政策,实施了一系列项目,在此我举几个比较有代表意义的现实例子。比如在中高职衔接方面,教育部颁布了《关于推进中等和高等职业教育协调发展的指导意见》《关于积极推进高等职业教育考试招生制度及改革的指导意见》《五年制职教改革的意见》，规定了具体的考试招生制度等十大任务，明确提出，必须明确中等和高等职业学校的定位：中等职业教育着重培养技能型人才，发挥基础性的作用，高等职业教育重点培养高端技能型人才等等。比如在校企合作方面，我们已经颁布了《关于充分发挥行业指导作用，推进职教改革发展意见》，同时拟制定《职业教育校企合作促进办法》《促进职业教育集团化办学的指导意见》。新西兰的朋友可能对中国职业教育的一些专业术语还不太了解，但随着合作的深入，大家对一些中国特有的概念，比如职教集团、集团化教学、职教资源库等，会有越来越深入的认识。同时我相信，你们对中国特有的经验会更感兴趣。

  在社会公平方面，中国政府采取了支持农村地区职业教育发展、支持民族地区职业教育发展和免学费、助学政策。在此我重点介绍一下我国的助学政策。2008年金融危机以来，世界有很多国家职业教育经费削减，而且很多国家开始收学费，但是中国职业教育依然实施并且扩大实施免学费和助学政策的范畴。自2009年开始，中国开始逐步推动中职免学费政策，到2012年秋季，中职免学费范围扩大到所有农村学生、城市涉农专业学生和家庭经济困难学生，同时对涉农专业学生和非涉农专业家庭经济困难学生给予国家助学金补助。目前已经有13个省份将免学费政策扩大到所有中职学生，助学金资助范围也有所扩大。我们主要是通过专业课程和教材建设、综合改革试点和能力建设来具体落实这些政策。比如在专业课程和教材建设方面，我们颁布了《高等职业学校专业教学标准（试行）》，目前我们正在制定《中等职业学校专业教学标准》，建立高职专业教学库等。在综合试点方面，国务院专门颁布了《开展国家教育改革试点的通知》，通知包括52项职业教育改革试点项目，包括办学模式改革、职业教育综合改革。在能力建设方面，有很多项目，很多院校也参加了，包括基础能力建设，如示范院校建设、教师素质提升、校长培训、实训基地建设等。在能力建设方面我们还强调扩大职业教育对外交流与合作。我们目前的选择、所有的试点项目等，最后一定是要通过最平常、最基础的教学来落实和体现的。

  我回过头来再谈一下为什么这次论坛《高职教育优秀教学法研讨》的主题选得非常好。教学是最基础的一项工作，它的基本要素包括学习者、教师、教学媒体和教学内容，所有这些都围绕教学展开。我国在注重宏观制度设计的同时，也非常强调职业教育教学改革。到目前为止，有三个文件与职业教育教学改革是密切相关的：

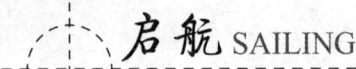

第一个是 1998 年《面向二十一世纪深化职业教育教学改革的原则意见》；第二个是 2000 年《关于全面推进素质教育、深化中等职业教育教学改革的意见》；第三个是 2008 年《教育部关于进一步深化中等职业教育教学改革的若干意见》。与高职相关的文件也有很多，很多原则性的问题与高职都密切相关。我国职业教育教学改革关注的内容主要包括以下两个方面：一是教学概念问题，比如要强调能力本位问题、人才培养模式问题、教学内容问题、教学方法择优问题，专业建设、课程改革、制度建设和教学评估等；二是强调能力本位，强调专业要服务行业企业实际需求，强调教学手段启发或者引发学生的主动积极性等。职业教育教学改革是职业教育改革的核心，但是如何进行改革、采用什么样的教学方法、什么样的方法是优秀教学方法等，到目前为止人们的看法并不一致。中新专家有必要坐在一起，对到底什么是优秀的教学方法进行研讨。对教学方法概念的内涵和外延、判断的逻辑框架、逻辑的依据，大家的认识也是不一致的。职业教育作为一种教育类型，本质是一样的，通过这个论坛，中新两国专家至少可以得到一个基本的结论——到底怎样判断一种教学方法是优秀的教学方法。这也是我个人对这次中新职教论坛的期待。

谢谢大家！

The Construction of Modern Vocational Education, the Path Choice of China

Liu Yufeng, Director of Comparative Education Research of the Institute of Vocational Education of Ministry of Education in China

Dear Friends, Respected Secretary-general Mr. Shao Wei, Respected President Mr. Qin Chuan, ladies and gentlemen,

Good morning! I'm very glad to have the opportunity to participate in Sino-New Zealand Vocational Education Forum. The topic of this Forum is brilliantly chosen, because all have to start from the base for vocational

colleges. This is the first Sino-New Zealand Vocational Education Forum. I will introduce some development thoughts on Chinese vocational education and strategic choice through this opportunity.

The topic of my speech today is "The Construction of Modern Vocational Education, the Path Choice of China". The speech mainly covers three aspects: the background, the path choice, and the expectation for the cooperation of Sino-New Zealand Vocational Education in the future.

China undergoes rapid economic development since the reform and opening up. China's GDP and per capita GDP increased rapidly since 1978, with per capita GDP growing from a few hundred yuan in 1978 to nearly forty thousand yuan in 2012. During this period, China realized the two big leaps. According to the statistics of World Bank, economic development is divided into four stages: lower-income countries with per capita GDP at 975 dollars and below; lower-middle-income countries between 976 and 3,855 dollars; medium-high income countries between 3,856 and 11,905 dollars; high-income countries above 11,906 dollars. In 2001, China's per capita GDP achieved the leap for the first time, with per capita GDP topping 1,000 dollars, stepping out of the stage of low-income countries. Afterwards, the second leap turned up in 2010. Therefore it is pleasant and encouraging to see that currently China's GDP ranks the second around the world. We rejoice at the improvement of China's national competitiveness ranking the 29th in the world. But at the same time, we are clearly aware that China is not a developed country yet. The reason why I said this lies in the per capita GDP. We are aware from the international reports that China's per capita GDP ranks 80th in more than 140 countries. According to the global competitiveness index, different stages of economic development are divided. Now China's economic development belongs to the project-driven economy stage. Compared with the developed countries, we lag far behind, even belonging to different stages of development. So we know from Swiss national development report that our country's economic development stays in the second stage, while many developed countries, including New Zealand, belongs to the third stage. Therefore it is safe to conclude that on the one hand, China's economic development is rapid, on the other hand, our development is not satisfactory, and we paid a high price for this development, such as environmental pollution, energy consumption problems. We need to solve all of these issues. First of these problems is what is the development direction of China. "The twelfth five-year plan outline of the national economy and social development" in our country clearly puts forward the development target and development requirements. These goals include fast yet steady economic development, significant progress of structural adjustment, obviously promoted of science and technology, achievements in resource saving and environmental protection, continuing improvement of people's living standards, obvious strengthening of social construction, the deepening of reform and opening-up, etc. Each target has a lot of detailed numbers. The plan and outline also include strategic adjustment of economic structure, the progress of science and technology innovation, and ensuring and improving of people's livelihood, and so on. The Chinese government has already noticed that the development of vocational education facilitates the achicvement of these goals, so putting forward to vigorously develop vocational education, with the eighteenth national congress proposing to speed up the development of vocational education.

What is our direction in the development of vocational education? The Eighteenth National Congress clearly points to the modern vocational education. Then what is modern vocational education? Personally, I think the modern vocational education is not only a concept of time but also a concept of nature. From the concept of time, the modern vocational education contribute to meet the social individual demands; from the concept of nature, the modern vocational education is the vocational education in modern society, which reflects the demands for vocational education put forward by the parties involved in the modern society. Therefore to meet the demands of the subject in the modern society is the attribute of the modern vocational education.

Modern vocational education attributes include three aspects: the adaptability of the development of society, economic adaptability, adaptability of the requirements for learners. Concerning the suitability of the social development, for example, the development of our modern society emphasizes fair, green, environmental protection and sustainable development, all these are what should be considered as the elements of vocational education development; concerning economic adaptability, vocational education closely relates to economy. Therefore, how to make vocational education match our industry development needs, is the main indicator of whether the attributes of modern vocational education have economic adaptability. Adaptability of the requirements for learners emphasizes system cohesion, flexibility, openess and the ability to meet the requirements of different learners and of different periods. Last year, the Chinese government proposed the construction contents of modern vocational education and the sketch of its attributes. This fully corresponds to the train of thought of the evaluation of vocational education—"three lens", which was put forward by the third world conference on vocational education, scientific and cultural organization (UNESCO). We emphasize the adaptability of economic, while educational, scientific and cultural organization emphasized the lens; we emphasize the people's satisfactory education, while educational, scientific and cultural organization emphasizes fair lens; we emphasize economy adapting to the development of the society, vocational education adapting to the development of the society, accordant to UNESCO emphasis on the reform of the lens perfectly.

How shall China choose the path of the construction of modern vocational education? Personally I think there are three paths to choose—cohesion of the middle and higher vocational education, cooperation between colleges and enterprise, and social justice. In order to carry out each path, the Chinese government has issued a series of policies, and implemented a series of projects. Here I will give you several examples of typical significance. Concerning the cohesion of the secondary and higher vocational education, the Ministry of Education promulgated "Guidance about promoting coordinated development of secondary and higher vocational education", "Guidance about promoting the higher vocational education enrolment system and the reform of examination", "The opinions of the five-year vocational education reform", as well as the provisions of ten big tasks like the specific test enrolment system and so on.

In "Guidance about promoting coordinated development of secondary and higher vocational education", it is clearly put forward that, the positioning of secondary and higher vocational schools must be clarified. Secondary vocational education focuses on cultivating skilled talents, playing a fundamental role, while higher vocational education focuses on training high skilled talents, etc. In college-enterprise cooperation, for example, we have already issued "Guidance about giving full play of the industry conduct, to promote vocational education reform and development", and at the same time formulate "the promoting methods for university-enterprise cooperation in vocational education", and "Guidance to promote vocational education collectivization school-running". Perhaps New Zealand friends are not familiar with some professional terms of Chinese vocational

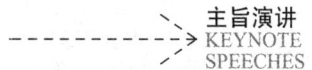

education. Through the deepening of the cooperation, there will be more and more in-depth understanding for some of China's unique concepts, such as vocational education group, group teaching, repository, etc. At the same time, I believe you might be more interested in China's unique experience.

In terms of social justice, the Chinese government supports vocational education development in rural areas and national regions, free tuition and financial aid policies. Here I mainly introduce the financial aid policies of our country. Since the financial crisis in 2008, vocational education in many countries of the world confronts national funding cuts, and many countries begin to charge fees. But in China, free tuition is still in implementation and financial aid policies are in expansion. Since 2009, China has begun the gradual implementation of tuition-free policy in secondary technical schools. Until the fall of 2012, tuition-free policy is expanded to all rural students, urban students majoring in agriculture, and financially difficult students. Besides, at the same time, countries grant subsidies are offered to students majoring in agriculture and financially difficult students. At present, there are 13 provinces that will expand the tuition-free policy to all secondary vocational students, with countries grant subsidies widened. The specific implementation of these policies is mainly carried out through the professional courses, teaching materials construction, comprehensive reform pilot and ability construction. In professional courses and teaching materials construction, for example, we issued the "professional teaching standards in higher vocational schools (trial)". Besides, we are working on the teaching standards in secondary vocational schools, and establishing a teaching library of higher vocational majors, etc. We implement these policies mainly through the professional courses and teaching materials construction, comprehensive reform pilot and ability construction. In professional courses and teaching materials construction, for example, we introduced the "professional teaching standards in higher vocational schools (trial)", now we are working on the secondary vocational schools teaching standards, establishing a library of higher vocational specialty teaching, etc.

I will continue to talk about why the topic of this forum "research and discussion on excellent teaching methods in higher vocational education" is brilliantly selected. Teaching is a basic work, the most basic elements of which include learners, teachers, teaching media and teaching contents, all of which center around teaching. Same as the macroeconomic system design in our country, vocational education teaching reform is also specially emphasized. So far, there are three documents that are closely related to vocational education teaching reform, "Opinions of the principle of deepening the reform of vocational education teaching toward the 21st century" in 1998, "Opinions of the promotion of the all-round quality education, deepening of the reform of secondary vocational education teaching" in 2000, "Several opinions of the Ministry of Education on further deepening the reform of the secondary vocational education teaching" in 2008. There are also many documents which are associated with higher vocational, with many fundamental problems closely related. China's vocational education teaching reform mainly focuses on the following two aspects. The first one is the problem of teaching concept, such as the emphasis on competence-based teaching, problems of cultivating talents, teaching content, choice of teaching methods, professional construction, curriculum reform, the system construction and teaching evaluation and so on. The second one is the emphasis on professional service to the actual demand of industry enterprise, the emphasis on the inspiration of teaching methods or how to trigger students' initiative enthusiasm, and so on. Vocational education teaching reform is the core of the reform of vocational education, but so far, people don't agree on how to reform, what kind of

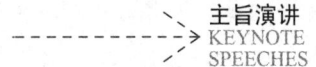

teaching method should be adopted, and what kind of method is an excellent teaching method, etc. Therefore, it is necessary for Chinese and New Zealand experts to gather around the table to have a research and discussion about what are good teaching methods. There are different understanding as to the concept connotation and denotation of the teaching method, the logical framework of judgment, the basis of logistic. As a type of education, the nature of vocational education is the same. Through the Forum, Sino-New Zealand experts at least could get a basic conclusion about how to determine which teaching method is first-class way of teaching. This is my personal expectation for Sino-New Zealand Vocational Education Forum.

Thank you.

学教做合一，让每位学生成为最好的自己

青岛职业技术学院教授　覃川

各位领导、各位嘉宾，女士们、先生们：

大家下午好！

下面，我发言的题目是"学教做合一，让每位学生成为最好的自己"。

众所周知，人才培养模式是每一所高职院校在学生培养方面所遵循的一种范式，是教育理念的表达方式。有怎样的人才培养模式，就会有怎样的教育手段和教学方式。19世纪末，美国教育家、哲学家杜威提出"做中学"，将生活纳入教育范畴；20世纪初，中国教育家陶行知将这一理论加以继承发展，创立以生活教育为主线的现代教育理论，即"生活即教育""社会即学校"。受杜威、陶行知教育思想的影响，这些年来，青岛职业技术学院在教育教学实践中，积极探索"学教做合一"人才培养模式，取得了一定的成效。

探索"学教做合一"人才培养模式，让每位学生成为最好的自己，需要思考以下三个问题：

一、为什么要提出"学教做合一"

实际上，教育本身就是一个生活的过程，教育离开生活就是一种虚幻的、没有意义的行为。对职业院校的学生而言，抽象逻辑思维能力和对陈述性知识的学习能力较弱，而动手操作能力、形象思维等其他智能有可能比较突出。面对这样的一个群体，学校应该提供更加丰富的学习资源和其他学习的条件，通过激发他们的智力潜能，发现和引导他们在符合自身个性特征的智能领域，自主地、探究式地学习，从而较好地掌握所需要的知识和技能。然而，受传统教育学的影响，长期以来，高职院校的教学活动主要是以教师、教材和课堂为中心，学生的主体地位和成长需求

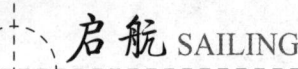

在一定程度上受到忽视。高职院校中的这种僵化、陈旧的人才培养模式,禁锢了学生的思维,打击了学生的信心,压抑了学生的潜能。人才培养模式改革势在必行。

2012年以来,青岛职业技术学院秉持"以人为本""让每位学生成为最好的自己"的人才培养价值取向,以全新视角重新审视教育教学理念,着力探讨并开始构建"学教做合一"人才培养模式,力图以"学"为根本建构起一种新型的人才培养模式,即在教学活动中,面对学生的成长需求,凸显为"学"而"教"的理念;同时,体现学生的主体地位,彰显学习的主导要素,实现"教与学""学与做""教与做"之间的紧密互动。

二、什么是"学教做合一"

顾名思义,"学"是指学生的学习活动,"教"是指教师的教导行为,"做"是指在学和教过程中的实践活动。其中,"学"是目的,是内因;"教"是手段,是外因;而"做"是"学"和"教"的载体。学、教、做在人才培养的过程中,是一个互相联系、互相作用的统一体,是一个强调"学生"主体地位、突出"学习"优先顺序的理念和价值取向。换句话说,无论是从动词上讲还是从名词上看,"学教做合一"强调的是"学生""学习"处于首要的位置,相比较而言,"教师""教学"处于相对次要的位置。

在教学活动的实施过程中,要求做到面向学生未来的职业生涯,通过引进职场真实工作任务,以项目或案例等为载体创设学习情境,训练学生掌握学习、研究、工作的思维方式与行动方法,不断提升自身专业能力的深度与专门化程度,而不是以教师自己的习惯和方式来包办学生的学习方式和学习进程,更不是一味地采取"黑板灌""电脑灌""笔记灌"的形式来强迫学生被动学习。

三、怎样实现"学教做合一"

"学教做合一"人才培养模式的构建是一个系统工程,涉及学校办学功能及教学组织运作等诸多方面,在这当中,课程尤为重要。从某种意义上讲,课程是学校的"产品",而这种产品能否适销对路,能否成为"学习商品",能否让学生这些"客户"欣然接受,关键在于课程这个产品是否与"客户"的需求相一致。因此可以说,课程改革是探索"学教做合一"人才培养模式的主要途径和基本保障。

首先,要将"人人成才"的理念真正融入到教育体系、教学环节和育人实践中。通过关注生命、关注生长、关注能力、关注智慧,将素质转变为能力、将方法转变为文化，打造"品牌课程"，培养"品牌学生"。

作为培养工作一线基层管理者的高职院校，在学生培养过程中，应着力培养其"职业领导力"，一方面要给学生创造可持续接受更高层次专业理论与技能学习的可能，另一方面还要为学生提供横向转岗与择业的机会。也就是说，既要关心学生的当下，建立专业技能与职业素养导向；也要关注学生的未来，建立树立美好生活导向和生命意义导向。

其次，要以"适应学生需要"为本构建课程。学生成长，是一个全方位的综合过程。学校作为育人机构，不仅仅承担专业教育活动的育人功能，而且还具备自然环境、制度环境、文化环境的育人要素。要更新"只有教学计划中的、教材上的才是课程"的传统课程观念，重视隐性课程建设，提升学院文化品位，彰显教职员工示范行为，以此构建起尊重学生成长规律的、有效的"大课程"系统。

第三，要坚持课堂教学的主渠道作用。课堂教学是将"学教做合一"人才培养模式落到位的关键。在课堂教学中，教师通过体现学生职业能力与人生发展的教学设计，以科学、有效的教学方法来呈现出和谐、生态的生命课堂。教师在课堂以引导者、参与者和协调者的角色，通过问题教学、专题讨论、案例教学、项目活动等方式，调动学生的主动性和积极性，激活学生的学习潜能。

第四，要建立科学、客观的评价体系。尊重学生天性和个性，树立全新"人才观"，帮助他们找到适合自己的成长之路。在学业评价中，转变"一考定输赢"的评价制度，建立多元、立体的评价制度，让拥有不同智力特征、不同兴趣和特长的学生都能脱颖而出，自信、自尊地成长。

第五，要建立全域性课程管理体系。要立足于"全人"培养，丰富并完善课程内涵，将学生社团活动、社会实践活动、文化素质教育、文学艺术修养、兴趣特长等教育内容，纳入课程管理；建立课程测评制度，促进课程质量的持续改善；提升教师课程意识，完善教师课程文化自觉，发挥教师课程素养作用，改变教师课堂教学行为方式；加强职业教育比较研究，引进世界发达国家的先进职教经验与课程标准，并着力进行本土化改造，提高课程的标准化、专门化和人本化等。

各位专家、各位同行，借鉴世界高职教育先进理念与教学方法，探索符合本国国情的高职教育人才培养模式，一方面需要高职院校长期的探索实践与积累沉淀，另一方面也需要高职院校之间的合作交流与分享双赢。青岛职业技术学院"学教做

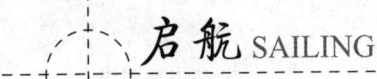

合一"人才培养模式的探索和实践，目前刚刚起步，今后的路还很长，希望能得到与会各位专家和同仁的不吝赐教。

我的发言就到这里，谢谢大家的聆听！

Teaching and Doing in One, and Let Every Student Be the Best of Him/Herself

Qin Chuan, Professor in Qingdao Technical College

Dear leaders, guests, ladies and gentlemen:

Good afternoon!

The topic of my presentation is "Teaching and Doing in One, and Let Every Student Be the Best of Him/Herself".

As is well known, talents training mode is a normal form that every higher vocational college follows on the perspective of student cultivation. This model is the method of expression of educational idea, which means the talents training mode is an echo of the education techniques and methods. At the end of 19th century, American educator, philosopher Dewey mentioned "learning by doing", which brings life into education field. At the beginning of 20th century, Chinese educator Tao Xingzhi inherited and developed Dewey's theory and set up modern education theory based on life education, which means "life is education" and "society is school". However, it is a pity that, till 1980s, Chinese educational teaching activities have long been affected by Kailov's pedagogy. Teachers, textbooks and classrooms become the center of teaching activities, which neglects students' dominant role and growth needs, and constrains teachers' teaching behavior to some extent.

Carrying out "Learning, Teaching and Doing in One, and Let Every

Student Be the Best of Him/Herself ", we need to think about the following three questions:

Why do we propose "learning, teaching and doing in one"?

In fact, education itself is a process of living. Without life, education is an illusory and meaningless behavior. In vocational colleges, students may be weak on abstract and logic ability and the ability of acquiring declarative knowledge, but their operation ability, imaginal thinking and other intelligence may be very outstanding. Facing this group, school should supply more abundant learning resources and other learning condition to discover and guide the students to study independently and in inquiry in order to let them have a better understanding on the knowledge and skill they need to grasp in the intelligent field that fit their own personal characteristics by motivating their intelligent potentiality. However, the rigid and obsolete talents training mode ties up students' thought, hurts students' confidence and suppresses students' potentiality.

Since 2012, Qingdao Technical College has adhered to the "people oriented" and "let every student be the best of him/herself" talent cultivation value orientation, reinspected education and teaching idea from a brand new perspective, made endeavor to explore and to start to set up "learning, teaching and doing in one" talents training mode, and established a new talents training mode based on learning, which means, in teaching activities, we need to meet students' growth needs and highlight the idea of "teach to learn". At the same time, we need to embody the dominant role of students and the leading function of learning to realize the close interaction between "teaching and learning", "learning and doing" and "teaching and doing".

What is "learning, teaching and doing in one"?

As is implied, learning refers to students' learning activities while teaching means teachers' instruction and doing is the practical activity in the process of learning and teaching, among which, learning is the purpose and internal reason while teaching is the external reason which means "teach to learn" and "doing is the carrier of learning and teaching". In the process of talent cultivation, learning, teaching and doing are interconnected and interacted within one unity, which emphasize the dominant role of students and highlight the idea and value orientation of learning-priority.

It is required in the implementation process of teaching activities that we need to face students' career in the future, to create learning context such as projects or cases as the carrier by bringing the real working tasks in career, to train students to grasp the way of thinking and behavior of learning, researching and working, and to improve depth and specialization degree of professional ability rather than monopolizing students' learning style and process according to teachers' own habit and methods or simply filling knowledge in students' brain by using blackboard, equipment and notes. By setting up the scaffold of assisting learning, teachers will let every students who live and study in the vocational college enjoy the happiness of obtaining knowledge, satisfy their own career interest, motivate their own potentiality and vitality and share the happiness of learning and life in the vocational college.

How to realize "learning, teaching and doing in one"?

The construction of "learning, teaching and doing in one" talents training mode is a project system, involving school-running function and organizational functioning of school and so on and so forth, among which curriculum is the most important part. To some extent, curriculum should be the product of school. Whether the product could become "studying commodity" and be good for sale, and let clients—students accept with pleasure, depends on whether the curriculum product could meet the clients' needs.

However, there are many curriculum problems in some of our colleges, which bring passive and negative affect for carrying out "learning, teaching and doing in one" talents training mode. Therefore, curriculum reform is imperative. Curriculum reform is the very basic insurance to construct "learning, teaching and doing in one" talents training mode.

Firstly, to integrate the idea of "everyone may become talent" in the education system, teaching process and cultivating practice. Through life concerning, growth focusing, ability highlighting and intelligence concerning, we turn quality into ability, transform methods into culture, create "brand course" and cultivate "brand student".

Vocational colleges, as administrator on the basic level for cultivation, should put effort to cultivate students' professional leadership in the process of students' cultivation. Therefore, we need to provide possible chance for students to accept sustainable professional theory and learning skill on a higher level, to train them to grasp the way of thinking and behavior of learning, researching and working and to improve depth and specialization degree of professional ability. Concurrently, we provide students the opportunity to hunt and transfer jobs crosswisely and broaden the field and width of employment. We concern both students' present by setting up professional skill guidance and students' future by establishing the direction of beautiful and meaningful life.

Secondly, to set up curriculum based on the idea of "suitable for

students' needs". Students' growth is an all-around comprehensive process. School, as the institution of cultivating people, is not only cultivating people on professional education and classroom teaching. The natural environment, institutional environment and cultural environment are also all key factors of cultivation. We need to break through traditional curriculum ideas, which considers that content shown merely in the teaching plan and textbook can be called curriculum. We also need to pay attention to tacit curriculum construction, promote cultural taste of college and manifest the model behavior of faculties and staffs to establish effective "big curriculum" system which respects students' instincts and law of growth.

Thirdly, to develop the main channel function of classroom teaching. Classroom teaching is the key to carry out the "learning, teaching and doing in one" talents training mode. During classroom teaching, teachers should use scientific and effective teaching methods to present harmonious and ecological class by using the teaching design which could embody students' vocational ability and development of life. Teachers, as the inductor, participator and coordinator, motivate students' initiative and enthusiasm, activate students' learning potential and create harmonious and ecological living class by multiple teaching methods such as problem-based teaching, seminar, case-based teaching and project activities.

Fourthly, to establish scientific and objective evaluation system. We should respect students' instincts and personalities, establish brand new view of talent and help them to find suitable course of growth. For the academic evaluation, we need to change the evaluation institution of determining winning and losing by only one exam, to set up multielement and stereo evaluation institution and let students who have different intelligent feature with different interest and specialty stand out and live with confidence and self-esteem.

Fifthly, to establish a global curriculum management system. For instance, we should enrich and perfect the connotation of curriculum, bring students' association activities, social practice, cultural quality education, literature and art quality, interests and specialty into curriculum management, formulate curriculum evaluation institution, promote curriculum quality with continuous improvement. We should also promote teachers' sense of curriculum, perfect teachers' curriculum cultural self-consciousness, give play to the function of teachers' curriculum accomplishment and change teachers' teaching behavioral pattern in class. We should enhance vocational education comparative research, bring advanced vocational education experience and curriculum standard from developed countries, make endeavor to localize them and increase the standardization, specialization and humanization of the curriculum as well.

Dear experts and colleagues, in order to explore talents training mode suitable for Chinese vocational education through using advanced curriculum ideas and teaching methods from vocational education in developed countries for reference, for one thing, vocational colleges need to accumulate exploration and experience, and for another thing, vocational colleges need to cooperate, communicate and share for mutual benefit. The exploration and practice of "learning, teaching and doing in one" talents training mode in Qingdao Technical College have just begun and still have a long way to go. So, dear experts and colleagues, please don't hesitate to offer your kind advice.

Thank you very much for your attention!

职业教育与培训的全球化——互相学习

新西兰怀卡托理工学院校长　马克·华

女士们，先生们：

早上好。

首先，感谢从中国职业教育研究所前来的各位领导，覃院长，企业领导，中国教育部官员，还有在座的出席今天会议的各位代表及发言人。

我非常荣幸能在此次中新职业教育研讨会上发言。本次研讨会为教学实习合作迈出了坚实的一步，并且巩固了2013年4月中国与新西兰双方政府和国家签署的教育声明。

我们两个国家在某些方面有着诸多不同，新西兰是一个400万人口的小国，中国是一个拥有14亿人口的大国。然而我们却拥有非常强大的纽带，正如在2008年中新双方签署的第一个自由贸易协定一样。

在过去的8年里，我拜访了中国20次。每次来，我都能学到新东西，同时也建立了新的关系网和友谊，开展了更多的合作。这应该是我们今天会议的目标。我本人非常荣幸能够站在今天研讨会的现场，此次会议标志着中新两国国际教育关系迈出了令人振奋的第一步。信息分享及相互学习教育方法是一个双向的过程，这也正是新西兰的教育理念。

今天在座的有11位从新西兰赶来的老师和研究员，随着今天会议的进展，我希望你们继续评估我们平时所学到的知识。通过评估我们可以获知事情进展的情况和各种不同的见解。相互学习必不可少。

在现代经济环境下，对可以为社会做贡献的技术类职工的需求日益增多。

在过去20年间，中国迅速完成了经济转型，经济实现全球化，为世界各地提供商品和服务。

　　同时，中国也经历了劳动力的快速城市化以及英语语言作为国际商业语言的不间断增长和发展。这些持续的增长需要连续投资和培养适应全球市场所需的技术工人。

　　当今中国经济的国际化和其与西方国家逐渐加强的紧密合作，使之完全改变了对技能需求的标准。其对劳动力的需求根据市场变成了需要语言能力、解决问题能力、数字计算能力和计算机能力过关的技术人才。

　　这些问题不是中国独有的，在新西兰，教育部门也总是肩负着开展学生技能和提高他们就业能力的责任。顺应这个改变的需求和达到产业部门的预期，需要教育部门建立起更强的产业联系，保证我们的学业学历在国内和国际上得到认可。

　　传统意义上讲，理工专科学院传授专修科目的课程，而在大学级学院传授本科和研究生级别的课程。可是这样一个严格的学历制度划分早已不能反映出现代产业对高技能工作人员的需求。在新西兰，我们看到了高质量教育的发展，确保理工学院和技术专科学院也同时传授本科和研究生级别的课程。

　　在其他一些国家，理工学院同时也被命名为科技大学。现如今在新西兰，您可以进入理工学院学习然后获得全国认可的与大学颁发具有相同标准的学位。这样一来也使理工学院类大学可以改变其教学方法，更好地与产业需求相结合，培养出适应今后社会发展需要的人才。

　　我们大家是如何着手实现的这个目标呢？新西兰职业教育部门是如何适应和面对这个挑战呢？

　　很显然，政府政策在这里起到决定作用。

　　国际教育产业是新西兰第五大出口产业。在2012年，教育产业为新西兰创造了24亿纽币的创收。我们的教育服务国际化，不仅仅表现为在新西兰日益增长的国际留学生的人数，还表现为我们把服务延伸至海外开展的合作办学、海外校区的建立和一些双学位学历的颁发。新西兰政府部门非常支持愿意承担这些工作和制定有效目标的学院。这些都在国际教育首脑声明中列成了规划。

　　更重要的是，新西兰总理承诺并渴望看到新西兰的教育院校在中国寻求愿意彼此学习的合作伙伴。

　　这些院校若要国际化发展，必须拥有政府强有力的支持。我们非常高兴地看到，新西兰教育部制定了明确的目标和发展蓝图来支持此项工作，并且提供了专门的资金投入和专家团队，以确保其起初阶段的顺利进行。

使一所学院国际化需要时间及人员上的投入，建筑物、基础设施和工作体系也会有显著和永久性的改变。新西兰已经有一部分学院开始了国际化的进程，同时也已经看到国际化为学生群体多样化与课程及内容设置带来的各项益处。

在哈密尔顿市，我们学校拥有1 000多名国际留学生，其中550名来自中国。这些留学生为学校的社区结构与城市和地区的经济发展起着至关重要的作用。据城市人口调查报告显示，有15%的人口为亚裔，其中很多都已在怀卡托省区取得商业成功。

中国职业教育发展有力地响应着其持续增长的经济和对人才劳动力的需求，同时也适宜新西兰的院校与中国模范技术学院合作，共同寻求双方感兴趣的课题，特别是在新西兰和中国技能市场需求方面彼此学习。

了解产业需求是我们设置任何课程时考虑的重要因素。现代产业不断寻找技能与特质都有所提升的毕业生。国际化大环境下，我们也注意到市场对毕业生学历的期望从证书、专科文凭，到本科和研究生级别的递增。作为理工学院，我们适应了这种需求的改变，提高了我们的学历级别并传授多项本科课程。

提供本科学历教学带给了我们益处和挑战。其中一个积极的方面是教学能力的提高，包括传授高级技能和培养具有判断性思考能力及问题解决能力的毕业生。当然，这也需要学校多方面的大力投入，如在职工进修与招聘、校内科研文化的发展、为保证学生成功而提供的支持服务方面。在一所学院学习从专科、本科到研究生级别的多项课程，也是接受新西兰职业教育课程的独特方面。

比例上，49%的在校学生就读于本科或者研究生课程，72%的学生年龄超过20周岁，学校在保证现有学生数量的同时一直在不断扩大招生。

我们在确保帮助学生进入更高级别课程学习、保证他们学习的课程方面是领域中最优秀的。

中国在职业教学领域和本科级别课程学习之间仍然划分界限。在理工专业学校开展资质和开发能力的同时，针对专业领域强项开发本科课程，也许是在座的各位及贵校获得声誉的一个契机。

在一所国际化的学院学习从专科到本科课程，发掘及培养学生能力带给我们的是挑战和奖励。行业中寻找的是那些具有独立操作、横向思考、解决问题和跨文化环境工作能力的毕业生。

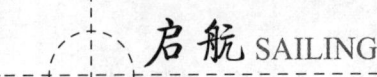

这些技能需要通过一系列的工作策略去传授给学生，包括团队合作、学生科研项目、课堂学习及把科学技术嵌入到教学大纲里。当设置课程或者修建硬件设施时，这些有意识的决定就会随着战略目标执行，以确保我们创造的环境使学生能够学到所需的技能，并能鼓励他们进行跨文化交流。

这些都是关键技能和我们毕业生成功的显著特点。为行业提供优秀毕业生，使他们具有IT技术、良好的计算能力、沟通能力、能够遵循复杂的指令、问题解决能力和独立上手能力。培养这些毕业生需要我们对如何传授课程和运用什么手段的工作加以改变。

此次研讨会将会共同探讨多方面的方法与手段和如何将它们应用在职业教育培训领域中。

另一方面，在新西兰学习的国际留学生通常需要额外的英语语言支持、写作报告的帮助和适应一个更加以学生为中心的教学风格的转向。这些方面都将会在今天和明天晚些时候由新西兰方面的发言人做出阐述。

当您在新西兰学习的时候，其中一个最大的不同将会是从传统笔试教育到一个以学生为中心教学方式的转变。这方面对于我前面所提及的技能发展有着诸多优势，但是对于国际学生来讲，将是对他们学习方法的一个转变。我们必须加强双方合作，找到双方教学风格各自的特点，寻求一个适合新西兰和中国的教育解决方案。

我们当然还需要理解和看到学生们自己也在改变和适应着这个社会。他们有着诸多围绕在新西兰学什么和怎么学的问题及期望，我们已经注意到他们在新科技领域的兴趣和所寄予的厚望。我们的学生有很强的电脑操作能力，愿意在网络上获得信息，自在地使用电子书籍和在线资源，在课堂外也自主地使用不同科技产品与同学沟通，总是期望我们学院能够提供无缝且可靠的网络覆盖以实现他们个人移动设备的信息沟通。这样就需要我们学院投入很大精力去改变和重新设计信息科技的基础设施。随着我们学院国际化，我们还进一步发展信息科技，提供多语言支持，进行电话会议并综合利用不同资源。

那么，在座的各位能够相互学习什么呢？

很明显，我们在通过职业化培训提高员工技能的道路上有着共同的目标。新西兰已经选择了质量有保证的高等学府使之可以传授最高学位和研究生学历，并向政府部门展示，他们可以给毕业生高质量的教学体验。当前产业发展迅速，顺应着不断变化的世界。各所学院需要以当前产业所需改变和调整自己的课程。灵活的课程设计和审批是至关重要的，尤其是当我们期待着国际化教学发展时。

学生期望的是学院提供优质的服务，期望学院可以积极响应、参与和客户为中心，并最终使他们具备技能拥有就业机会。他们注重教育排名、学院业绩和成绩表，十分在意来自社区网络的反馈和来自朋友、家人的意见。他们的投资是相当巨大的，并且在这个日益相互联接的世界里，学院本身必须率先培养能在世界范围工作的毕业生。

这次会议是我们中新两国建立承诺、相互分享和学习的重要里程碑。通过分析技能需求和现有的最佳实习模式，我们希望最终在各自的国家提供给学生需要的服务和引领时代的职业教学。我衷心希望大家能够喜欢本次教育研讨会并且相互学习。

谢谢。

Internationalisation of Vocational Education and Training—Learning From Each Other

Mark Flowers, President of Waikato Institute of Technology

Ladies and gentlemen:

Good morning.

I would like to start by acknowledging Senior Officials from CIVTE, President Qin, Industry Leaders, Officials from China MOE and of course the Delegates and Presenters here today.

It is my pleasure to speak at this inaugural Sino-NZ TVET symposium. This symposium is a great step forward in collaboration around teaching practice and underpins the Educational Statement signed between our two governments and countries in April 2013.

In some ways we are so very different: NZ is a small country of 4 million, China is a large country of 1.4 billion. However, we have very strong ties, as was shown when we signed the first free trade agreement back in 2008.

During the past eight years I have visited China 20 times. Each time I learn something new. I also form new relationships and friendships and these lead onto forming new links. That is what we should all aim to get out of today. I'm proud to be standing here at today's symposium, which marks the first step in an exciting new relationship between China and New Zealand for international education. The sharing of information, and learning from each other about different approaches to education is a two-way process, and very much a New Zealand approach to education.

Today we have 11 teachers and researchers presenting from across New Zealand, and I'd encourage you all to continue to evaluate what we've learned as we go through the day. It is through evaluation that we gain progress and insights. Learning from each other is essential.

We live in modern economies, with growing demands on our society to maintain and develop skilled employees who can contribute to society.

China has in the past 20 years seen a rapid transformation of its economic base, into a global economy, contributing goods and services across the world.

It has also seen a rapid urbanization of its workforce and the continued growth and development of English as an international business language. Sustaining that growth requires an ongoing investment in and development of a skilled workforce capable of meeting the demanding needs of a global market.

As China internationalizes its economy and promotes stronger links to western countries, it ultimately changes the skills required from its workforce to support those markets including increased language skills,

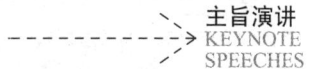

problem solving, numeracy and IT literacy.

These issues are not unique to China, in New Zealand we see continued pressure on Institutions to improve students' skills and increase their employability. Adjusting to the changing needs and expectations of industry requires Institutions to build stronger linkages into Industry and look to ensure that our qualifications are nationally and internationally recognized.

Traditionally, Polytechnics taught to sub degree level and Degree and Post Graduate levels were taught by Universities. However such a strict separation of qualifications does not reflect the workforce of today, with the increased demand by modern industries to have highly skilled staff. In New Zealand we have seen the development of quality assured Polytechnics and Institution of Technology that teach at Degree and Post Graduate levels.

In other countries such Institutions would be known as Universities of Technology. Today in New Zealand you can attend Institutes of Technology and study and gain a nationally approved Degree of the same standard as that given by a university. This has allowed the Polytechnic sector to change its approach to teaching and also better align to the changing needs of industry creating students capable of contributing to today and tomorrow's society.

So how did we get there, how has the New Zealand VET sector adapted and met this challenge?

Clearly, Government policy is critical.

International education is our 5th largest export industry generating $2.4 billion dollars in 2012. Internationalizing our educational services will not only see us grow student numbers in New Zealand, it will also see us extend our services offshore with joint programmes, off shore campuses and dual awards being offered. The Government is supportive of Institutions who want to undertake such work and have set appropriate targets for the sector to reach. These were set out in the Leadership Statement for International Education.

More importantly, the Minister made a clear commitment and desire to see the educational providers in New Zealand stretch out their hands into China to find partners who wanted to learn from each other.

For Institutes to develop internationally, there has to be strong support from Government and we are pleased to see that Education New Zealand have strong objectives and targets to support such work and where appropriate suitable funding and expertise will be secured to help start the process.

Internationalizing an Institution takes time, investment in staff, buildings, infrastructure and systems that will significantly and permanently alter the way they operate. It's a process that a number of institutes in New Zealand have started and are already seeing dividends in the diversity of their student population and in the design and content of their programmes.

In Hamilton, we have over 1,000 international students, 550 from China. They contribute immensely to the social fabric of our Institution and increasingly to the City and regional economy. Our city has 15% of its population who describe themselves as Asian and have set up successful businesses in the Waikato region.

China's VET sector is growing strongly responding to continued economic growth and workforce demand. It's appropriate for New Zealand institutions to align with model polytechnics in China, looking for areas of mutual interest and to learn from each other especially where they align to New Zealand and China's skill demand areas.

Understanding the needs of industry is a critical component in the design of any programme. Industry are constantly looking for their graduates to have improved skills and attributes. Internationally we have seen professions increase their qualification expectation of graduates from certificate to Diplomas to Degrees and in some cases to Post Graduate level. As Institutes of Technology we have had to adapt to these changing demands by raising our qualification levels including the important threshold of offering Degrees.

This move to degree level teaching brought rewards and challenges. A positive aspect was the ability to teach highly technical skills and develop graduates with critical thinking skills and problem solving abilities. Of course it also required significant investment in staff development, recruitment, the development of a research culture within the organization and an overhaul of our support services to ensure students were successful. It is part of the unique perspective of New Zealand vocational education that you can study at a Diploma, Degree and Post Graduate level within one organization.

49% of students study at Degree or Post Graduate Level, 72% are over 20 years of age, we retain and progress a significant number of students.

Indeed when it comes to supporting students into higher level study and ensuring they stay studying we are among the best in the sector.

China still has a demarcation between vocational level teaching and degrees level study. As your Polytechnics develop their capacity and capability perhaps there will be opportunities for a number of you to gain accreditation to offer degree level programmes in specialist areas.

Developing the capabilities of our students to study at Diploma and Degree level within an internationalized institution has been challenging and rewarding. Industry are looking for graduates who can operate independently, think laterally, problem solve and work in an intercultural environment.

These skills need to be taught to students through a range of strategies including group work, student based projects, class work and the embedding of technology into the syllabus. These are conscious decision taken at a strategic level when designing programmes or building facilities to ensure that we create an environment that supports students to learn such skills and encourage cross cultural exchanges.

These are critical skills and are a significant part of the success of our graduates. Producing graduates, who are IT literate, have good numeracy skills, can use IT competently, can communicate and follow complex instructions, problem solving and act independently are skills identified by Industry. Creating graduates requires a change in how we teach and the tools we use.

This symposium will look at a range of these tools and how they can be applied to the vocational sector.

In addition, International students who study in New Zealand generally require additional support with English language, report writing and a shift to a more student centric teaching style. These aspects will be discussed by some of the New Zealand presenters later today and tomorrow.

One of the key differences when you study in New Zealand will be the shift from a traditional teaching style of "wrote learning" to a more student centered approach. This has its advantages in developing the skills I have mentioned earlier but for international students it's quite a change in their learning style. We all have to look at ways that we can learn from each other to incorporate the best of each style and find a solution that can be applied in New Zealand and in China.

Of course we need to understand that students themselves are also changing and adapting to society. They have expectations around what and how they will learn and in New Zealand this is clearly seen in their interest in and expectations around new technology. Our students are very IT literate, want to access information on the web, are comfortable using e-books and online resources, want to stay engaged with their fellow students outside the classroom and expect our Institutions to deliver a seamless reliable mobile service. That has put considerable strain on our Institutions to change its IT infrastructure to meet these needs and building these into new building designs. As Institutions develop internationally this extends into IT support in other languages, video conference delivery and collaboration around resources.

So what lessons can we share with each other?

Clearly, we are both on a similar journey wanting to develop highly skilled staff across a range of vocational disciplines. New Zealand has taken the approach that select quality assured Institutes can teach up to Degree and Post Graduate level where they can demonstrate to government that the graduates will have a quality teaching experience. Industry continues to develop rapidly in response to the changing world we live in, and Institutions need to adapt and change their curriculum to meet industry needs. Flexibility in course design and approval is critical, especially as we look to internationalize our teaching.

Students are looking for a quality service from Institution, both in terms of being responsive, engaged, customer focused and to ultimately equip them with the skills that will allow them to gain employment. Students look at educational rankings, performance and league tables, feedback on social networks and feedback from friends and family. Their investment is sizeable and in an increasingly connected world it is the Institutions themselves who have to take the lead in providing relevant services that develop graduates that can work internationally.

This conference is an important milestone in our China and New Zealand's commitment to sharing and learning from each other, to look at the skills and best practice available and ultimately provide the types of services to students that place us at the forefront of vocational teaching in our respective countries. I hope you will enjoy the educational symposium and learn from each other.

Xiexie.

行业指导 校企合作
是高职人才培养的有效途径

天津轻工职业技术学院　戴裕崴

各位领导，各位专家，各位来宾，各位同仁：

大家上午好！

我是天津轻工职业技术学院院长戴裕崴。天津轻工职业技术学院非常荣幸得到教育部国际合作与交流司批准，和中国教育部职业教育研究所、青岛职业技术学院一起，借助这个项目成为新西兰职业教育的合作伙伴。今年6月我也非常有幸为这个合作项目专程到新西兰怀卡托理工学院进行了专题访问。刚才马克校长谈到，校企合作是中国职业教育的特色，我在新西兰怀卡托理工学院访问的时候，恰恰赶上了他们的校园开放日，他们把雇主（合作企业）请到学校与在校生以及即将报考他们学校的学生见面，场景非常热烈，我想这也是新西兰校企合作的一种方式。今年8月，我们学院8位教师又专程到新西兰怀卡托理工学院进行了为期两周的专业方面的学习与培训，效果非常好。

天津轻工职业技术学院坐落在海河教育园区，目前占地面积50多万平方米，建筑面积16万平方米，是2011年3月整体入驻的新校区。目前学院有六大专业群，29个高职专业，一个技能型本科专业，在校生7 600余人。学校从2008年开始连续六年承办全国职业院校技能大赛模具类和新能源类两项比赛，这两个专业也是学校重点投入建设的专业。学校是教育部财政部批准的100所示范性骨干高职院校的建设单位。中国的职业教育有一个显著的特点，就是要和经济发展相匹配、相适应。中国经济现在正从经济大国向经济强国迈进，经济发展方式要转变，产业结构要升级与调整。这种形势下，我认为培养技术技能型高职专门人才，需要政府主导、行业指导、企业参与。我个人有一个观点，一个高职学院存在的价值，关键在于对区域经济发展的贡献度。如果一个高职学院对区域经济发展贡献度不高，它的存在意义就不大。本次论坛主题是教学法，这个主题设置得非常好，从最基本的教学法开始讲起，让学生了解教学内容。但是有一个前提，就是学校教给学生的知识和技能，应该是企业或区域经济发展所需要的。

我今天演讲的题目是"行业指导、校企合作是高职人才培养的有效途径"，内容分为以下四个部分：

一、依托行业指导，创新校企合作的体制机制

天津轻工职业技术学院在校企合作体制机制方面有两个层面：第一是在轻工行业层面，学院组建了天津轻工职业教育集团；第二是在学院层面，成立了学院校企合作董事会。轻工职教集团以我们学院为龙头，核心层包括轻工行业内的中等职业技术学校、行业内骨干企业，还有行业内的科研院所以及行业其他高职院校，还有一些外围的企业，但是紧密层是行业内的。轻工职教集团的主要作用是整合轻工行业资源，包括中高职的衔接和企业、科研院所以及学校在轻工行业内的合作培养，优势互补。我们学院层面校企合作的董事会单位来自全国7个省市，共14家企业。进入董事会的成员单位遴选原则有三条：第一是能够指导学院现有专业及专业群的发展；第二是学院相关专业相对应的行业的龙头企业，当然这些企业还必须与学院有紧密的、深层次的、全方位的合作关系；第三是这些企业能够将行业最先进的技术和最先进的行业标准，以及对职业人才的要求带入专业建设和课程建设。

董事会能起到什么作用呢？我们把校企合作的体制称为"三级贯通式"。在学校层面，最高层是校企合作董事会，是校企合作的决策平台；二级学院层面为校企合作的执行委员会，是贯彻落实的平台；在29个专业层面，是专业建设委员会，它是专业建设和课程建设的操作平台。校企合作董事会成员一般情况下是企业总裁或分管专业教育的总裁，校企合作执行委员会成员是企业负责培训或教育的副总裁或部门经理，专业建设委员会由企业技术人员组成，因为专业层面涉及具体专业、特别是课程合作问题。校企合作董事会成员单位绝大多数来自我们行业以外，所以我们还面临形成互利共赢局面的问题。我们配合校企合作的体制，出台了19项制度。

二、校企合作模式

我院与校企合作董事会14个成员单位的合作有四种模式，分别是指导性的合作模式、双主体育人合作模式、共建校内实训基地模式、递进式合作升级模式。我院与天津模具工业协会、天津新能源协会合作属于指导性的合作模式，这是因为模具和新能源是我们的重点专业，所以和地方的行业协会的合作是非常紧密的，同时也是一种指导性的合作关系。

双主体育人合作模式很典型的案例是我们与数控机床龙头企业大连机床集团的合作。大连机床集团和我们合作在天津投资20亿，建立了大连机床研发制造基地，同时在基地与我们合作设立了企业培训中心，这也是我院学生学习的另一个课堂。同时，大连机床在我院内设立了大连机床天津地区技术服务中心，由我院教师和学生共同来完成产品在天津地区的售后维修，我们称之为"校中厂"。再举一个案例，我院和中国汽车模具行业第一名——天津汽车模具有限公司合作。天津汽车模具有限公司是目前中国最大的汽车模具企业，是上市公司，我们跟它的合作基本也属于双主体育人合作模式。当然，两者合作专业不同，大连机床集团和我们数维专业合作，天津汽模是我们的模具专业合作。

三、校企合作共建校内实训基地

这里有两个比较典型的案例，第一个案例是和上海三菱电梯的合作，上海三菱电梯是中国电梯行业产销量第一的企业，与它合作的形式是它在无偿为我院提供价值500万元的四部电梯和相关实训设备，在院内建设实训基地。这个基地既是我院机电一体化专业电梯维修方向学生的实训基地，又是上海三菱电梯华北大区的员工培训中心。第二个案例是和中国最大也是全球新能源产业光伏发电最大的企业英利集团的合作。我们与英利集团共同投入，同时借助了天津滨海新区的资金支持，共建了全国高职院校首个校内真实的光伏发电站，这个光伏发电站同时也是我们和英利集团在天津共建的光伏产业研发中心。

四、递进式合作模式，即传统的合作企业如何递进升级

举一个案例，我们和德国菲尼克斯公司的合作。德国菲尼克斯公司是世界现场总线技术的发明者，我们跟菲尼克斯的合作已经有十年的历史了。过去，合作模式是共建校内实训基地，十年前，它们投入了产品和现场总线技术，在学校内建设了现场总线一体化实训基地。在过去合作的基础上，菲尼克斯公司在我院建设了中国华北地区产品展示中心和技术服务中心，公司最新的产品、技术在我们这里向用户

展示。借助它最新的产品和技术，我们的专业教师和公司的技术人员共同开发教材进行师资培训和员工培训，菲尼克斯公司还在学院设立了菲尼克斯专门的学生奖学金。近几年，我们贯彻校企合作的人才培养模式，学院人才培养质量提高的效果是非常明显的，我们专业的社会影响力和专业对区域服务的能力也大幅度提高，同时也大幅度提高了企业对我院学生的满意度以及学生就业的竞争力。

2012年天津市教委委托第三方对天津市所有本科和高职院校进行了学生就业方面的调研和测评，我院毕业生就业竞争力在天津市26所高职院校中排名第一。我院还连续两年被评为天津市普通高校创新创业教育与就业工作示范学校。2013年，有关方面对全国高职院校进行了用人单位满意度测评，经过各省市推荐，在优选后的26所高职院校中，我院排名第13位。

以上是我关于校企合作培养高职人才有效途径的发言。欢迎各位领导，各位同仁，各位来宾和朋友莅临天津轻工职业技术学院指导工作。

谢谢！

Industry Guidance and School-Enterprise Cooperation is the Effective Way of the Vocational Education

Dai Yuwei, Tianjin Light Industry Vocational Technical College

Respectable leaders, experts, guests, teachers,

Good morning!

I am Dai Yuwei, president of Tianjin Light Industry Vocational Technical College. The title of my speech is "Industry Guidance and School-Enterprise Cooperation is the Effective Way of the Vocational Education". It is honored for Tianjin Light Industry Vocational Technical College, together with the Vocational Education Institute of Chinese Ministry of Education, Qingdao Vocational College, to build up the vocational cooperation relationship with New Zealand. In June this year, I visited Waikato Institute of Technology.

President Mark just mentioned that School-Enterprise Cooperation is featured in Chinese vocational education. There was the School Open Day during my visit. It was very impressive to see the active scene, in which the school invited the employers to come to the campus meeting the students who would be enrolled. I think this is one of the NZ ways of the School-Enterprise Cooperation. In August this year, our 8 teachers had professional study and training for two weeks in Wintec which already had very good feedback. The following are my report.

  The campus of Tianjin Light Industry Vocational Technical College moved to Haihe Education Park in March 2011, covering an area over 500,000 square meters with 160,000 square meters in construction area. There are 7,600 students covering six professional groups, 29 professional majors, 1 professional major at bachelor level. We successfully held the National Vocational Skill Competition for 6 years since 2008 in the Mold Design and New Energy areas. These two majors are also the important developing areas in our college. We are approved as the national vocational excellent constructive school by the Ministry of Education and the Ministry of Finance. Vocational education is regarded as the best service education type which has very close connection and direct contribution to the development of the economy society. With the trend of the transition from the big economic country to the powerful economic country, the changing of the economy developing, upgrading and adjusting of the industry structures, I think training skillful vocational college personnel needs government support, industry guidance and enterprise participation. I have a personal opinion that the value of a vocational college depends on how much she can contribute to the regional economy development. A worthless college is the one without any contribution. The theme of our forum is "Teaching Method". It is a very good one. We discuss from the basic teaching methods in order to let our students understand what they are learning. But we need to remember that the knowledge and skills our students are learning should be what are needed for enterprises and regional economy development.

There are four parts for my speech:

I. Relying on Industry Guidance and Innovative School-Enterprise Cooperation System

There are two platforms of School-Enterprise Cooperation System at TLIVTC. One is at the light industry level which establishes the Tianjin Light Industry Vocational Education Group; the other one is at the college level which set up the board of the School-Enterprise Cooperation. Our college is the leader in the vocational education group. The core participants are the vocational schools in light industry, leading companies, industry research institutes, other colleges as well as other related industry companies. The main task is to integrate resources, cooperate and train the skilled professionals for industry need. We achieve geographical and spatial complementary advantages. The board of the School-Enterprise Cooperation consists of 14 companies covering 7 provinces in China. There are three principles to be selected into the board: guiding the current major and major development for college, leading industry companies which have close relationship with the college and bring the advanced skills, industry standards and the professional personnel requirements into professional and curriculum constructions.

What's the function of the board? We call it "Three-level reforms" which sets up the school-enterprise cooperation executive committee and the professional construction committee to make effective decisions on the professional development and the personnel development. At college level, we set up school-enterprise cooperation executive committee which involves the implement for the Board's decisions. At the 29 majors, we call it professional construction committee which is the professional and construction and operation platform. The member of the School-Enterprise Cooperation Board consists of CEO or the manager who is in charge of education. The vice CEO, the manager or director who is in charge of education in the companies are the members of the executive committee. Skilled personnel from the companies participate in professional construction committee due to the specific areas and curriculums. The members of the School-Enterprise Cooperation Board are mainly out of our industry. So we set up 19 regulations for win-win policy.

II. School-Enterprise Cooperation Model

There are 4 models to have cooperation with 14 companies from the board of School-Enterprise Cooperation. They are the Model of Guidance, the Model of Double-Subject Education, the Model of Establishing Training Centers and the Model of the Progressive Cooperation Upgrade. We have close cooperation with Tianjin Mode Industry Association and Tianjin New Energy Association. Both are our important majors. The industry associations also offer guidance.

Double-Subject Education Model is mainly applied in CNC equipment application and maintenance, cooperating with Dalian Machine Tool Group Co., Ltd. Dalian Group has cooperated with us and invested 2 billion to establish Dalian Equipment Research Manufacture Base and Enterprise Training Center. It is regarded as another classroom for students and Dalian Equipment Service Center in Tianjin Area. It is called "the company in the school" according to which our teachers and students are responsible for the repairing in Tianjin area. Another case is the cooperation with Tianjin Mold Association which is the top one in Chinese car mode industry. Our TMA is the largest car mode manufacturing company. The cooperation with Dalian focuses on the CNC maintenance while with TMA is on Mold area.

III. Establishing Training Centers

One of the two typical cases is the cooperation with Shanghai Mitsubishi Elevator Co., Ltd. Shanghai Mitsubishi Elevator Co., Ltd. holds the number one sales percentage in domestic market. They donated four elevators and related equipment which are worth 5 million yuan. This center not only serves students in Mechatronics, but also is the training center for Mitsubishi Employees in North China area. The other typical case is the cooperation with Yingli New Energy Group Co., Ltd. Tianjin Yingli Group is the largest vertically integrated photovoltaic manufacturer both at home and abroad. Our cooperation with Yingli New Energy Group Co., Ltd. supported by Tianjin Binhai New Area set up the first real solar power station in Chinese college campus. This station is also the research center for both of us.

IV. Progressive Cooperation Upgrade, which means upgrading the traditional cooperation.

For instance, the cooperation with the cooperation with Phoenix Contact (Nanjing) Inc. for more than 10 years. Phoenix invented the field bus control system. In the past, they invested products and bus control system and established a field bus control integration training center, which is the previous cooperation mode. Based on the past cooperation, Phoenix set up North China Production Exhibition Center and Professional Service Center on our campus. With the latest production and technology, our professors and their experts work together to develop teaching materials and undertake teacher and employee training. Phoenix also set up Phoenix scholarship. In recent years, we implement the School-Enterprise Cooperation in personnel training mode, and the quality of personnel training has effectively improved. Our professional social influence and professional regional service ability have also increased

significantly. Meanwhile, the industry evaluation of students and the students employment competence have also greatly improved.

2012 Tianjin Education Commission commissioned a third party to conduct an employment survey on undergraduate students evaluation, and our graduate employability and competitiveness ranked the first place in Tianjin among 26 vocational colleges. Our college has continuously been rewarded as the Excellent Tianjin innovated employment education college for two years. In 2013, the authorities conducted a nationwide vocational colleges employer satisfaction survey, in which we ranked 13th place among the 26 vocational colleges which were recommended by different provinces.

Such is my speech for the Effective Way of School-Enterprise Cooperation. Invitations to leaders, distinguished colleagues, ladies and gentlemen and friends to visit our school.

Thank you!

三、优秀教学法研讨
Symposium: Excellent Vocational Teaching

学徒制教学法

新西兰基督城理工学院教育发展中心　Selena Chan

背　景

工作场所的学徒学习涉及学习专业从业者身上广为认可和体现的行业实践。学习基于行业的职业技能除了能力以外，还要边干边学，刻意练习和学会思考，与同行、同事和导师一起构建或创建专业知识。该报告站在学徒的角度介绍了他们如何学习技术。

工作场所对学习者来说有时候是一个比较困难的学习环境，因为学徒们不确定有多少参与共创性学习的机会。对实际技巧的获取也知之甚少。在新西兰，顺利完成学徒阶段的人数一直很少，且不同行业之间也存在明显差异。

文献基础

学徒的主要目的是确保通过适当的培训和以实践为主的学习后能够成为合格的从业人员，可以胜任技工或工匠的工作及承担责任。

社会教育者强调在学习过程中个人和社会两者同等重要。因此，在学习如何成为行业从业人员时，学习过程中学习互动的作用不可忽视；人们通常通过对非言语信号的潜意识的解读和对周边环境的细心观察来达到对主体间关系的理解。从社会生物学和社会文化的角度来看，学习起源于本体论，比如天生的才能和亲和力与在后天生活中学到的技能、知识和性格相结合。

除此之外，当代的学习理论现在承认学习的社会物质性，该观点对目前理解人类如何学习提出了挑战。社会物质性将历史焦点从认知、个体和社会，如社会文化方面，转移到了学习者与工具、科技、团体（包括人类和动物）、行为和物体的相互作用。学习和其他人类行为应该被理解为是流动的、动态的和复杂的，而不是静止的。

近期关于职业教育学的研究对学生学习实用技能和知识的方式进行了总结。此项目运用 Lucas 等人提出的学习方式把学徒们用来学习行业知识的学习方式进行分类。学习方式包括：

• 单独的学习方式：通过观察、模仿、实践来学习和快速学习。

• 学习者用来理解并提高学习成果的策略：批判性思维方式、聆听、抄录和记忆、画草图、打草稿和反思。

• 由其他工作人员、培训人员和上司通过下列方式所提供的直接帮助：辅导、提供反馈信息、交谈和解决现实工作中的问题。

• 间接帮助：参加技能比赛，教他人学习和帮助他人。

• 运用科技手段加强的学习和教学方法：虚拟环境、模拟场景、角色表演和游戏。

重要的是一定要明白在工作场所的学习是多样的、复杂的，并且会受到多种社会文化因素及工作场所的局限，所以从正规院校教学派生出来的学习理论并不能完全适用于职场学习。对上述概念的总结见下面的图1。

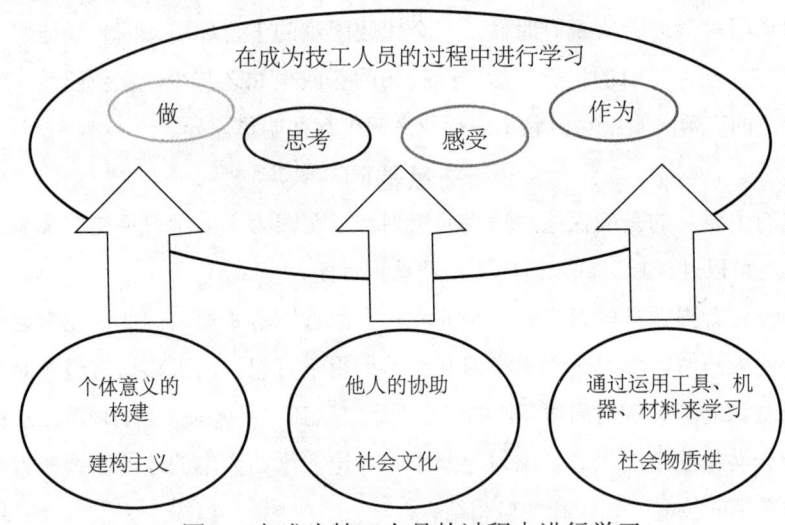

图1 在成为技工人员的过程中进行学习

研究方法

对学徒们进行了电话采访以找出他们是如何学习技能的。我们运用了现象解释学的方法来了解学徒们在工作场所的学习体验。

我们做了一个文献综述，在前面章节简单介绍了当代学习理论，旨在让职业教育者可以将参考文献融入到实际教学中。对学习成为技工人员的过程中的很多方面都难以进行量化统计，因此，核心的分析方法是理解学徒们是如何学习行业技能的，并找出特征教育学或一些专业职业技能行业采用的主要学习方法。

此项研究发现学徒学习大多采用多种"学习方式"，辅以极频繁的辅导，通过观察和实践来学习等方式，该结论与其他一些研究结果相似。学徒通过观察、实践、辅导和提问的方式学习在调查数据中出现的频率最高（参见表格2a和2b中的简介）。有趣的是他们提到信息反馈这一学习方式的频率非常低，尽管提问、交谈和教他人学习被认为是学徒们很重要的学习方式。

表格2a　每个方法和策略在学徒回答中的出现频率

观察	模仿	实践	批判性思维	聆听、抄录和回忆	画草图&打草稿	思考
15	3	21	1	4	1	4

表格2b　与其他人一起学习或向其他人学习的方式在学徒回答中出现的频率

辅导	信息反馈	对话	解决问题	提问	教授其他人
16	1	5	4	14	7

指南的制定主要围绕两个对学徒学习起重要作用的因素——学徒机构和工作场所为保证工作场所学习效果所提供的条件。两者需要保持同步以便能进行"共创性学习"。所以，对于学徒来说，他们可以运用此指南提供的工作程序让自己成为一名尽职的从业者，能够进行反思性学习从而成为有能力的问题解决者。相应地，该指南能协助辅导人员运用提供有价值的反馈信息的策略，通过模型化、辅导、支持框架和退出帮助学徒学习。在辅导过程中，必须帮助学徒看清行业技能学习中的许多细微的差别，且培训人员和辅导人员要多注意新手工人的学习需求。

图2和3是该指南的图解。

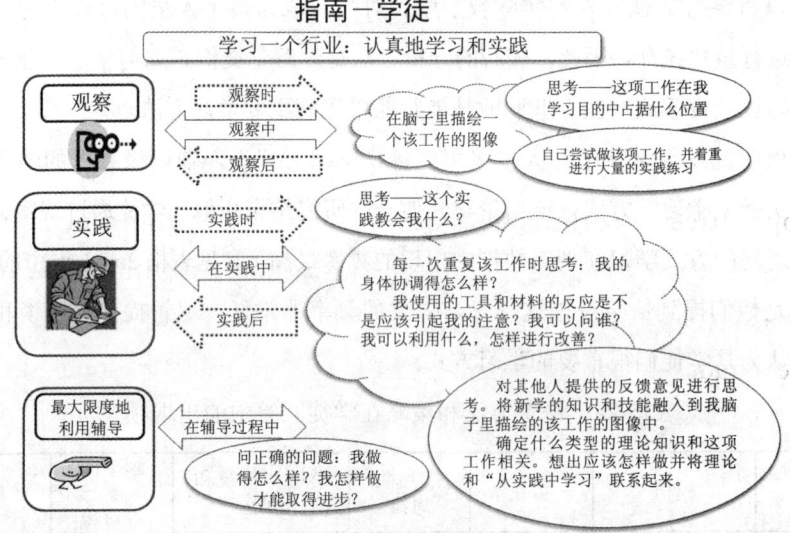

图2 学徒的指南

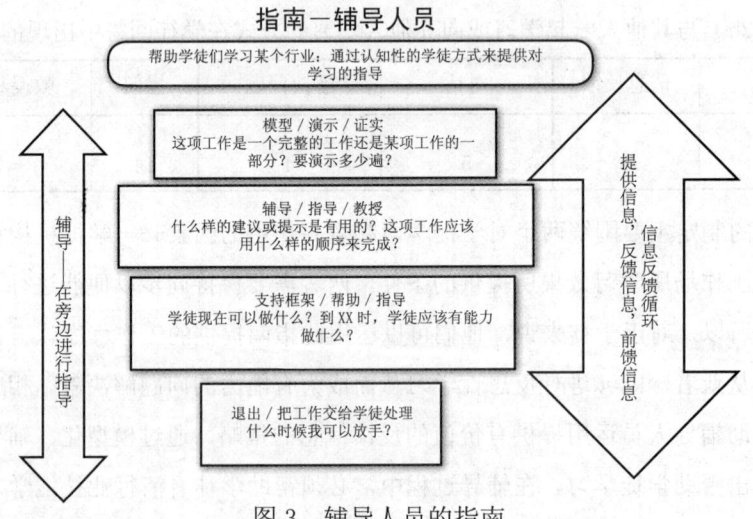

图3 辅导人员的指南

Learning a Trade Through Apprenticeship

Dr. Selena Chan, Centre for Educational Development, Christchurch Polytechnic Institute of Technology,
New Zealand

Background

Apprentices' workplace learning involves learning occupational practices as recognised and embodied in expert practitioners. Learning trade-based occupational skills goes beyond competency. Learning to become a trades person encompasses aspects of learning by doing, deliberate and reflective practice, and co-construction or co-creation of specialist understandings with peers, co-workers and mentors.

There is recognition that the workplace is sometimes a difficult environment for learners with apprentices having variable access to expansive participative learning opportunities. Additionally, the attainment of practical skills is still poorly understood. In NZ, completion rates of apprentices have been low with marked variability across industry sectors.

Literature Foundation

The main objective of apprenticeship is to ensure apprentices have access to adequate training and practice-based learning to become competent practitioners, entrusted with trade workers' or crafts persons' work tasks and responsibilities.

Socio-culturists advocate the importance of both the individual and the social in how learning occurs. Therefore, in learning how to become, there is the contribution of learning interactional expertise; attaining inter-subjective understandings often through subconscious interpretation of non-vocal signals and learning through circumspection or by looking around.

The socio-biological and socio-cultural perspectives considers learning to have ontological origins, i.e., innate talents or affinities combined with skills, knowledge and dispositions learnt through the life course.

Additionally, contemporary learning theory now recognises the aspect of socio-materiality which challenges current understandings of how people learn. Socio-materiality shifts the historical focuses from the cognitive, individual and social, i.e., socio-cultural, towards learners' interactions with tools, technologies, bodies (including human and animal), actions and objects. Instead of static relationships, learning and other human activities are to be understood as being fluid, dynamic and complex.

Recent work on vocational pedagogy summarises the ways in which students learn practical skills and knowledge. The ways of learning as suggested by Lucas et al. are used in this project to categorise apprentices' perceived approaches to learning their trade. Ways of learning include:

•Individual approaches: learning by watching, imitating, practising and learning on the fly.

•Strategies used by learners to make sense of and improve learning: learning to think critically, listening, transcribing and remembering, drafting and sketching and reflection.

•Direct assistance from other workers, trainers, supervisors through: coaching, providing feedback, conversation and real-world problem solving.

•Indirect assistance: competing in skills competitions and teaching and helping others.

•Technology enhanced learning and teaching methods assisting learning: virtual environments, simulation, role play and games.

A proviso is to understand workplace learning as multimodal, complex and influenced by diverse socio-cultural nature and boundaries of workplaces. Therefore, theories of learning derived from formal education may not be fully transferable.

A summary of the concepts is provided in Figure 1 below.

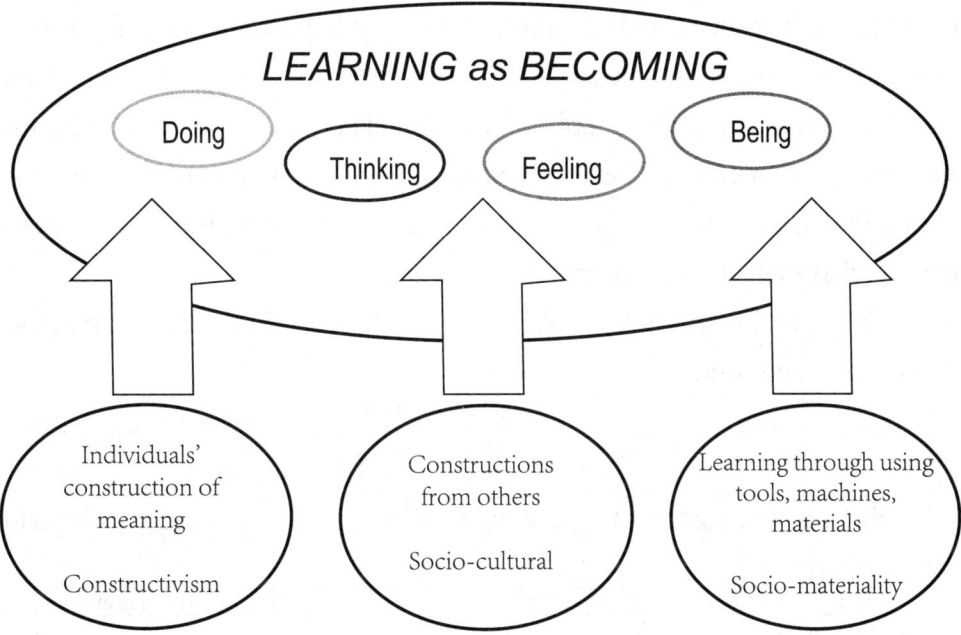

Figure 1 Learning as Becoming

Research Methods

Apprentices were interviewed by telephone to discuss how they learnt their trade skills. A phenomenographical approach was used to understand how apprentices experience workplace learning.

A literature review, as briefly summarised in the previous section, was conducted of contemporary learning theories with the aim of contextualising the literature for vocational educators. Many of the aspects of learning through becoming are difficult to quantify, therefore, the central analytical approach is to understand how apprentices approach learning a trade and to identify signature pedagogies or the main learning approaches of specialist trade occupations.

This study found the frequency of the various "ways of learning", with high frequencies of coaching, learning by watching and practice, is similar to other studies. In particular, the hallmarks of apprenticeship learning–learning by watching, practising, coaching and through enquiry–occur with the highest frequencies through the interview data (see Tables 2a and 2b for summary). Of interest is the very low frequency of commenting on aspects of feedback, although enquiry, conversation and teaching others were identified as important ways apprentices learn.

Table 2a: Frequency of Apprentices' Responses on Individual Approaches and Strategies

Watching	Imitation	Practice	Critical thinking	Listening, transcribing Remembering	Drafting & Sketching	Reflection
15	3	21	1	4	1	4

Table 2b: Frequency of Apprentices' Responses on Learning With and From Others

Coaching	Feedback	Conversation	Problem solving	Enquiry	Teaching others
16	1	5	4	14	7

The guidelines centre round the two main contributors to apprentices' learning, the agency of the apprentice and the affordances provided by the workplace for effective workplace learning. Both need to be in synchrony for "expansive learning" to occur. Therefore, for apprentices, the guidelines provide processes apprentices can use to become mindful practitioners who are able to reflectively learn to become effective problem solvers. In turn, the guidelines for coaches are to assist apprentices through modelling, coaching, scaffolding and fading supported by sound feedback strategies. The coaching process needs to help make visible the many nuances of trade skills learning and trainers and coaches need to be more attuned to the learning needs of novice workers.

Figures 2 and 3 provide diagrammatical summaries of the guidelines.

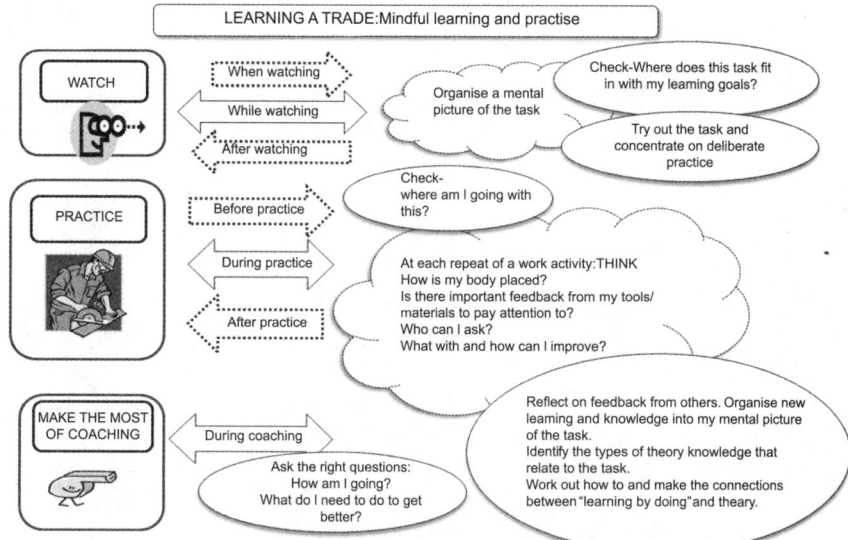

Figure 2 Guidelines for Apprentices

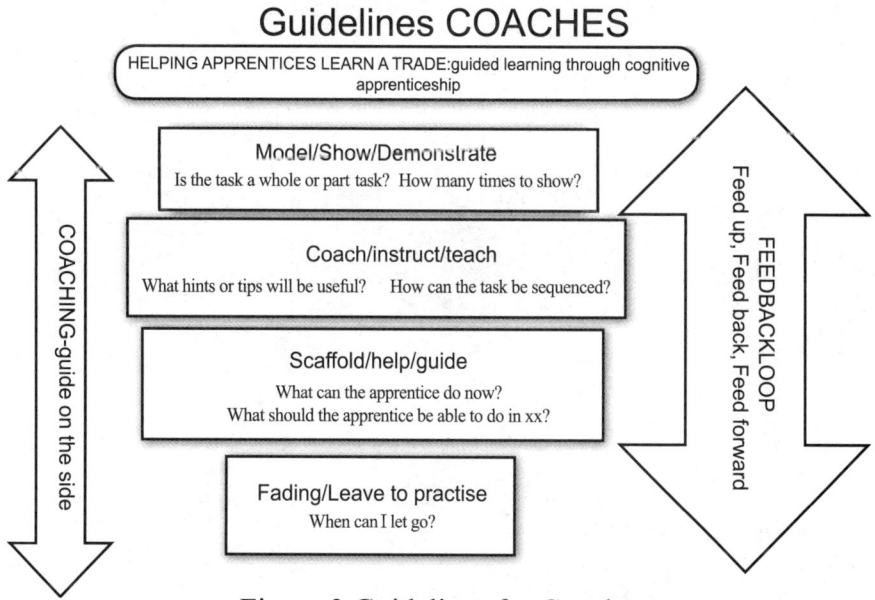

Figure 3 Guidelines for Coaches

逆向教学强化知识应用 考核改革提升自我认知

包头职业技术学院 张毅

教育部[2006]16号文件的出台，为广大高职院校的发展提供了制度与纲领保证，高职院校迎来了难得的历史发展机遇。其中提到，课程建设与改革是提高教学质量的核心，也是教学改革的重点和难点。包头职业技术学院作为全国百所示范院校之一，在课程改革中做了有益的探索，取得了非凡的成绩。笔者作为我院焊接专业的教师，现将在教学过程中的一些经验与体会和大家进行交流。

1. 项目教学法在焊接设备的使用与维护中的应用

首先介绍一下焊接设备的使用与维护这门课程。焊接设备的使用与维护课程是焊接自动化专业的一门核心课程，其教学目的是培养学生焊接设备使用及维护能力，并为后期的焊接工艺实施和焊接结构生产学习打好基础。根据这门课程所对应的职业能力培养要求，我们提出了"会安装、懂操作、能维护、讲安全"这一总体教学目标。

焊接设备的使用与维护教学团队在我院的示范性院校建设中引入项目教学法，取得了良好的教学效果。在项目教学中，广泛被采用的"六步法"（即资讯、计划、决策、实施、控制、评价）非常适合于在理实一体化课程中开展"以工作过程为导向"的项目教学法。这种方法改变了传统的教学模式，突出学生的主体地位，有效发挥教师的指导作用，模拟实际工作环境，激发学生的学习兴趣，培养学生的团队意识和创新能力，提高学生的综合素质，帮助学生习得扎实的实践技能，争取实现学生学习和就业的零距离上岗。

但是，焊接设备的使用与维护这门课程难点在于课程偏电，与电工学联系紧密。

尽管本着"必需、够用"的原则，减少了理论教学时数，强化了实践教学，突出基础理论知识的应用和实践能力的培养，但在专业的基础理论与基本知识时，学生畏难情绪较重，总怕学不会。而且，学生的生源问题导致这些年来学生素质有所降低的问题确实困扰着教学工作。怎样解决这个问题？为此，我们对六步法进行了改进，即采用基于结果的逆向教学法。该教学法在资讯步骤之前加入导入环节并将后面六个步骤加以整合，形成由导入、资讯、实践和评价四个环节组成的逆向式教学法。

2. 基于结果的逆向教学法

2.1 导入环节

2.1.1 导入的作用

在以往的教学中我们遵循六步法教学，学生首先要学习和工作任务相关的基础理论知识，在实施环节才会在实训基地见到真实的工作情境。这样，当学生首先接触到相关的基础理论知识时，就会遇到两个问题：第一，知识点抽象难懂；第二，理论到实践过渡困难，衔接差。而采用基于结果的逆向教学法很好地解决了这样的问题。在工作任务学习之初的导入环节，主要目的有两方面：首先，明晰能力目标，增强直观认识；其次，减少畏难情绪，激发学习热情。让学生实现从"我怕学不会"到"我一定要学好"的心理转变。

2.1.2 导入环节做法

先将任务引导文发到学生手中，学生首先从中了解需要掌握的学习目标，接下来教师通过现场演示或视频、图片展示的方法，使学生对学习目标有更直观的了解和认识。

案例分析：

典型工作任务：埋弧焊设备的使用

埋弧焊对于绝大多数学生来说是比较陌生的，据此教师提出两个问题：

（1）埋弧与明弧的区别？

（2）自动焊与手工焊的区别？

经过学生讨论，最终明确埋弧焊基本工艺特点；接下来教师去引导学生思考怎样来完成这样一个工艺过程，并在理实一体化教室由教师展示埋弧焊操作基本展示，让学生通过非常直观的视角学习到结果（学习目标），从而激发好奇心与求知欲；学生自然而然逆向去思考要达到学习目标需要的知识储备，所学的知识不再抽象，变得具体生动。在此基础上再开始资讯部分的学习，可以克服学习的畏难情绪。实质上这种基于结果的逆向式学习是将原先的"理论——实践"的学习过程转化成"实践——理论——实践"的过程。当然，导入阶段的现场演示部分目的在于激发学习兴趣，因此，它与六步法的实施阶段有着质的区别。在该阶段，教师应选择恰当的内容与形式来作为引导，否则就会本末导致，给学生造成很大的困扰。而且在此阶段的实践环节，其实基本以教师操作为主导。教师选择的视频及图片资料也要直观易懂，而非只是生涩的原理介绍。

2.2 资讯环节

有了导入环节可以使学生更快更好地进入到资讯环节的理论部分学习。资讯环节中，我们对此学习任务采用"模块化"教学方法，即根据"必需、够用"的原则对理论知识做了"模块化"处理。

案例分析：

埋弧焊设备的结构与使用

在以前的教学中，我们侧重于焊接设备结构原理的学习。比如说，焊接控制系统中，要学会分析电路原理图，如图所示。

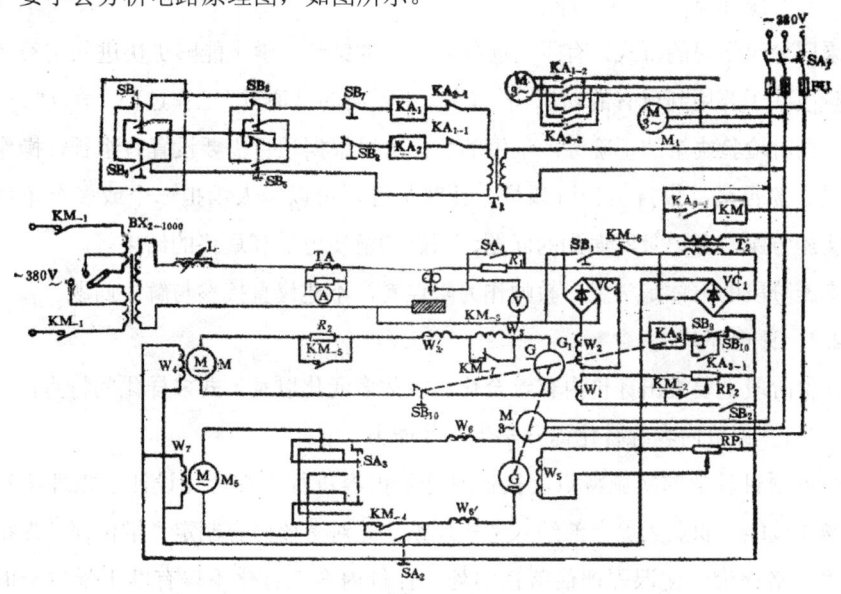

MZ-1000 型自动焊机电路原理图

但根据我们对岗位工作任务的调研，焊接操作技术工人无需掌握设备控制系的设计,只需掌握焊接设备的操作,了解设备控制系统组成模块并熟悉每一模块功能,能够熟练调节各个焊接参数。基于此我们将埋弧焊自动控制系统分为焊接电源控制系统、送丝控制系统、小车行走控制系统三个模块,并说明每一模块功能及参数设置和调节方法,如图所示。采用模块化教学方式取得了良好成效。这样的学习过程目标明确,重点突出,实用性强。

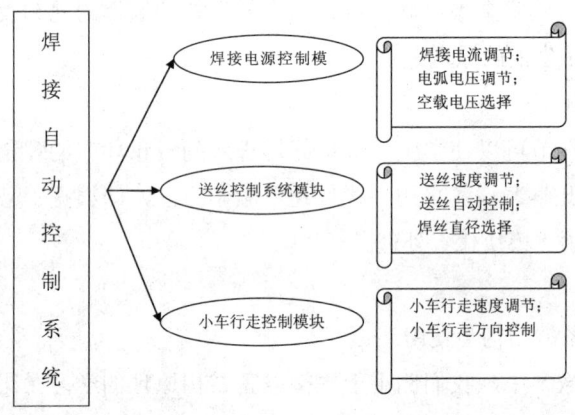

2.3 实施环节

采取分组学习的方式,有了之前导入环节的铺垫,学生能够更快进入实践环节。实施阶段除了要用到已有的知识、技能外,更重要的是通过"工作过程"学习"过程性"知识,同时检验决策的正确性。学生的角色可以根据项目需要设置有组长、操作员、记录员、监督员、报告员、协调员、计时员等,可以每人承担一个或多个角色。学生在实施方案时要记录所遇到的问题、问题的解决方法和最终的结果等。

实施阶段的主体是学生,教师作为陪伴者,不建议直接参与解决问题。

2.4 评价环节

评价阶段主要突出评价内容综合化、主体多元化以及形式多样化的特点。

2.4.1 评价内容综合化提升学生职业能力

根据项目教学的实施特点,我们对评价内容进行了综合化设计,将理论知识、实际操作技能、职业素养全部纳入考核体系,并对考核内容制定"量化评价"指标,采用"表格评价"使课程评估落在实处。评价内容综合化不仅有助于学生全面、健康地发展,符合学生的长远利益,更能激发学生学习的积极性和主动性,使他们有意识地提高自己的职业素质和职业能力。

2.4.2 评价主体多元性提升自我认知能力

多元评价主体包括教师评价、学生评价、学生互评等。将这些评价加以综合总结，使得学生与教师之间、被评价者与评价者之间达成互动；在实施过程中既保持客观性又具有鼓励性，帮助学生增加自信、获得成就感，使学生主体能够更有效调控自己的学习过程，培养现代企业迫切需要的合作精神与自主学习能力。

实施学生主体评价是在评价主体中加入学生自评与学生互评。学生自评是学生对自己完成工作任务最直接的检验。在学生自评过程中，有两个问题需要重视。第一，教师在制定任务评价标准时，评价指标易于量化，具有可操作性。能够把教师主观评分转化为客观评分，使评估考核更趋于公平，这样学生自我评价才易于操作。第二，教师要充分理解学生在自评过程中自我认知能力的发展规律。认知过程包括体验的启发、反思训练，直接在实践过程中发挥作用，作为教师不仅要有足够的耐心，更要充分信任学生，给予学生足够空间与时间。

学生互评环节，则是对学生团队合作精神的体现。在小组学习中，每一个小组均有一个组长，组长是分组学习的组织者，一方面要安排各个成员在工作任务中的分工，同时还要管理和监督成员完成工作的质量，并在互评中给出每个成员的成绩。

在实施新的评价体系中，我们发现学生在最初的工作任务评价时，会有对评价标准理解的偏差，也会有对自己给自己评价的不适，因此，其评价结果与教师评价结果会出现较大的不吻合，但随着更多工作任务的学习，我们发现二者评价结果会越来越接近。可见，这样的评价方式不仅仅是简单的打个分数，更是对工作任务的再学习。

2.4.3 评价形式多样化激发学生创新热情

采用多样化的评价方法对学生进行测评。如在考试形式上，采取多种考试形式，除笔试外，还有口试、开卷和实验能力考核、操作、作品等。通过丰富多样的评价形式，可以很好地促进学生开放的个性和创新意识的形成。

3. 总结

采取基于结果的逆向式教学法，可以明显提升学生的学习热情，在明确学习目标的基础上突出知识的应用；同时在评价中，充分调动学生自身的作用，通过学生的自评、互评、小组评价以及教师评价等多种形式，综合考察学生对知识的掌握能力。

Outcome-based Inverted Education and Comprehensive Assessing System

Zhang Yi, Baotou Vocational Technical College

Curriculum construction and reformation is the core of the education quality. Baotou Vocational Technical College, as one of China's 100 model vocational institutions, explored positively and made great achievements by curriculum reformation. I, a teacher from material engineering department, would like to share some teaching experience with everybody.

1. Application of Project Teaching Method in "Operation and Maintenance of Welding Facilities"

"Operation and Maintenance of Welding Facilities" is one of the core courses in welding major. The teaching purpose of the course is to train the capability of operating and maintaining welding facilities and to lay a foundation for the courses of welding process and welding structure production.

Our instructing team used the project teaching method which is always realized by six-step method (information, planning, deciding, practicing, controlling and assessing). This method is very effective to reform the conventional teaching mode, emphasize student-centered role, simulate real practical environment and improve the comprehensive quality.

However, the difficulties of "operation and maintenance of welding facilities" are the fact that the basic knowledge is closely connected with electrotechnics which is hard to learn for students. Hence, students are always afraid that they can't learn well. Therefore, we perfect the six-step method and apply a new one which is called outcome-based inverted education method. Connecting process is added before the information process and the six steps are integrated into four processes which are connecting, exploring, practicing and assessing.

2. Outcome-based Inverted Education Method

2.1 Connecting Process

2.1.1 The Function of Connecting Process

In the six-step method, students learn basis theory before they see real work situation at practicing process so that they have two difficulties—firstly, knowledge is too abstract to understand. Secondly, it's hard to transit from theory to practice. It's very effective to solve the problem with applying the outcome-based inverted education method. Connecting process which is at the beginning of learning plays an important role in clearing learning objective and stimulating learning emotion. As a result, students' psychology can transit from "I'm afraid not to learn well" to "I can do it well".

2.1.2 Perform Connecting Process

In short, in connecting process, students know learning objective from the task leading text and then understand the objective intuitively by teachers' showing on site, or through video and picture.

Case:

Working Task: Apply SAW (Submerged Arc Welding) Facility

SAW is very strange to most of students. How to solve the difficulty? Firstly, the instructor will ask students to think over two questions:

(1) What's different between submerged arc and open arc?

(2) What's different between automatic welding and manual welding?

After discussing on the above questions, students can know something about SAW process and then ask such a question curiously: how to perform it? And then teachers will show the SAW operation on site to make students see the learning objective to stimulate their learning emotion. So in this way students will make an inverted thinking naturally about what knowledge they should have. The basic knowledge learning at the exploring process will not be abstract any more. Hence, the outcome-based inverted learning changes the procedure from "theory—practice" to "practice—theory—practice". Of course teachers should select proper content and forms to guide students.

2.2 Exploring Process

Students can plunge themselves into exploring quickly after the connecting process. The module teaching method is adopted in which theory knowledge is modularized.

Case:

Working Task: List SAW Facility

The former learning objective focuses on the SAW structure theory. For example, students should learn the electrical schematic diagram of control system shown by the following picture.

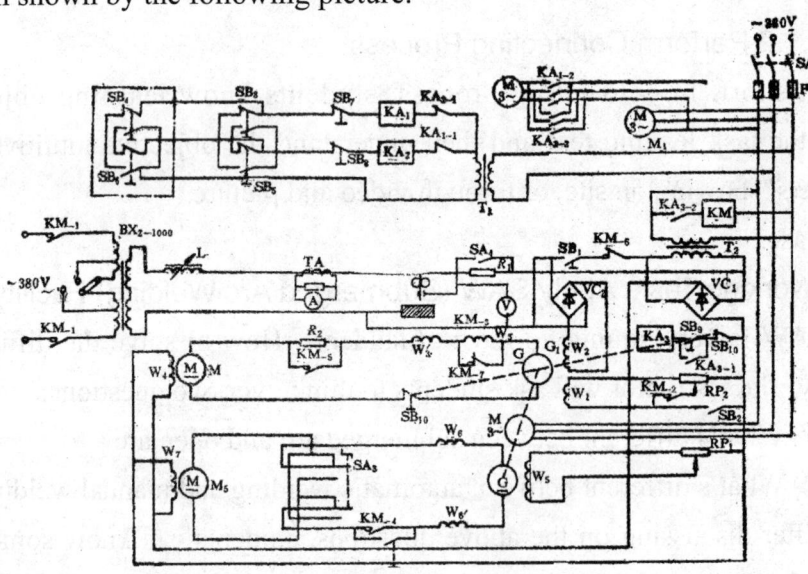

But welding technician needn't design the control system according to the investigation of the working post. The objective is changed into listing

the modules and their functions of controlling system and adjusting welding parameters. As a result, we change the content as the following picture.

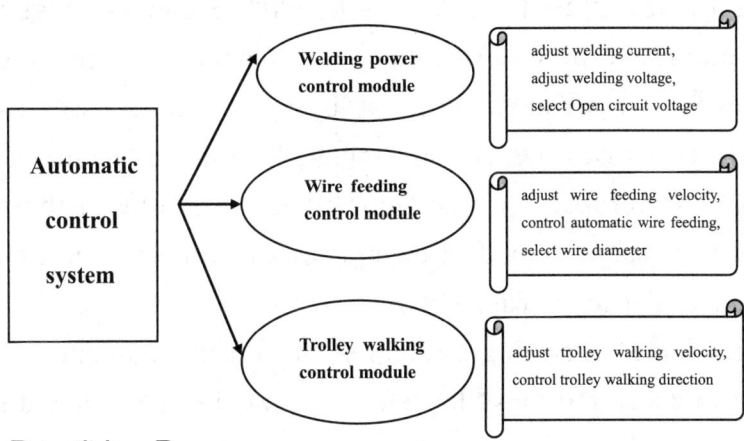

2.3 Practicing Process

In this process students should learn procedural knowledge and check the correctness of decision-making. Students' role can be set as the group leader, operator, recorder, supervisor, coordinator and timekeeper and each one can take one or more posts. It's necessary to record problems, solutions and results when students perform their work task.

The subject of the practicing process is the student while the teacher is the object just like an escort, who is not suggested to solve problem directly.

2.4 Assessing Process

Assessing process stresses on content integration, multi-subject and diversified forms.

2.4.1 Improving Students' Professional Capability by Content Integration

Assessing content is comprehensively designed according to the performance of project teaching method. Theory knowledge, practical operation and professional quality are all included in the assessing system in which content is quantized and table-structured. Content integration can not only help student develop professional quality and capability, but also stimulate their learning initiative.

2.4.2 Achieving Self-Knowledge by Multi-Subject Assessing

It's interactive between students and teachers, students and their teammates to assess comprehensively by multi-subject assessing which includes teacher assessing, self-assessing and students' mutual assessing. Students can increase their self-confidence and obtain the sense of achievement to adapt to modern enterprises which need cooperation spirit and self-directed learning capability.

Student-subject assessing includes self-assessing and mutual assessing. It's direct to check their task by self assessing. Teachers should set out a standard and objective assessing system to make self-assessing operate easily. Additionally, teachers should understand sufficiently that students need enough time to improve their self-knowledge capability, so that what teachers should do is to give students absolute confidence and enough time and space.

Mutual assessing among students focuses on team work spirit. Each group has its own group leader who is both the organizer to arrange each group member's work and the evaluator to give team members score.

We found that students didn't understand assessing standard well initially in the new assessing system. Hence, there was a bigger gap between teachers' assessing and students' assessing result, but as more work task was studied, their self-assessing capability could be improved gradually. In fact, this assessing method is a re-studying form rather than giving a score simply.

2.4.3 Stimulating Students' Creation by Diversified Assessing Forms

Diversified assessing forms are applied, such as written examination, oral examination, open book examination, practical operation works and so on. It's very effective to promote students' open personality and creation consciousness.

3. Summary

It's very efficient to accelerate study emotion, make clear learning objective and emphasize knowledge application with outcome-based inverted education method. In the new assessing system, students' learning capability is examined comprehensively by multi-subject and diversified forms.

英语教学要适应时代发展
职业英语

怀卡托理工学院　Jo Thomas

下述讨论包括两个主要观点：

根据职业教育学生的特定需求，我们在传授什么样的知识；

介绍2013年5月在广东省举办的在职教师培训课程。

英语教学要适应时代的发展，尤其是职业英语教学——什么变了？

我们经常听人说我们现在生活在一个全球化的时代；英语是商业领域、互联网和许多研究领域共同使用的通用语。良好的英语能力确实能赋予人们一种优势。然而，全球化尽管重要，但当地学生的学习需求也同样重要。

现代英语教学应该清楚了解学习者和当地社会的需求。比如说，为什么您的学生需要学习英语？他们全部都会前往西方国家留学吗？他们日常生活中需要英语吗？他们在当地工作中需要英语吗？英语对当地社会有益吗？作为教师，我们需要思考学生需要学习什么，不需要学习什么。

英语人口

新西兰与加拿大、澳大利亚、美国和英国为一组英语国家，其大多数人口说英语。还有一组国家，虽然英语不是第一语种，但却是官方语种。最后一组国家，英语越来越多地被作为主要外语语种使用——中国是其中国家之一。

世界上有81个国家和民族的人们说英语，英语为母语的人口为3.6亿，但说英语的总人口超过10亿。显而易见，在不同国家使用的英语会有所不同，且各个国家

的英语学习者会因为不同的原因学习英语，也会以不同的方式在他们的日常生活中使用英语。

因此非英语国家说英语的人比英语国家说英语的人还多，这在以前从未有过。

世界英语

英语是历史上唯一一个非母语人口比母语人口还多的语种。在中国，大约有1亿孩子学习英语。

也就是说世界上只有少数人说的是"标准英语"，而更多的人说的是各种各样的地方英语。这些不同的"世界英语"归根结底还是英语，但与美国或英国教科书中介绍的不同用法不完全相同，且大家相互之间使用的英语也不尽相同。现代世界不同地理区域有如此众多的人使用英语，这种情况当然在所难免。然而我们的教科书和课程内容可能无法反映这种现状。我们做不到传授学生方方面面的英语知识，因此，作为英语教师和教学大纲编写人员，我们需要思考学生真正需要学习什么，然后决定我们需要教什么。我们需要传授学生就业、走入社会或进一步深造最需要的英语知识和技能。

重点是在了解学习者的需求后，教学才最有效。

在新西兰政府出资的众多职业语言学校中，学生生源主要为移民和国际留学生，我们发现学习者的需求为：

- 培养自主性（独立学习），因为所有教学机构和工作场所均看重这一点。
- 可转换态度和技能（他们可将珍贵的技能用于其他课程学习或工作场所）。
- 职业教育或继续深造，语言教学目标明确（学习内容与学生的实际需求相关联）。
- 适时教学（学生在需要时学习所需知识，不要过早或过晚）。
- 在培养学生达到英语母语水准时要切合实际。因为它需要大量的时间和努力，而且还可能做不到。相反，我们需要将重点放在可理解性、效率和效果方面。说话的人在与人交流时需要用上述三种方式以便让他/她的听众听懂。

新西兰职业教育学校的英语教学

新西兰职业语言教学有五大要素，它们是教师、学生、教学方法、教学大纲和教学针对性。我将逐一介绍上述五大要素。

首先，让我们了解一些新西兰的教师。在新西兰，教师均有教师资格，就像中国的教师一样。对教师在教学中教什么、如何教均有明确规定，但与此同时，教师在日常教学工作中，在选择如何教方面也有一定的自由度和自主性。我在教学中，经常采取小组备课和小组授课的方式。教师还定期地、不时地免费接受专业培训。学院尽最大努力保证教师的专业知识技能水平与所从事的教学难度和风格相符。

我所从事教学的语言学院目前60%的学生为移民，40%为国际留学生，其中50%的国际留学生来自于亚洲国家。学生有着不同的文化、年龄、教育和生活背景。学生学习语言的目的为与人交流、工作或深造，因此，我们的课堂教学和大纲必须反映这些不同的需求。

我们采取的教学方法为混合式，但更多采用的是任务型教学方法，边做边学，在课堂教学中尽可能使用贴近生活的语言。教学方法为以需求为主，以学生为主而不是以教师为主，学生进行大量的双人学习、小组学习和独立自主学习。教师会一直观察学生的学习表现，如果效果欠佳，我们会研究如何针对不同学生的情况调整教学方法。

教学大纲是政府批准的。我们根据毕业生标准，思考一个语言课程的毕业生在完成学业后必须具备什么样的能力。它必须达到继续深造要求的语言水平和工作需求。下一步考虑的是学习成果，思考学生通过学习必须掌握的知识和技能以通过相应的等级考核。除了上述内容，大纲还需包括其他单元如课程内容介绍、课程评估方法和教学方法。

语言教学必须有针对性。在课程拟定后，要根据学习者的需求编写大纲内容，然后决定使用的教材和媒体技术以更好地帮助教学。

社区环境中使用的英语（英语作为外语）；

工作场所英语（专用英语）；

学术用途英语（学术英语和专用英语）；

境外使用的英语（英语作为外语和专用英语）。

中国的在职教师培训

今年5月份，我与另一位资深教师一起，采取这种教学方法，在广东省对来自于8所职业院校的21名在职教师进行了专业培训。

我们进行了为期一周的强化教学，随后通过Yammer社交网站进行了3周的在线教学。我们在Yammer上专为这组教师开发了一个私人、封闭式的交流网站，然后分别邀请这些教师加入。

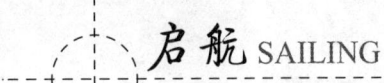

强化教学周采取基于原则为主的教学方法，该方法要求重视主要原则，比如教与学的自主性和教学内容的关联性。

教学目的是留给教师们一个教师工具箱，使他们在课堂教学中能马上应用，同时邀请教师们探索自己对语言教学的看法。

以下为在职教师培训中讨论的话题及教师们对其提出的反馈意见。

第一点是让学习者参与，也就是说让学习者对学习感兴趣进而积极参与。它包括帮助教师想办法让学生保持大脑清醒并对学习外语感兴趣。教师们对这一话题非常感兴趣，因为他们经常对缺乏学习积极性的学生束手无策，他们非常愿意讨论这个话题以及如何让语言教学更加生动有趣。

第二点是课堂管理。新西兰教室与中国教室不同，而且有些东西很难改变，但有些想法的确值得教师尝试，比如使用语音控制和安静的教室。这一想法也被广泛接受；他们发现这一想法很有趣，但实施起来相当困难。这一想法的主要内容之一是教师授课时间和学生发言时间的分配。我们的目的是让教师少说，学生多说，并依此事先计划每一活动以使学生有更多的机会发言和发表自己的看法。

第三点是重要的学生学习自主性和独立学习能力。教师仍然引导和实施教学，但学习者也有自己的任务，需要他们通过独立思考来完成。教师们非常赞成这一观点。他们喜欢培养更多具有独立学习能力的学习者，只有这样，学生才能通过经常与他人分享自己的看法真正为创造良好的学习环境做出自己的贡献。然而教师很难让学生在安全的教室环境里犯错误，包括体验轻轻摔倒以便从错误中学习。

第四点是以学生为中心，学生是教学的主体。关于这个观点似乎根本不存在争议，但实际上作为教师的我们经常会忘记在课堂活动中以学生为中心。我们经常会忙着讲课以至于忘记去想学习者的实际需求。我们应该反问自己什么样的教学方法对学生最有帮助，而不是什么样的方法对老师最有利。教师们对这一点非常感兴趣，也很乐意接受它。

第五点介绍的是个人学习风格。即老师应该意识到不同的人会偏爱不同的学习方法，有些学习方法对某些人来讲会比其他的学习方法更有效。例如，从一般意义和广义上来讲，有些人是视觉学习者，有些是听觉学习者，还有些是动觉学习者。更具体地讲，7种多受偏爱的学习方法可以描述为：

视觉法（空间／图片，图像，空间技能）；

听觉法（听觉，音乐/声音和音乐）；

口头学习法（口头和书面的语言/文字）；

感知法（动觉/身体，手，触摸感）；

逻辑法（数字/逻辑，推理，系统化）；

合作法（人际交往/小组，或与他人交流）；

内省法（内省/独自工作或自学）。

教师们对此极为感兴趣，非常喜欢自我尝试以弄清楚他们自己属于哪种学习者且可能成为哪种教师。

第六点是关于有针对性地开发教材，编写教材，选择课本和网络资源，使它们与教学相关联且符合学习者的学习需求。教师们对这一观点反响热烈，因为他们意识到要做到这一点需要做大量工作，但这也正是为什么小组备课，及希望做到小组授课的重要性。这样教师们能教材共享，不需要自己做所有该做的工作。

第七点是课程评估，以保证测验该测验的内容。同时要理解学习评估和评估为了学习二者间的区别，将评估作为宝贵的辅助学习工具，而不是学期结束时单一的占分比重很高的考试。这是一个关于学习测验的非常另类的观点，有些测试占分不高，只是为了弄清楚哪些知识需要着重讲，以及检验学生到目前为止对知识的掌握情况，并不是所有的重要考试都会让学生紧张。有些考试不是老师能左右的，然而对于如何授课，如何帮助学生准备考试我们教师却有更多的决策权。

最后一点是在教学中要遵守相关性原则。当学习者明白他们为什么需要学习某些知识及当教师深信该知识对学生有用时，那么教与学会变得更有效、更深入、更有意义。教师们明白这一点，且对此产生共鸣。有时当国外课本中含有不恰当的内容时，教师们不知道舍去他们不想要的文化观点后，如何讲解语言知识，或语言的哪些方面的内容比其他内容更重要，因此探讨有关这方面的教学方法对他们很有用。

最后，教师们在强化专业培训周的最后一天，在广东省采取小组备课和讲课的现场教学方式，对自己进行了评估。要求他们在教学中使用一些在培训中学到的教学方法和观点，但也有一定的自由发挥空间。在随后的3周里，通过他们在Yammer在线网站活动中的表现，对他们进行了进一步评估，评估结束后，他们每个人都收到了证书，说明他们已经成功完成了专业培训课程。教学培训课非常有趣和宝贵，教师们冥思苦想了不同的语言教学方法使其尽可能地适合学生的学习需求。

回到新西兰后，各种讨论、问题和建议一直在 Yammer 网站上持续，教师们一致要求保留该网站以方便小组成员之间以及与我们进行对话。我们上传了链接、短片、文章、文件、幻灯片演讲等，要求他们阅读，发表自己的意见，并在教学中尝试培训中介绍的教学方法，就取得的新发现提供反馈意见。

中国的教师非常乐意接受新观点，愿意在教学中尽自己最大努力，非常高兴有机会参加专业培训，然后在回到各自的工作岗位后与同事分享所学知识。培训周同时为已经掌握最新教学方法的教师提供与小组中其他人员分享自己知识的机会，并相互学习他人的优秀教学方法。这是一个非常宝贵的机会，使得来自于不同但密切合作的两个国家的英语职业教育者能够分享教学观点和教学方法。

English Language Teaching for a Changing World

VOCATIONAL ENGLISH

Jo Thomas, Waikato Institute of Technology

Two key ideas are covered in this discussion:
- What we are teaching our vocational language students for their particular context;
- The description of an in-service course for vocational language teachers taught in Guangdong Province, China in May of this year.

English Language Teaching for a Changing World and especially vocational English language teaching—what has changed?

We hear with increasing frequency that we now live in a globalised world; English is the lingua franca, the world language of business, of the internet, and of much research. Good English ability can indeed be empowering. However, while globalisation is important, so is the local context of the learner.

Modern English language teaching needs to recognise both the learner and local community needs. For example, why do your students need to learn English? Are they all going to travel overseas to a Western country to study? Will they need English in their daily lives? Do they need it for work locally? Will it be of benefit to your community? As teachers we need to think about what our students need to learn, but also what they do not need to learn.

English Speakers

New Zealand, along with Canada, Australia, the United States and the United Kingdom, is one of a group of countries where English is spoken by most of the population. There is another considerable group where English is an official, but not a first language. Finally are the countries where English is used increasingly as the main foreign language—China is in this group.

English is spoken in 81 countries and small nations across the world, with only 360 million native speakers, but more than one billion speakers in total. Clearly, the way English is used in these different groups of countries will be different, and the learners of English in these countries may have different reasons for learning English and different ways to use it in their lives.

World Englishes

English is the only language in history to have had more people speaking it as a second language than as a first language. In China approximately 100 million children are studying English.

That means that "standard" English is only spoken by a small number of English speakers worldwide and actually most people who speak English speak local varieties of English. These different "World Englishes" are still English, but might not be exactly the same as that variety used in textbooks from the United States or from England, or exactly the same as one another. This is inevitable with so many people speaking English across so much of the modern world. However, our textbooks and programme content may not reflect this reality. We cannot teach our students every aspect of English, which means that as English language teachers and curriculum writers we need to think about what our students actually need to learn and what we need to teach them. We want to prepare our students with the English language knowledge and skills that will be most useful to them for joining the local workforce, the community, or for higher study.

The key point is that teaching is most useful when we know our learners' needs.

In my New Zealand context of a large government vocational language school, made up of both migrants and international students, we have identified the learners' needs as being:

• To develop autonomy (independence in learning) as this is valued in all types of education and in the workplace.

• Transferrable attitudes and skills (valuable skills they can take into other study or the workplace).

• Targeted language teaching for clear vocational or study pathways (so their learning is relevant to students).

• Timely teaching (so they learn what they need when they need it, not too soon or too late).

• To be realistic about attempting to train students to use English exactly like native speakers. This would take a large amount of time and effort and not be successful. Instead we need to think about focusing on intelligibility, efficiency and effectiveness. The English language user needs to be able to communicate in these three ways to be understood by his or her audience.

The New Zealand Vocational Context

There are five key elements to the New Zealand vocational language context. These are the teachers, the learners, the approach, the curriculum and the targeted language. I will address each of these in turn.

Firstly, let us look at the teachers in New Zealand. In New Zealand teachers are well-qualified, just as in China. Teachers have very clear guidelines to what and how they teach, but also have some freedom of choice, and some autonomy in how they do that with their daily lesson planning. In my context, the teachers always team plan and often team teach. They have regular, frequent, free, professional development. Every effort is made to match the teachers' specific skill area to their level and style of teaching.

The learners in my New Zealand language department are currently made up of 60% migrants and 40% international students. Of those international students 50% are from Asian countries. Among students we have a wide mix of cultures, ages and differing educational and life experiences. The students' language needs are for the community, the workplace or for higher education, therefore, our classes and syllabi must reflect those different needs.

The approach to teaching is mixed, but is mostly task-based, learning by doing, by using the language in as realistic a context as possible within the classroom. The approach is need-based, student-centred, not teacher-centred, and involves a lot of pair work, group work and independent, autonomous work. The teachers are always watching student outcomes, if it's not working we think about what adjustments can be made for different students.

The curriculum is Government approved. We begin with a Graduate Profile, with thinking about what a graduate of this programme must be capable of doing by the end of the programme. That needs to match closely with what is required for the next stage of study or workplace. Next in the process are the Learning Outcomes, thinking about the skills and knowledge that the students must develop, to be able to pass at the appropriate level. The curriculum also has other components including the overview of content, assessment, and the approach to teaching, among other aspects.

The language to be taught is specifically targeted. After the curriculum is developed, the syllabus content is written to match the learners' needs, and decisions are then made on the materials and technology to best support the learning. We match the syllabus content specifically according to whether the learner is studying:

• EAL for community (English as an Additional Language);

• ESP for the workplace (English for Specific Purposes);

• EAP and ESP for higher study (English for Academic Purposes and ESP);

• EFL and ESP for offshore delivery (English as a Foreign Language and ESP).

A Teachers' In-service Course in China

In May of this year, with another senior language teacher, I delivered a professional development in-service course based on this approach to teach vocational English language, to twenty-one teachers from eight vocational colleges in Guangdong Province.

We did thirty hours over one week of intensive teaching followed by three weeks of online teaching using Yammer, a social networking site. We established a private, closed network within Yammer especially for this group of teachers, which teachers were individually invited to join.

The week was based on the idea of principle-based methodologies that requires that key principles be decided as important, such as learner autonomy, and relevance of content in teaching and learning.

The topics covered in the in-service course, and teachers' responses to those topics are as follows:

1. The first was engaging learners, which means getting the learners interested and involved. It involved assisting teachers with ideas for how to keep students wide awake and interested in learning a foreign language. Teachers were very interested in this topic as they regularly struggle with unmotivated students and were eager to discuss this and how language teaching can be made more interesting.

2. The second was classroom management—NZ classrooms are quite different from Chinese classrooms, and some things are difficult to change, but there are other ideas that might be useful for the teacher to try, such as the use of voice control and quiet classrooms. This idea was also well received by the teachers; they found it quite amusing, but also quite difficult. One of the key ideas here is Teacher Talk Time as compared with Student Talk Time. We were aiming to have the teachers talk less and the students talk more and to put that into each activity in advance to enable students to have more opportunity to speak and share their ideas.

3. The third topic was this important idea of learner autonomy and expecting independence from our students. The teacher is still guiding and teaching, but the learners also have tasks which require them to think independently to complete them. Teachers embraced this idea eagerly. They liked the idea of developing more independent learners, where they really are contributing to the classroom learning environment through sharing their ideas constantly. It can however be difficult for the teachers to allow students to make mistakes in a safe classroom environment, so that they have the chance to learn through experience, including the experience of failing in small aspects, so as to learn from mistakes.

4. The next topic was student-centredness, where the learner is the focus of all teaching. This might seem very obvious, but actually as teachers sometimes perhaps we forget to put the students at the centre of our

classroom practice. We can be so busy teaching content that we can forget to think about the learners' actual needs. We should ask ourselves, what the best way is for the student, rather than what the best way is for the teacher. Teachers were very interested in this idea and very receptive to it.

5. The fifth topic addressed individual learning styles, which means being aware that different people may have a preference for a particular approach to learning, that some ways might work better than others for different people. For example, in general and broad terms, some learners are more visual, some more auditory, or others kinaesthetic in their approach to learning. In more detail, the seven specific styles used to describe possible preferences in learning are:

- visual (spatial/pictures, images, spatial skill);
- aural (auditory, musical/sound and music);
- verbal (linguistic/words in both speech and writing);
- physical (kinaesthetic/body, hands, sense of touch);
- logical (mathematical/logic, reasoning, systems) ;
- social (interpersonal/groups, or with others);
- solitary (intrapersonal/work alone or self-study).

The teachers were extremely interested in this and really enjoyed trying this out to see what sort of learners they were themselves and also what sort of teachers they might then be.

6. The sixth topic was about developing materials that specifically suit the learners, creating materials and choosing and adapting textbooks and online resources, that are relevant and appropriate for the learning context. This topic caused a lot of discussion as teachers realised it meant there was quite a lot of work involved, but this is why team planning, and hopefully team teaching is valuable. Teachers can share materials and not do all the work involved in this by themselves.

7. The seventh topic was assessment, and ensuring that the testing conducted, does test what it needs to test. Also appreciating the difference between assessment of learning and assessment for learning, so using assessment as a valuable learning aid, not just a single high-stakes examination at the end of the students' course. This is quite a different concept of testing, where some testing is low stakes, and the test is to see what needs to be taught again, to see how the students are progressing so far, not always very high stakes testing that is stressful for learners. Some tests are beyond the teachers' control. However, how students are taught and prepared for tests we can potentially control more.

8. The last topic was ensuring the principle of relevancy is followed in our teaching. When learners understand why they need to know something, and when teachers are convinced of the value to their students, then it makes for better, deeper, more meaningful teaching and learning. The teachers understood this idea and it resonated with them. Sometimes when foreign textbooks have unsuitable topics in them teachers can be unsure of how to teach the language without the cultural idea they do not want, or which elements of language are more valuable than others, so it is useful to discuss approaches to this.

Finally, the teachers were assessed themselves on the last day of the intensive week in Guangdong Province, with a live teaching practice which they had to plan and deliver in teams. They were required to incorporate some of the ideas and techniques covered during the week together, but were also given some autonomy. They were then further assessed on their online contribution to the shared Yammer site over the following three weeks, and at the end of that time each received a certificate to say that they had successfully completed the professional development programme. The teaching sessions were interesting and valuable, and teachers had given significant thought to different ways of approaching their language teaching to best suit their learners' needs.

After our return to New Zealand, the discussions, questions and suggestions continued on the Yammer site with the teachers voting to keep it open for their collaborative "community of practice" conversations with one another and with us. We added links, videos, articles, documents, PowerPoint presentations and so on, and the teachers were asked to read, to give their opinions, and to give feedback about anything new from the course that they had tried out in their classes.

The Chinese language teachers were very receptive to new ideas, keen to do their best for their learners, and excited about the opportunity to be involved in professional development for themselves, and then to be able to share that with their colleagues on their return to their teaching environments. The week also provided the opportunity for those teachers who were already quite current in their language teaching to share what they knew with others in the group and to learn from one another's best practice. It was a valuable opportunity that allowed sharing of ideas and practice between English language vocational teachers from two very different but connected countries.

多种教学法在物流管理专业课程中的应用

宁夏工商职业技术学院商贸经济系　邵宁平

一、导入

当前物流管理专业教学模式的改革应当以企业的需求为基础，在与企业深入合作的基础上，通过对企业工作流程的认知和对企业岗位需求的了解，有针对性地开展专业课程的教学改革。行动导向教学是物流管理专业教学改革的一个创新点。我院物流管理专业定位于培

养能从事现代物流管理工作的应用型高技能人才，由此决定了我院的物流管理专业的教学以培养学生实践、实用、实干能力为特色。为此，我们将行为导向教学模式中的各种教学方法应用在许多专业课程的教学中。

二、多种教学法的应用分析

行为导向教学的具体教学方法主要有情景模拟、角色扮演、案例教学法、项目教学法、任务驱动法、引导文教学法、"头脑风暴"教学法、张贴板法等。现就本院物流管理专业课程教学中几种常用的教学法进行简单的介绍。

（一）项目教学法

项目教学法是将一个相对独立的项目，交由学生自己处理，信息的收集、方案的设计、项目的实施及最终的评价都由学生自己负责；教师起到咨询、指导与解答疑难的作用；学生通过项目的进行，了解并把握整个过程及每一环节中的基本要求与整个过程的重难点。

操作性项目在物流综合实训课程中是常用的教学法之一。它给出情境、工具，让学生利用所给的情境和材料完成指定的作业并展示，主要训练学生的操作性、能

动性和合作能力。例如，在学习配送管理实务与仓储管理课程某些知识点时，可以让学生到配送中心或企业的仓库，根据企业的要求进行拣货、配送等或者在校内实训中心进行模拟捡货、配货等作业环节。

在第五学期开设了综合实训课程物流案例与实训、电子商务与物流。综合实训的主要任务是通过学生组建物流和销售公司，实体进行物流及销售作业，教师则进行企业业务操作指导。在项目进行前期，教师先进行了相关的专题培训，培训内容包括市场调研、公司组建、业务管理、财务管理以及相关业务单证的填写。专业为每个公司提供实训项目启动资金3 000元。学生自主成立公司，设立相关的组织机构，主要成立仓储部、采购部、运输部、销售部和财务部，实体完成物流管理、采购管理、销售管理、库存管理等多个子项目。每个子项目的完成均以完整真实的业务为载体，整个过程由真实的企业模拟单证作为信息的记录。公司的所有业务往来，包括资金与货物要全部有单证先行，并由相关的负责人进行签字盖章完成，一旦出了问题全部由直接负责人负责。

学生拿到启动资金之后，先进行前期的市场调研，确定采购计划，然后到东环批发市场进行采购，之后由实训基地的仓库工作人员进行相关的库存管理。随后公司的销售部门制订销售计划，选取合适的销售场地进行产品销售。教师对整个项目实施过程进行全程监控，包括每日早上各个公司的考勤、公司晨会以及每日公司运作过程相关单证的填写。在一轮运作结束后，教师通过对各个公司业绩的考核评出本轮的优秀企业、优秀经理及优秀员工并进行奖励。

物流综合实训项目以工作过程为导向，指导设计实训内容体系，充分体现了我专业"三共建、三融合、三阶段、三能力"的人才培养模式要求和"课岗融合""双证融合""学战融合"的课程体系思路，体现了最新的高职教育理念。通过实训，充分调动了学生的积极性和创造性，一方面使学生在理论课上所学到的物流作业知识得以实际应用，通过公司运作掌握了物流管理技巧，感受到了管理真谛；另一方面让学生在真实公司的操作与掌控中体验了企业运作的成功与失败，明白了团队协作的重要性。

（二）案例教学法

案例教学法是目前我院物流管理专业教师在授课中普遍采用的教学方法，为此还为8门核心课程编写了案例集。在物流信息技术与应用课程教学过程中，案例教学法具体分为以下三步：第一步，在进行项目训练之前安排一个案例，介绍案例涉及的背景、实际采用的管理方法、技术，由学生结合以前所学分析该企业存在的问题，既可以有效运用其他课程所学知识，又可以为后续教学做铺垫；第二步，分析实训项目内容及要求，查找、理解完成项目内容所需的理论知识点，而后进行实际操作，既可以深化学生对书本知识的理解，又可以考察其对理论知识的实际应用情况；第三步，总结实际操作中遇到的问题，并提出解决问题的对策，考察解决实际问题的能力。

另外，我们采取动态的方式来选取教学中所用的案例，经常将实习基地的企业在运营过程中碰到的一些实际问题编成案例融入日常教学中。如在讲授仓储管理中，我们将众一物流的仓库建设、使用的实施设备、仓库布局等实际资料给学生，让他们自己查资料，分析其中的问题，并提出解决问题的方法。通过案例教学，使物流相关理论与实践很好地结合起来，使学生能更好地了解物流企业实际运作中的情况及问题，进而培养学生综合运用知识分析问题和解决问题的能力，达到为今后职业做准备的目的。

学生应该运用逻辑思维方式。教师应该首先帮助学生清楚地了解优势、劣势、机遇和挑战，然后通过案例教学的方式对理论知识加以总结。

（三）角色扮演教学法

在教育教学领域中，"角色扮演法"又称"情景模拟教学法"，它在虚拟而又逼真的情景中进行，要求教师根据教学内容和背景材料设计场景。学生根据情节在仿真场景中扮演一定的角色，身临其境地按设定岗位的职责、任务、工作程序、人际协调等提出观点、方案或进行实际操作，从而掌握一定的知识和技能。

在供应链管理的课程中，"啤酒游戏"通常被用来让学生更好地理解供应链理论。供应链的三个环节包括制造商、批发商和零售商。学生可以在供应链环节中扮演零售商、批发商、顾客、生产者和原材料供应者。例如，接到订单以后，供应商应该先考虑库存情况，再对生产和原材料进行管理。

在供应链管理的教学过程中引入角色扮演教学法，针对高职学生的学习风格与特点，让学生通过主动实践来认识、掌握所要传授的知识或技能，彻底改变过去以"填鸭式"为主要特征的传统教学模式中学生被动地接受知识的低效问题，有助于激发学生学习的积极性与主动性，并且能够实现理论联系实际促进学生提高创造性解决实际问题的能力。这种教学法不仅加强了学生预测和决策的能力，还增强了学生的团队意识和系统性思考问题的能力。

（四）任务驱动教学法

任务驱动教学法是指在学生学习的全过程中，以若干个具体任务为学习主线，学生在完成任务的过程中，学习基本知识和技能，同时提高分析问题、解决问题和综合应用所学知识的能力。任务驱动教学法强调以任务为主线，以学生为主体。学生在完成任务的过程中，逐步加深对学科知识的理解、进行经验性知识的累积以及分析、解决问题能力的锻炼。

以国际货运代理实务课程中从中国深圳出口至美国洛杉矶的货物运输为例，首先需要分析现实岗位的工作任务和工作情境，整理出学生要适应该岗位所需要具备的职业能力。经分析，本案例中工作过程包括查询贸易条款，了解货物生产情况，确定运输方式（包括拖车运输、铁路运输、海洋运输以及多式联运等），预订运输工具，准备出口文件、报关、报检工作，完成实际交货，银行结汇等。如果将整个流程作为一个大的"任务"，这对于刚接触实际操作的学生来说难度过大、所需要的时间也过长，不利于学生对相关知识的掌握。因此，可以考虑将整个工作流程分割成若干个"子任务"，让学生分步进行练习。

之后创设任务情境。课堂上教师给出任务。在该案例中，我们截取从"接受客户订单"到"预定运输工具"一段作为训练任务。客户的要求及货物情况如下：

1. 该票货物在 FOB 贸易条款下，起运港为 FOBSHENZHEN, CHINA；目的地为 LOS ANGELES, USA；到港日不能超过 2011/9/10，运输方式为海运。

2. 工厂位于东莞，货物将于 2011/8/20 完成，货品名称：皮鞋，货物约为 $60m^3/18T$。

3. 买方指定船运公司：CSCL（中国海运有限公司）

接到任务后，学生根据顾客的需要和实际情况分为不同的小组。

各个小组经过认真分析之后，就按照工作顺序逐步完成"任务"。首先，要与工厂确认货物在规定时间是否能够完成。有时货物出厂之前还需要买方派出代理在工厂验货，如果验货不合格也可能导致无法按时装运，所以学生要将各种可能存在的风险纳入考虑之中。同时，进一步与工厂确认货物的重量与体积，以保证所选择的装载工具适用。第二步，与船公司确认船期、舱位以及集装箱设备情况，将具体的准确的信息反馈给进口方，以得到对方对以上信息的书面确认。第三步，安排拖车前往工厂装运货物，同时准备报关资料、联络报关员在货物进入海关监管区域后进行报检报验。

在阶段性任务完成之后，教师应组织各个小组将本小组完成任务的情况对大家进行展示。对学生完成出色的部分进行表扬，对出问题的环节作为案例进行全班范围的分析。对每个小组的操作时间和操作步骤安排的合理与否进行点评，对是否符合操作流程、是否符合客户要求、是否符合行业惯例等方面进行认真的总结，从而使学生能切实地得到训练并掌握实践经验。

（五）技能训练教学

我们在物流专业学生前两年的教学中所开设的课程中，实训学时所占比例达到50%，在实训课程中学生通过对物流实验中的各个模块的操作，明晰地理清整个物流企业的流程，熟悉物流企业各岗位如何利用信息平台相互协作。实验实训课程也是集案例教学、角色扮演和情景模拟为一体的教学设计。

以采购管理为例，其教学目标设置如下：

（1）采购管理技能包括一般性的基本技能和综合性的技能训练。通过技能练习和训练将书本课程中的知识技能转变为学生自己的工作技能。

（2）以智力技能训练为主，并从解决问题角度将智力技能分为问题发现技能、问题分析技能和问题解决技能。着重训练学生掌握采购和供应管理中的认知技能、分析技巧和方法应用。

（3）要求学生通过说（讨论、口头表述）、写（撰写文件或报告）、做（实验操作或模拟实施）等表现方式将训练项目的结果展示出来，培养学生的实际工作能力。

在实际操作中，以当地某知名百货零售连锁企业为案例，老师提供企业规模、发展战略和采购现状等背景资料。要求学生从采购匹配企业战略的角度出发，结合企业实际，运用战略计划过程，研究提出企业未来5年的采购战略和持续改进计划。学生按班级分成若干个小组，每个小组8~10人，每个小组代表一个管理咨询团队，以战略方案可行性和创新性为评价标准。本次技能教学的目的是训练学生科学合理的采购决策思维和分析技巧，熟悉和掌握采购战略计划流程。教学时间：课内1学时用于各团队陈述方案及评比，其他准备工作在课外完成。

（六）赛式教学法

赛式教学法是指在教学活动中，把学生必须掌握的各项专业知识及技能融入比

赛项目,并安排专业教师进行指导、组织学生参加具有较强针对性和高度逼真性的专业竞赛,如专业理论知识、实践操作技能大赛等,通过让学生自主处理一个完整独立的比赛项目,使他们在比赛过程中学习理论知识的同时掌握实践操作技能,最终培养出具有良好的专业素养与实践能力的应用型人才。

自从全国举办大学生物流大赛开始,我们已经在学院成功举办了两届物流大赛,学生通过参加物流大赛不但巩固了已学的物流专业的知识,还在与其他专业学生的配合交流中学到了其他专业的知识,另外也培养了他们与人交往、合作和自学的能力。

在仓储与配送实务、运输管理实务、物流信息技术应用、物流成本、物流技术与设备等多门课程中开展赛事教学法,依托实验实训基地,通过搭建物流竞赛平台的方式,来为全体学生提供在竞赛中学习的机会。具体做法:一是充分发挥实验实训基地的作用。实验实训基地有效地将理论与实践、教学与生产、学校与社会相结合,是提高学生专业竞赛能力的重要场所;二是根据课程设置举办专业竞赛。组织学生利用课余时间围绕专业课程进行针对性较强的技能培训,并通过物流竞赛的方式对培训效果进行考核;三是借鉴全国物流专业竞赛的项目,分解后较好地融入到物流专业课程的实践教学中,通过举办校级竞赛,考察学生对物流专业技能和知识的综合运用能力,同时也为全国性专业竞赛优秀参赛选手的选拔工作打下了一定的基础。

通过赛式教学法,一是以赛促学,通过竞赛对学生进行考核,检验学生的专业知识和技能水平,促进学生积极自主地学习专业知识并进行技能训练;二是以赛促教,通过知识和技能的相互渗透和补充,促进指导教师教学水平的提高,从而推动"双师型"教学队伍的建设。

(七)企业调研实践法

物流行业的蓬勃发展,也给物流管理类课程的教学实践提供了更多的实践机会。学生通过独立的行动来进行企业实践调研。

三、思考

要想提高课堂教学质量,首先要创新教学理念,我们首先要认识到"学生是课堂的主人,教师是学生学习的引路人"。把学生放在课堂的主体地位上,可以调动学生学习的积极性,培养学生的学习兴趣,教师还能在教学时考虑学生的实际情况,根据学生的实际掌握情况进行教学,改变"压制、强迫"的手段,会使课堂教学效果有明显的提高。学生不能完全依赖教师的课堂教学学会全部知识,我们要通过培养学生的学习习惯和能力，来提高学生对知识的掌握程度，提高教学质量。可以根据学生的学习情况、知识的难易程度，安排学生预习、学习、复习，有利于学生学会学习方法。但是，使用各种教学法时，还需要把握以下几个方面。

（一）把握各种教学方法的比例关系

课堂教学中，要选择合适的教学方法。大学一年级的新生不仅要学习有关课程的基础理论知识，还要拿出一部分时间进行实践训练。同时，根据自己的兴趣选修部分课程，体验不同的教学方法。

（二）把握理论课与实践课的比例

实践教学是课堂教学的延续，能弥补课堂教学理论与实践联系不强的缺陷，在制订教学计划时，要合理安排实践教学的比例；在课程设置时，也要合理考虑课程内实践教学的比例。合理的实践教学环节有利于学生对理论知识的消化，也有利于培养学生适应社会的各种能力。

（三）合理选择多媒体教学和视频教学的手段

现代教学中多媒体的应用比较普遍，使用这种教学手段能给学生提供更多的信息，是方便教学的一种手段，但是，如果教师对多媒体教学过分依赖，会产生相反的效果。所以，我们要根据课程的特点和讲授内容的特点合理使用多媒体。视频教学形象、直观，可以帮助学生更好地理解和消化课程内容，适当的视频课程可以提高学生的学习兴趣，从而提高教学效果。

（四）加强校企间的合作

校企合作重要的是落实就业，是能力本位课程体系的根本保障。构建工学结合，是解决教育资源的手段和措施，更是创新人才培养模式的重要内容，采用物流认识实习、现场教学等手段，通过校企合作，能够给学生以充分的技能训练和实践机会，有效延伸教学空间。

四、结语

多种教学方法合理而有效的运用，能够培养满足社会需要的物流管理高素质人才，使学生具备分析和解决实际问题的多方面能力，能够应用先进的管理理念和科学的管理方法，对物流活动进行计划、指挥、协调和控制，使各项物流活动实现最佳的协调与配合，以降低物流成本，提高物流效率和效益，最终使物流管理专业学生的通用技能和专业技能得到大幅提高。

The Applications of Various Teaching Methods on Logistics Management Courses

Shao Ningping, Ningxia Vocational Technical College of Industry and Commerce

1. Introduction

The current reform of logistics management teaching mode should be based on the talents demands of enterprises. As an in-depth cooperation with enterprises goes on, through the understanding of enterprise workflow and the awareness of the position requirements of enterprises, a teaching mode reform should be carried out on specific point. Ningxia Vocational Technical College of Industry and Commerce should orient on the education of high skilled talents engaged of modern logistics management, deciding that the logistics management professional teaching should be practical. Therefore, we will use a variety of teaching methods oriented on professional teaching.

2. Application Analysis of a Variety of Teaching Methods

Behavior-oriented teaching methods include simulation, role-playing, case study, project-oriented teaching methods, task-driven approach, guiding text approach, brainstorming method, board and the like. The contents as follows shall give the brief introduction of the commonly used teaching methods of the logistics management courses.

(1) Project Oriented Teaching Method

The project oriented teaching method is to deliver a relatively independent project to let the students handle the project independently, including information collection, program design, project implementation and final evaluation. The teachers shoulder the responsibility of guidance and advice. Through the performance, the student should handle and manage the whole project, especially every single point.

The operation project is one of the most frequently used teaching methods that provide scenario and tools to students and to let them finish and present their assignment. Students are trained in operation, initialization and cooperation. For example, in the "Distribution Management Practices" and "Warehouse Management" courses, according to some of the knowledge points, the students can be assigned to distribution center or warehouse of enterprises, to pick up the goods, to distribute goods or to perform the simulated goods up-picking in school training center.

In the fifth semester, the courses of "Logistics Case Study and Practice" and "Electronic Commerce and Logistics" are opened with the tasks such as organizing a logistics or sales company to perform the practical logistics and sales assignment under the guidance of teachers. Early in the project, the teacher first carried out special training that includes market research, company formation, business management, financial management and business documents preparations. Each company is provided with professional training project with a budget of plan of 3,000 yuan. With the money, the students set up the company or relevant organizations, including warehouse department, purchasing department, transportation department, sales department and financial department, to perform the entity logistics management, purchasing management, sales management, inventory management and the like. While recoding company information, the whole business process is recorded with stamp signed.

When they get the loan, the students should start their business with a marketing investigation and then, a purchase plan. Warehouse staff training is followed afterwards based on inventory management. In the sales department of the company, students should make sales plan, and select the appropriate business site for product sales. The teachers, in the meanwhile, monitor the whole process of the project, including the attendance of the company's daily business process and the check of daily operation process and related documents. The teachers will supervise the whole process and generate an overall appraisal to the class and to each student according to their performance.

Logistics comprehensive training programs are work process oriented on training system generated from the new ideas of higher vocational education. Through training, the students should learn to be creative, not only learn logistics knowledge based on practical trainings, but also master logistics management skills, experience and success and failure of the enterprises operation, and the importance of teamwork.

(2) Case Study Teaching Method

Case study teaching method is a teaching method commonly used in lgistics professional teaching. Three steps are included that include a case designed with a background, the introduction of the background and the case analysis. Through a case study, the students will be tested with the application of theoretical knowledge and be trained with the ability to solve actual operation problems.

In addition, a dynamic method is selected in case teaching. For example, as teaching the course of "Warehouse Management", the teachers will start up the course with a logistics warehouse construction, afterwards, the actual implementation of equipment, warehouse data layout and information analysis. Through the case, relevant logistics theory and practice work are well combined together, so that the students can better understand the scenario and problems of the logistics enterprises so as to have a comprehensive use of knowledge and the ability to analyze and solve problems, based on future occupation purposes.

Students should pay attention to the analysis of the process with a logical way of thinking. The teachers will firstly help the students know clearly the advantages, disadvantages, opportunities and threats. The teacher will sum up the knowledge pints after a case discussion and case analysis.

(3) Role Play Teaching Method

Role play is frequently used in teaching process. The teacher, according to the teaching content, will design a scene according to the background and let the students perform a role to better understand knowledge and to learn skills.

In the course of "Supply Chain Management", "Beer Game" is commonly used to let the students better understand the theory of supply chain. Three components are included, manufacturers, wholesalers and retailers. When the students join in the supply chain, each person, performed as retailer, wholesaler, consumers, producers and suppliers of raw materials, is engaged in their business activities. For example, when customer orders are received, inventory should be considered and then the supplier should learn how to manage the enterprise production and material changes.

In the teaching process of "Supply Chain Management", a role play teaching method is used to let the students master impart knowledge or skills with enthusiasm stimulated but not "cramming". The approach shall strengthen the ability of forecast, decision-making and the ability to solve problems.

(4) Task-Driven Teaching Method

The task driven teaching method are used to let the students learn skills, improve the ability of analyzing problems and solve problems with an aim. With a task as the main line, the students should complete the task to gradually deepen their understanding of knowledge, increase their accumulation of experience knowledge and the ability to solve problems.

In the course of "International Freight Forwarding Agent", a case is designed as goods to be exported from Shenzhen, China to Los Angeles, USA. Students should analyze the case, including the goods production timetable, the best mode of transport way to save money, export document preparation, customs declaration, inspection work, completion of the actual delivery and bank settlement. The entire work process is divided into a couple of tasks to let the students solve problems step by step.

Take the case as follows for example:

1. Under the term of FOB, the departure port is SHENZHEN, CHINA; and the destination Port is LOS ANGELES, USA; ETA is before 2011/9/10, ocean freight.

2. Factory is located in Dongguan, the cargo will be completed in 2011/8/20. Product Name: Leather shoes about 60m^3/18T.

3. Shipping Company: CSCL (China Ocean Shipping Co. Ltd.)

After receiving the tasks, the students are divided into several groups according to customer requirements and the actual situation.

Each group, after careful analysis, will firstly confirm the order within the stipulated time. If time is not enough for the products, the shipment will not be successful. At the same time, when the factory confirms the weight and volume of goods, the shipment should be confirmed and then, shipping and container equipment. Furthermore, the students should prepare the documents for customs clearance, contact the customs and so on.

When the task is closing, the teachers should check if the students complete it successfully with customer requirements and industry practice. Also, teachers should give a summary to let the students know their weak points during the practical training.

(5) Skill Training Based Teaching

Training hours in our school will take up to 50% of the whole program of 2 years. The students are trained to understand the logistics process, to familiarize with the logistics business and to utilize the information platform collaboration. The training courses are a combination of a variety of teaching methods.

In the course of "Procurement Management" as an example, the teaching goal is as follows:

(1) Procurement management skills including basic skills training and general skills training.

(2) The students should focus themselves on skills and methods practices.

(3) Students are trained with working ability.

In actual operation, provided with strategy and procurement situation, background information, the students are asked to design an enterprise strategy combined with the actual business, and then, in the next 5 years, purchasing strategy and continuous improvement plan should be carried out. The students are divided into several groups to be trained with scientific and purchasing strategic thinking, decision-making thinking and analytical skills.

(6) Competition Oriented Teaching Method

Competition oriented method is to let students master the professional knowledge and skills through teachers' guidance. When participating in competitions, the students are eager to learn knowledge and practical skills under a pressure so that the method can be carried out successfully.

Since our school has successfully held two sessions of logistics competition, students are trained with logistics professional knowledge to solve actual problems and to communicate with students from other schools to share experience.

In the course of "Warehousing and Distribution Practices", "Transportation Management Practices", "Logistics Information Technology", and "Logistics

Cost", "Logistics Technology and Equipment" through the up-building of the logistics competition platform, the students are provided with the learning opportunities. The students are organized to focus on professional training and a national-level logistics professional competition for better skill training.

Through the competition teaching, professional knowledge and skills of the students are trained properly and promoted. The students actively learn professional knowledge and undertake skills training so as to meet the teachers teaching level improvement.

(7) Enterprise Survey Practice

With the vigorous development of the logistics industry, the school provides more opportunities for practice teaching.

Enterprise survey practice is to let the students do independent research by going outside.

3. Considerations

In order to improve the quality of classroom teaching, the teachers must firstly recognize that "students are the masters of the classroom; the teacher is to guide students to learn". The students should master the class while teachers cultivate the interest of the students in learning. The teachers should also consider the actual situation of the students in teaching. The students can't depend on teachers completely; however, teachers should improve the students' mastery of the knowledge.

(1) Proportion of Various Teaching Methods in a Class

In the classroom teaching, an appropriate teaching method should be carefully picked up. The first grade university students should not only learn the basic theory of the course, but also, take a proportion of time for practical training and other elective courses according to their personal interest, with a variety of teaching methods.

(2) Course Proportion for Theory and Practice

Practice teaching is the extension of classroom teaching. In teaching plan, to arrange the proportion of practical teaching, the teachers should consider how to distribute the proportion for theory and practice courses that will be helpful for students' career future.

(3) Selection of Multimedia Teaching and Video Teaching Method

Multimedia is widely used in modern teaching. It can provide the students with more information. A teacher cannot rely too much on multimedia but should adjust teaching content to help students better understand the course content, and improve their interest in learning.

(4) Strengthening School-Enterprise Cooperation

School-enterprise cooperation is important for a higher employment rate of the graduates. Teaching innovation is also important for an enterprise cooperation that can give students adequate training and practice opportunities, thus effectively extending the teaching space.

4. Conclusion

Through the use of various teaching methods that are reasonable and effective, the course can meet the requirement of logistics management talents and the students can be trained with the ability to analyze and solve practical problems, especially the advanced management concepts and scientific management methods to plan, command, negotiate, control and take all the logistics activities to the best advantage to reduce cost and enhance logistics effectiveness.

通过体验式教学激发学生的学习动力和学习热情

丰盛湾理工学院　Kelly Pender

　　Hatton 解释说，教学主要是根据教师在学校和社会的经验塑造出来的；教育工作者在准备执教前，他们的"经验已经塑造了他们的态度和价值观，因此他们的态度和价值观可能会有意无意地影响他们的教学"。我觉得这个观点对于我的教学理念、对他人的态度和人生观的形成意义尤为重大。

　　我对教学的激情、热情、积极性和尊重均受到了我生命中非常重要的人的影响，因我想要通过教育来试图改变人们命运的决心而燃起，这是我与我的学生分享的理念。我认为在本次发言的开头来说明我的观点很重要，因为它是我之所以成为我的原因。我在一个非常和谐的家庭环境中长大，我的父母和祖父母对我的成长有着难以置信的影响，他们随时准备向我伸出援助之手。我的妻子、两个可爱的孩子和家庭是我的一切。我想不出比我如何学习做一个父亲和丈夫更好的体验式学习的例子。对于我来说，在生活的大课堂学习成长的过程，过去是，而且将来也一直会是团队合作、解决问题、犯错误和取得成功的不断学习的过程。

　　我所从事的是"健身证书"的课程教学，为健身行业提供健身教练或为毕业生打好基础以便继续深造。课程为期一年，从 2000 年开始直到今天。我们的学生人数一直为 35~44，他们就像是一盘由各种水果组成的"水果沙拉"，来自不同年龄阶层，分属不同种族，经历和身体条件各异并具有不同的受教育经历。我认为这些都是学习环境中的积极因素，虽然有时也很有挑战性。作为一名教师站在教学和教育角度来讲，这个"熔炉"提供了完美的学习环境供学生成长，使他们学会欣赏和理解他人，

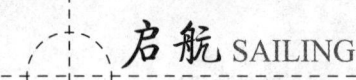

学习在一个以人为本的行业工作所需的知识。在工作中，客户也会带给他们相似的挑战。

McEwan解释说，一名好的教师在一定程度上代表了热情、乐观、有使命感和真实，且以身作则。教学不仅是我的职业，更是我的爱好，我深深地被教学所激励，并对教学充满激情。

我的目标是用实际行动做努力工作的表率，用经验、态度和热情去武装学生。Jim Henson介绍说："学生不会总记得你教过什么。但他们记得你是什么样的人。"

我计划在整个课程教学中使用的体验式学习方法是培养团队精神，鼓励思考和反思，加强个人和专业知识的增长和学习。正是这些学习体验让课程变得与众不同，这一点和多年来高学员保持率和学业完成率有直接关系，尤其是考虑到学习者多样化这个特点。通过激发学习动力、积极性，鼓励学生参与各种活动来加强学习是我的教学原则。我尊重学生带给课程的知识，并利用每一个机会来促进大家分享这些知识。

我的教学态度是，教学只会受到想象力和安全因素的限制。在学习过程中重要的是要学会打破条条框框思考才会有新的发现。我相信在安全的环境中，这是有效的成人教育必不可少的教学方法。在开学初期我们就清楚每个学生的学习风格。学生分析和讨论自己的学习风格和哪种教学方法最适合自己，然后哪种方法适合整个班级。从这时开始，我尽量采用适合学习者需求的教学方法。在整个学习过程中，我会重新审视这个教学方法，并根据需要做出调整。健身课程从性质上来讲主要采取动觉学习法，外加部分视觉和听觉学习法，我确保通过有效的教学方法和评估活动照顾到所有学习者的需求。

Chickering和Gamson解释说，一个好的教师的特点是鼓励学生主动学习，他们还指出"学习不是一个旁观者的运动"。简单地说，如果学生只是坐在课堂上听老师说教，记住老师的话，以后简单地进行复述，那他们等于什么都没学会。在学习中，学习者必须用嘴说、用笔写、用笔画、对知识进行创新和经常运用。

去健身场所实地参观与教学是一个不可分割的整体，能帮助学生学习现场知识和对健身行业有更全面的了解。我们参观当地和其他地区的健身中心，请行业人士有的放矢地说明现场实践为什么和在哪方面可以运用于教学。

这些都是有效的学习体验，既令人鼓舞，又提高了学生的理论知识，同时向学生展示了好的行业规范。去许多当地健身中心参观的内容包括会见以前的学长、检查学生的学习情况和帮助学生寻找灵感。

有效的综合评估策略在我的教学理念中占很大的比重。Bensemen 和 Sutton 指出,"我们对学习者评估时所设计和使用的评估方法的质量,会影响教学质量和学生的学习体验质量"。通过总结多年来从学生、同事、行业和 ITO 那里收到的意见反馈,对学习成果的要求集中为增加现实生活中公平的、适当的、有效的和反思式评估活动。最根本的一点是要让学习者了解评估活动并为设计出最佳的评估规范献计献策。我尽可能多地设计真实、接近行业现实工作环境的综合评估活动以反映课程的教学成果和行业标准。NZQA 说:"最好的证据往往都是最直接的。如果你想知道某个人是否知道如何做一项实验,那就让他们去做,而不是让他们用嘴说或用笔写。"

Empowerment and Compassion Enhanced Through Experiential Learning

Kelly Pender, Bay of Plenty Polytechnic

Hatton explains that teaching is shaped, predominantly, by teachers' experiences in school and society; that before educators enter teaching preparation they have had "experiences that have shaped their attitudes and values, which may, wittingly or unwittingly, influence their teaching". I feel this perspective is particularly significant in the development in my teaching philosophy, attitude toward people and outlook on life.

My passion, enthusiasm, motivation and respect for learners has been influenced collectively by significant people in my life and ignited by seeking to make a difference with people through education. This is the philosophy I share with my students. It is important to describe my perspective early on in this document, because this is the "why" for me. I have grown up in a close family environment, where my parents and grandparents have been incredibly influential on me, always there for support. My wife, two beautiful children, and family are everything to me.

I cannot think of a better illustration of experiential learning than to use myself as an example as a father and a husband. For me this has been, and will continue to be a journey of collaboration, problem solving, mistakes and successes as I learn my way through the university of life.

My programme is a "Certificate in Fitness" that provides graduates entry to the fitness industry as a Fitness Trainer or helps lay the foundation to a continuation of higher level learning. A year-long course that has been running since 200, we have always hosted 35-44 learners who are a "fruit salad" in diversity. Variety in age, ethnicity, experience, physical capabilities and educational history I acknowledge as positive features in our learning environment. Whilst at times challenging as an educator, in terms of teaching and pedagogy, this "melting pot" environment provides the perfect setting for students to grow, learn to appreciate, empathise, and develop the required understanding necessary to work in a people-centred industry, where clients will provide them with similar challenges.

McEwan explains that an effective teacher is partly personified by being passionate and positive, mission-driven and real, who leads by example. Teaching is not only my profession, but a hobby to which I am deeply motivated by and passionate about.

My aim is to role model a strong work ethic and to empower students with experiences with attitude and passion. Jim Henson describes that "students don't always remember what you try to teach them. They remember what you are".

Learning experiences I plan throughout the programme are to develop team spirit, stimulate thought and reflection, and enhance personal and professional growth and learning. It is these experiences that create programme uniqueness, which have direct connection to high retention and completion rates over the years, particularly considering the diverse range of learners. Energy, enthusiasm, student involvement and activities to reinforce learning are principles in my delivery. I respect the knowledge students bring to the learning environment and I promote the sharing of experience at every opportunity.

My attitude to delivery is that you are only limited by imagination and safety. It is essential to think outside the square to gain a different perspective in learning. I believe this approach, in a safe environment, is essential to effective adult education. At the start of the programme, individual learning styles are identified. Students analyze and discuss their own learning styles and how delivery may best suit them as individuals, then, collectively as a group. From this process, my teaching is styled to suit the needs of the learner. This exercise is revisited throughout the programme and adjustments made as required. Fitness students are predominantly kinaesthetic, part visual, part auditory learners in nature and I ensure all learning styles are catered for through effective delivery techniques and assessment activities.

Chickering and Gamson explain an effective characteristic of a teacher as one that encourages active learning, identifying that "learning is not a spectator sport". Quite simply, students do not learn much just by sitting in classes listening to teachers preaching, memorising information to simply regurgitate at a later time. Learners must verbalise what they are learning, write about it, draw about it, create with it, relate it and frequently apply it.

Industry relevant field trips are an integral part of delivery to assist real world preparation and appreciation. We visit local and out of region fitness facilities and engage speakers with clear cut goals and purpose as to why and where the experience fits within the learning context.

These are effective learning experiences that are both motivating and theory enhancing for the students as well as showcase good practice. Many local fitness centre visits involve meeting graduate students, providing reality checks and inspiration to current learners.

Effective integrated assessment strategies are a strong ingredient in my teaching philosophy. Bensemen and Sutton cite that the "quality of the assessments we design and use with learners affects the quality of the teaching and learning experience they have." Through feedback over time from students, colleagues, industry and ITO, learning outcomes are clustered to grow real life fair, appropriate, valid and reflective assessment activities. It is essential for learners to understand and contribute to best practice assessment. I design as many integrated assessment activities as possible to be authentic to the actual performance conditions required in industry to reflect programme outcomes and required unit standards. NZQA describes the "best evidence is usually the most direct: if you want to know if someone knows how to conduct an experiment, get them to do it rather than just talk or write about it".

化工单元操作及设备维护课程教学创新

新疆轻工职业技术学院　陈晓峰

摘要：专业核心课程的开发与"岗位导向"课程不同，它要兼顾职业性和技术性，具有全面性、发展性的特点。本文就化工类专业核心课程化工单元操作与设备维护的开发过程从教学模式、方法、手段等七个方面的创新进行了总结。

关键词：岗位导向、创新课程、教学模式

一、对课程创新的认识

进入本世纪以来，随着职业教育的改革，职业教育区别于学历教育，在"以就业为导向"的思想指导下，一度比较强调职业教育课程内容的"岗位导向"，在订单班中尤为明显。我校化工专业结合新疆化工大发展的优势，与企业开展大量的订单教育，开发了部分"岗位导向"课程，在实施的过程中发现了一些问题。

"岗位导向"课程设置，其积极意义在于岗位技能强，特别是学生毕业后的"首岗"技能，学生直接上岗适应期短，受企业欢迎，但是从用人单位对毕业生质量反馈角度看，也存在着学生素质不够全面的现象。"岗位导向"的课程设置，存在先天不足的缺陷，"岗位技能"与"终身发展"之间的矛盾无法解决，这就要回到这两个问题：什么是职业教育？什么是技术教育？两个概念的内涵都相当丰富，从简单、直观的角度来理解，技术教育侧重于专一性、岗位性的特点，而职业教育应该具有全面性、发展性的特点，目标指向人的一生。学校教育应该思考这样的问题："我们让学生带走什么？"在建设国家示范校的过程中，这个问题显得更加重要。因为"示范"包含着质量、榜样、创新的全面要求。从学生个性发展的角度，恰当选择自主

发展的课程，是职业教育必须做到的。课程是专业的灵魂。课程改革，已经成为专业建设的重要问题。

二、课程内容的开发

课程开发是在专业课程体系建设基础上进行的，不能脱离整体要求。我们对新疆境内近十家以上的大型企业进行了调研，对化工操作人员的岗位能力进行了分析，基于化工产品生产过程，将化工操作人员从事的岗位工作，分为物料准备→装置运行→装置维护支持→装置异况处理→质量检测→HSEQ管理7大工作领域、30个工作任务，凝炼出156项职业能力。根据工作任务的相关性和学生的认知规律，将它们分为专业核心课和专业方向课程。课程体系由三大模块组成，即基本素质模块、专业核心能力模块、专业方向模块（订单模块）。专业方向课程在订单培养的过程中可以作为"岗位导向"课程开发，而专业核心课程要结合岗位能力需求以项目导向方式来开发，同时必须保证内容的完整性、全面性及学生今后的可持续发展。

目前，在国内本科院校和职业院校化工类专业都开设有化工单元过程或化工原理课程，但课时量较少，以理论教学为主，讲求理论的系统性和计算，理论与实践脱离，同学们学完后不懂得如何去运用这些理论解决生产中的实际问题。

现代化工企业需要大批掌握化工工艺生产操作又懂系统维护、工况分析工作的高技能复合型人才。因此，我们邀请企业专家参与了本课程的开发，8名来自企业的专家和专业教师对化工企业运行员岗位进行分析，得出该岗位的工作流程，进而列出该岗位的职业能力和知识要求。有专家提出要把单元操作与设备系统维护放在一起开展教学，用更为完整的项目来带动教学。该提议得到企业专家和教师们的一致认可，因此，课程组决定将单元操作与设备维护融于一门课程之中构成化工单元操作及设备维护这门课，将过去的化工原理、化工设备、化工装置运行三门课程的内容融合在了一起。

在完成岗位能力分析后，课程组进行课程的整体设计。课程组的成员查阅了大量文献，到企业考察生产流程，听取企业专家的意见和建议，最终完成了化工单元操作与维护课程的整体设计和部分教材的编写。课程中，单元操作与设备维护知识被运用到6个实际生产项目之中，每个项目都以产品为载体，学生在完成典型的工作任务中学习知识和技能。工作任务的设置由简单到复杂，由单项到综合，实现学生认知、实践、再认识、再实践的螺旋上升。学生在教师指导和带动下完成训练项目，使学生在实战中训练操作能力，并获取相关的必备知识。在新的专业人才培养方案中，本课程的课时数从化工单元过程与操作的 160 课时逐渐提高到化工单元操作与维护的 280 课时，形成理论实践一体化的"项目导向、任务驱动"的教学模式。所培养的学生技能熟练，并善于分析和解决问题，实现综合发展。

三、课程教学方法的突破点

以课程中的精馏项目为例，重构后的课程从 7 个方面挑战传统教学模式：

一是打破传统先理论后实践的授课顺序，同学们可以直接按仿真操作指南，进行精馏，出现一系列错误学生开始质疑时，引入精馏的简单原理，再实践。

二是通过团队合作完成工作，学生在掌握了精馏仿真操作后，分组进入实验室，老师简单介绍流程和阀门位置后，开始进行乙醇水的分离，同学们先分组制订方案，查阅资料，然后讨论，期间可以请教老师，当方案合理时，开始上装置操作。

三是竞赛方式可以促进学生的学习兴趣和探究意识，目前 90 后的职校学生普遍没有自主学习意识，但有极强的表现欲，因此，竞赛可以使他们超常努力，课堂中可以经常设竞赛项目，在操作结束时，安排竞赛，把优秀的选手推荐为学校大赛的种子选手。

四是打破传统教学方式中实践课由实习指导教师来上，理论课教师只上理论课。开始有些教师不敢上实操和仿真课，但我们只给了一年的时间培训锻炼，所有教师都已实现理实一体化的授课，教学质量明显提高。

五是考核方法改革，课程采用形成性考核，成绩主要包括四部分：职业道德、工作过程质量、实训项目报告、操作质量。其中：

(1) 职业道德：在课程总成绩中倒扣分 0～50 分。包括遵纪守时、认真负责、积极主动、踏实肯干、团结协作、严谨求实、爱护公物等方面。由教师评定。

(2) 工作过程质量：包括实训操作能力及表现和课堂交流讨论表现。

实训操作能力及表现：占 30%，考核内容包括实训前的准备情况、方案的制定、操作的规范程度和熟练程度。由教师和小组内成员根据标准评定，小组内成员互评占 30%，教师评分占 70%。

课堂交流讨论表现：占 30%，包括获取信息、语言表达、自学、提出问题、分析问题、解决问题等能力。由小组互评和教师评分组成，项目汇报时根据标准进行评价，互评占 30%，教师评价占 70%。

(3)实训项目技术报告:占10%,每小组提交技术报告。报告格式按要求撰写,写作符合规范。由教师评分。

(4)操作质量:占30%,按岗位操作规程,对每次操作过程和结果进行评分。操作质量的评分由教师评分。

六是在教学过程中必须留给学生知识拓展的内容。在精馏项目教学中掌握基本理论和基本操作的基础上,必须有学生拓展的内容。如精馏项目,塔的设计就是拓展的内容,不是所有学生都需要完成,完成的可以加分。

七是创新课程必须有实训作为支撑,化工单元操作及设备维护课程建设有1 300平方米工厂化的单元实训车间,仿真机房工位数150个,配备单元操作仿真软件,化工管路拆装实训工位齐全,完全满足学生理实一体化教学需要,教学内容大部分在实训场所完成。

四、课程实施过程中的问题及突破

创新课程的实施对教师的执教能力是一个极大的挑战,要求他们必须能够驾驭课堂,将知识和技能融会贯通。老教师可能能做得到,但年轻教师由于经验不足、实践能力欠缺,可能难以把握。在我校化工专业教师年龄梯队中,年轻教师占多数,为了能让改革的思想成果贯彻和实施,我们组织专业带头人和骨干教师和部分年轻教师对化工单元操作与设备维护进行了全程288堂课的课程设计,包括教案、典型任务的选取、教学案例资源、PPT、习题、竞赛方案、阅读材料等,边设计,边研讨,在这个过程中教师的理念得到了极大的更新,由开始的排斥发展为接受和积极参与,使教学改革得以实施。

五、创新课程的建设效果

本门课程设计和实践,为今后化工专业的建设和发展打下了坚实的基础。

(1)由于创新课程的实施,我专业学生在历次疆内技能大赛中获得一等奖并代表新疆参加全国技能大赛获得二、三等奖。

(2)由于创新课程的实施,企业对学校和学生的认可度进一步提升,毕业生出现供不应求的局面。我们还为企业举办技能大赛,为企业培训人数每年达3 000人。

(3)学校成为全疆煤化工师资培训基地,并举办全疆化工技能大赛,为新疆煤化工石油化工的发展输送了大批合格人才。

The Teaching Innovation of "the Chemical Engineering Unit Operation and Maintenance"

Chen Xiaofeng, Xinjiang Institute of Light Industry Technology

Abstract: The development of the core curriculum differs from the job-oriented curriculum which gives consideration to both occupational and technical capabilities. It possesses the characteristics of comprehensiveness and expansibility. This article summarizes seven aspects of the innovation about the teaching methods and models in "the Chemical Engineering Unit Operation and Maintenance".

Keywords: job-oriented; curriculum innovation; teaching mode

1. The Understanding of the Curriculum Innovation

With the reform of the vocational education in the 21st century, the vocational education is distinct from academic education. Under the guidance of the employment-oriented, the chemical engineering in our school took the advantage of the rapid development of Xinjiang chemical industry, established order education with enterprises and developed job-oriented curriculum. However, we discovered some problems in the process.

The significance of the job-oriented curriculum is that the students can strengthen their technical abilities in their jobs, especially their first posts after their graduations. It is able to shorten the adaption period which gains favorable comments from many enterprises. Nevertheless, we learned from the feedback from these enterprises, the qualities of these students are insufficiently comprehensive. There are defects in the establishment of the job-oriented curriculum. The contradiction between job skills and lifelong development can't reach a proper solution. This situation leads us back to the concept, "what's vocational education?" "What's technical education?" The connotation of these two concepts is fairly abundant. From a simple perspective, technical education pays more attention to specificity and job performance. While vocational education emphasize on comprehensiveness and expansibility, which intents on the students' life planning. It appears to be more important that in the process of establishing the national demonstration school, we should question what we are able to let the students to take away from the school. Since demonstration school contains comprehensive requirements of qualities, models and innovations, the vocational education must choose proper self-development courses for the prospective of personality development of the students. These courses are the soul of the specialized subject. As a result, the reform of the curriculum is the major problem of the construction of the subject.

2. The Development of the Curriculum Content

The development of the curriculum content is based on the system of the chemical engineering curriculum. In the research of nearly ten enterprises in Xinjiang, we analyzed the capabilities of the chemical operators. Based on chemical production process, we divided the chemical operators into 7 parts, including material preparation, plant operation, plant maintenance support, plant abnormal condition treatment, quality inspection, and HSEQ management. 30 tasks covered 156 occupation abilities. According to the correlation of the tasks and the cognitive rules of the students, we divided them into professional core courses and professional orientation courses. The system of the curriculum is made up of 3 modules, including the basic quality module, the professional core ability module and the professional orientation module (the order module). The professional orientation development can be treated as job-oriented course in the procedure of order-form training, while the professional core course must combine the capability demands. Meanwhile, it must ensure the content integrity and sustainability.

At present, the chemical engineering in domestic colleges and universities and vocational colleges are all established "Chemical unit operations" or "Principles of chemical engineering" courses. However, with less class time and priority to theoretical teaching instead of operating practice, students aren't capable of applying these theories to solve practical problems in production.

Modern chemical enterprises need a large number of highly skilled talents who master chemical process and system maintenance and analysis of operating. Therefore, we invited 8 experts from chemical enterprises to participate in the development of this course; they worked with our professional teachers on the analysis of the chemical enterprise member post operation. They concluded the working process of the position, then listed the professional ability and knowledge requirements of the position. Experts raised the unit operation and equipment system maintenance should be put together to carry out the teaching, to drive the teaching with more complete project. This proposal was unanimously recognized. And the course group decided to take the unit operation and equipment maintenance to integrate into one course—"The Chemical Engineering Unit Operation and Maintenance". This course properly mixed "Principles of Chemical Engineering", "Chemical Equipment" and "Chemical plant operation" together.

Having completed the post capacity analysis, the course groups carried out the overall design of the course. Our course group members consulted a large number of literatures, reached to the enterprise to investigate their production process and listened to the suggestion from the experts, and finally completed the "chemical unit operations and maintenance" teaching design and part of the writing of the course. In the course, unit operation and equipment maintenance knowledge is applied to the 6 practical production projects; students learn knowledge and skills in the typical work task. With tasks set from simple to complex, and from single to comprehensive, students can accomplish progress from cognition to practice, renew and practice. Students are able to complete the training project under the teachers' guidance, and are allowed to operate in actual combat training. In the new scheme of talent cultivation, the capacity of the course of chemical unit process and operation gradually increased from 160 hours to "chemical unit operations and maintenance" which includes 280 class hours, thus forming the integration of the theory of practice of "project orientation, task driven" teaching mode. The students cultivated were skilled, and expert in analysis and problem-solving, so as to achieve a comprehensive development.

3. The Breakthrough of Teaching Method

To take rectification project as an example, the refractor course challenges the traditional teaching mode from seven aspects:

1) Break the traditional teaching order, so that students can operate directly according to the simulation operation guide to the rectification. After a series of mistakes students begin to question while we introduced the simple principle of rectification, and then practice.

2) Finish the work through the teamwork. As long as students master the rectification simulation, we divide them into several groups into the lab. Then the teacher briefly introduces the process and valve position, and let the students start the separation of ethanol water. Small group first make plans, access to information, and then discuss. They may ask teachers if the plan is reasonable and begin to operate on the device.

3) Competition methods can promote the students' interest in learning

and exploring consciousness. Now the 90's vocational schools students generally have no sense of autonomous learning, yet they got strong performance desire. Therefore their competition can make extraordinary efforts; competitions can be set up often in the class.

4) Break the traditional way of teaching that theory class teachers focus on theory, while practice guidance teachers only on practice lesson. All teachers have implemented the integration of theory to practice. The teaching quality has improved significantly.

5) Reform of assessment methods. The formative assessment mainly includes four parts—the professional ethics, the quality of the working process, the report of training project, the operation quality.

(1) The professional ethics. Deduction point of 0-50 points in the course grade. Disciplined to be punctual, responsible, active, solidary and cooperative, etc. Assessed by the teacher.

(2) The quality of the working process, including training operational capability and classroom discussions performance.

Training Operational capability and performance took up 30%. Examination content includes training preparation, program development and operating norms and proficiency, according to the standard assessed by the teachers and team's members, Mutual accounted for 30%, the teacher's evaluation 70%.

Classroom discussions performance accounted for 30%, including the access to information, language expression, ability to ask questions, analyze and solve problems, etc. according to the standard assessed by the teachers and team's members, Mutual accounted for 30%, the teacher's evaluation (70%).

(3) Training project technical report accounted for 10%. Each group should submit technical report. Report format should be written as required.

Graded by the teacher.

(4) Operation quality accounted for 30%. Score each operation process and result according to post operation procedures. Operation quality ratings graded by the teacher.

6) In the teaching process the expansion of the content of knowledge must be left to students. For example, in the rectification project, the design of the tower is the expanding content. Not all students have to complete it, but those who complete it gain extra scores.

7) Innovative courses must have training practice as a support. "The Chemical Engineering Unit Operation and Maintenance" curriculum are constructed with 1,300 square meters training workshop. 150 simulation computer workstation are equipped with unit operation simulation software. Chemical pipeline disassembling training location are complete. All the above fully meet the needs of the students to raise the integration teaching, Most of the teaching content are accomplished in training places.

4. Problems and Breakthrough in the Process of Curriculum Implementation

The implementation of innovative courses is a great challenge for teachers' teaching ability, who must be able to control the classroom, achieve knowledge and skills to a comprehensive level, which may not be a difficult task for the old teachers, but may not be easy to handle for the young teachers due to a lack of experience and practical ability. Young teachers took up a major part in chemical professional teachers in our school age echelon. To carry out and implement thoughts of the reform results, we organized professional teachers and the leading part of the young teachers of chemical unit operations and maintenance for the 288 class curriculum design, including teaching plans, the selection of typical tasks, case teaching resources, PPT, problem sets, competition plan, reading materials, edge design, discussion, and in this process, the idea of teachers got greatly updated, changing the previous attitude from reject to accept, even actively participating in it to implement the teaching reform.

5. The Achievement of the Innovative Curriculum Construction

Through the design and practice of this course, we laid a solid foundation for the future development of chemical engineering specialty construction.

(1) Due to the implementation of the innovation course, students in our major won the first prize in all previous skills contest in Xinjiang and on behalf of Xinjiang took part in the national skills competition and won the second and third prizes.

(2) Due to the implementation of the innovation course, our students and our school improved the recognition from the enterprises. Thus, graduates are in short supply. Our school helped hold skills contest for the enterprises. We trained 3,000 people per year for chemical enterprises,

(3) Our school became the coal chemical teacher training base and held the Xinjiang chemical skills contest. Furthermore, we transport a large number of qualified personnel for the development of coal chemical industry petroleum chemical industry in Xinjiang.

挑战性受教者的教学过程参与

怀卡托理工学院　Julia Bruce

生活共识是一个概念性框架，它将个人反思、文化探查和有意义的、具有相同价值观的小组协议相结合以建立质变学习环境。"生活共识"这个术语来源于我14年职业教育生涯和目前所从事的高等学校师资培训的经验。该框架囊括了我的许多教学和学习策略，它们已成功地帮助学习者不断提高自我意识和掌握可转换学习技能。这些教学和学习策略获得了2008 AkoAotearoa 高等教育教学成功应用优秀奖。从那时起，我受AkoAotearoa 的邀请帮助遍布新西兰的多个工作室向高等教育者介绍这些策略。我相信如果生活共识框架及其相关策略能够向其他成人教育机构介绍和推广，那它们可能会对更多的学习者产生积极的影响。目前正在进行的一项研究，重点测试在青年学习者从高中学校学习向成人工作场所学习过渡过程中这一理论的应用效果。

图1　生活共识的概念性框架

为了响应政府的新政策，我们看到越来越多的青年进入新西兰高等职业学校学习，但到目前为止，对在这个群体的教学中所采用的方法却几乎没有什么研究。许多青年在向成人学习环境过渡过程中经历了很多困难。生活共识框架包括了许多知名的教育理论，如 Malcolm Knowles 的著作。他的成人教育学理论认为成人与儿童相比有不同的学习需求。他对成人学习者的主要假设是，成年人有自主学习能力、有经验，这可以成为一种学习资源。他们的"学习准备就绪"与他们所扮演的社会角色密切相关，他们是"有目的的学习"，而不是"按书本要求来学习"。

生活共识框架和 Malcolm Knowles 的成人学习者假设理论相一致。该框架考虑到了许多青年在从学校学习向以 Malcolm Knowles 的成人教育理论为基础的学习环境过渡的过程中所遇到的困难。Selina Chan 研究了 27 位在新西兰选择通过学徒训练学习一门技术的学习者，他们中的大多数是青年。之所以给青少年提供选择通过学徒训练学习技术的原因包括个人行为不良和在校成绩不佳。Chan 提倡开发"元认知"和"学会学习"等技能，以帮助青年从学校学习顺利过渡到工作场所学习。这些技能包括批判性思维、反思，通过提问及与他人沟通学习如何解决问题。生活共识框架提供了一个支持性体系，实施后可以帮助学习者掌握上述及其他技能，同时为他们提供正面的、支持性的学习体验。

生活共识框架的基础由许多学习理论构成。这些理论可以划分为四种更广义的"定向学习"教学理论，即人本主义、认知主义、社会文化和行为主义理论（Smith, 2003）。生活共识框架能反映上述每种学习理论。

人本主义学习理论家，如 Carl Rogers，告诉我们，成年人有着丰富的生活经验、信仰和世界观，而这些可以丰富学习环境。Rogers 的理论重点是通过引导型实践、"真实性"、同感和接受来建立学习关系。Rogers 认为，"引导型学习方法"要做到教育与辅导二者兼顾，因为要想实现成功的学习体验，必须考虑人的整体需求。"真实性"是指主导者的真实性，Rogers 建议主导人"做真正的自己"，不要伪装，这样才能与学习者沟通，建立成功的学习关系。在这里，接受是指主导者承认和重视学习者作为个体具有独特的思想、经验和世界观，而且这些可以优化学习环境。当一个主导者能深刻理解学习者在学习过程中的感受时，他就与学习者之间产生了共鸣。

生活共识框架不仅建立学习者与教师／主导者的学习关系，同时还注重建立同学间的学习关系。根据研究人员的经验，鼓励学生做人要有诚信，重视多样化和理解那些在学习之旅中与自己同行的人，有益于建立一个包容的和转化型的学习氛围。

社会文化学习理论既重视个人学习，又重视学习者之间的学习关系的重要性。这些理论的基础是成人可以利用他们的多样化思维、文化和经验通过观察他人和社会对知识的建构来一起学习。Lave 和 Wenger 注意到，实践小组可以激励学习者全身心地投入到自己的学习中，成为小组活动的积极参加者。每个小组的社会文化实践不但要由每位组员参与制定，而且要人人遵守，以便做到人人参与。

根据这一理论创立的生活共识框架用于支持学习者去开发适合各自小组需求的社会文化学习实践。这些实践都是在每个小组的独特学习环境和大家共同认可的道德标准和正面行为准则的基础上建立的。学习者在整个学习过程中，不断探讨和调整他们的共识，以信守他们的共同价值观。与此同时，还对每位成员的价值观的真正意义和这些价值观的形成原因进行持续的调查。

学习者所参与的长期实验和反思过程，作为生活共识的一部分，体现在认知主义学习理论中。认知主义学习理论关心的是促进"学习过程"和对知识的深刻理解。Phil Race 的"池塘涟漪"的认知主义学习理论以体验式学习概念为基础，强调体验、实践、反思和理论化的重要性。然而，Race 将这些想法进一步发挥，指出人们通过体验式学习在这些阶段进进出出，而且主导者和同学的意见反馈在让学习变得"有意义"的过程中起着举足轻重的作用。在研究中，关于学习者为什么喜欢学习，Race 有了许多新发现。它们是：

收到他人的反馈；

看到他人的回应；

学习者能够帮助他人；

学习者看到他们所学知识对他人的影响；

看到结果。

为了整合这些发现，Race 在他的学习理论中包括了同行教学和同行评估学习阶段，并赞同采取小组学习方式。构成生活共识框架的教学策略是基于上述想法，根据不同的学习目的将众人分组。分组有利于学习，同时评估其他小组的学习以及反思自己小组的学习进展。小组不仅要思考他们课程学习的进展情况，而且还要思考如何管理小组。框架同时鼓励个人反思他们对小组所做的贡献以及他们在小组中所起的作用。设计这些自我反思实践的目的是为了提高学习者的自我意识，以培养他们的学习自主性，使他们在学习和工作中能进行自我调剂。

第四种"定向学习"是行为主义理论，是许多较为传统的教学方法的理论基础。行为主义学习理论认为，学习和行为都是由环境、重复和强制行为塑造的（往往是通过奖励和惩罚的做法）。早期进行的证明行为主义理论的研究主要注重研究学习者的可观察行为而不是研究学习者的认知思维过程或对知识的理解程度。

虽然行为主义理论在教育者心目中不如认知主义、人本主义和社会文化学习理论受欢迎，但该理论的许多方法仍然在当今成人教育中继续沿用。在遵守生活共识框架时，对于小组公认的不被接受的行为，小组成员要共同裁定处理方法。小组裁定的结果大部分是采取赏罚模式。违反约定共识的学习者往往受到诸如在早茶时间为同学泡咖啡的惩罚，甚至更糟——为大家提供早茶。采取惩罚方式的做法在今天的成人教育学习环境中可能显得有些严厉，然而，我所主导的使用生活共识模式的每个小组都表示希望将这样的处理决定写入明文规定。

也许这种愿望是因为适应行为主义模式下学习和工作的结果？通过我的实践，我注意到如果充分发挥生活共识框架的作用，激励学习者积极参与新形式下的共同学习实践，会变成一种取代奖罚做法的内在动力。

Yorks 和 KASL 在其最新的"全身心投入学习策略"的概念中包含了许多这方面的学习理论。这些策略是在"学习者相互间学习"、小组多样性与开发"全身心投入学习"策略的需要基础上制定的，目的是让所有学习者参与变革型学习过程。在我自己的教学实践中，生活共识提供了一个框架，它促进了这些学习策略的实施，并取得了令人满意的结果。笔者目前正在进行一项研究，目的是确认如果将生活共识框架和学习策略用于向成人学习环境过渡领域的教学，是否也能达到让学习者参与和实现质变学习的目的。

生活共识是一个框架，它可以在现有的课程教学中使用。该框架鼓励主导人去寻找"受教时刻"并利用这一机会去培养学习者的可转换学习技能，如自我意识、批判性思维、人际交往、合作建构实践和自主学习能力。框架一旦建立，如果有效地运用"五个重点教学策略"（表1），这些机会应该会更经常出现，也会更容易被主导人发现。

下面的表格介绍了教师如何将教学策略应用于教学实践、预期的学习效果以及作者目前项目的研究目的。

表 1　五个重点教学策略

教学和学习策略	预期效果	研究目的
道德协议：根据每个学生小组的特定学习内容和组织形式，通过不断的反思和讨论确定采取什么样的道德协议。学习者一开始可以采取小组形式每周、每两周或每月讨论一次，然后再让大家集体讨论。	这一战略旨在建立安全的道德学习氛围，鼓励学习者采用可转化的道德实践。在实施这一战略过程时，可培养反思性实践、批判性思维和解决问题的能力。	要回答的问题：主导者和学习者认为一个持续的道德协议讨论对建立一个转化学习氛围和可转化的道德实践会产生什么样的影响。主导人通过半结构式访谈的形式与研究人员讨论该策略的成果，学习者主要通过小组会议的形式进行讨论，并填写一份问卷调查表。
小组共同管理通过使用前面提过的道德协议来实现，并进一步讨论坚持或不坚持协议的后果。这包括通过定期召开会议的形式来监督反思学习环境的有效性以及解决问题策略的掌握情况（这些会议可以与道德协议讨论会议同时举行）。	小组共同管理模式鼓励学习者共同承担责任和共同拥有学习环境。可以通过实施这一策略培养批判性思维和解决问题的能力，并将其应用到今后的工作和终身学习中。	要回答的问题：主导者和学习者认为小组共同管理对建立一个转化学习氛围和学习者共同承担责任和共同拥有学习环境会产生什么样的影响。主导人通过半结构式访谈的形式与研究人员讨论该策略的成果，学习者主要通过小组会议的形式进行讨论，并填写一份问卷调查表。
自我反思性实践：鼓励学习者定期反思他们自己、整个小组和小分组的技能/知识掌握情况以及可转化人际交往和学习技能的提高情况。反思可以采取自我反思、小分组会议和前面提到的道德协议会议讨论的形式。	帮助学习者提高自我反思实践，增加自我意识。自我意识的增加可以发展成为自主工作和学习技能以及提高自我导向。	要回答的问题：主导者和学习者认为长期小组、小分组和自我反思实践对建立一个转化学习氛围和提高学习者的自我意识会产生什么样的影响。主导人通过半结构式访谈的形式与研究人员讨论该策略的成果，学习者主要通过小组会议的形式进行讨论，并填写一份问卷调查表。
基于项目的学习小组：促进学习者以小分组的形式学习。它是基于项目的学习，要求学生自己和同学间就技能、知识的掌握情况以及小组工作能力进行评估。	这些合作学习体验旨在培养可转化学习技能，如团队合作、批判性思维、解决问题的能力和共建实践活动。	要回答的问题：主导者和学习者认为合作学习体验对建立转化学习氛围，学习批判性思维，提高解决问题的能力，弘扬团队合作和共建实践会产生什么样的影响。主导人通过半结构式访谈的形式与研究人员讨论该策略的成果，学习者主要通过小组会议的形式进行讨论，并填写一份问卷调查表。
文化探查是了解每位学习者的文化和世界观。其中采用的一个方法是，邀请每位学习者带来和讨论一件能代表其某种特定文化的代表性物品来与大家分享，比如食物、歌曲、表演、视频或类似的东西。这种活动可以只限于10分钟，作为每节课或每天的插曲，还可以根据课程的设置循环举行。	文化探查可以提高学习者的自我意识及其他世界观意识。该策略旨在建立一个安全的文化学习氛围和包容性学习环境，使多样化受到重视并被视为一种有用的学习资源。	要回答的问题：主导者和学习者认为文化探查对建立一个安全的文化学习氛围和包容性环境，培养自我意识和其他世界观意识会产生什么样的影响。主导人通过半结构式访谈的形式与研究人员讨论该策略的成果，学习者主要通过小组会议的形式进行讨论，并填写一份问卷调查表。

Engaging Challenging Learners

Julia Bruce, Waikato Institute of Technology

The Living Consensus is a conceptual framework that incorporates self-reflection, cultural inquiry, and group agreement on meaningful shared values to build transformative learning environments. The term "Living

Consensus" comes from my own practice as a vocational trainer for 14 years and now a staff developer for tertiary teachers. The framework houses many of my teaching and learning strategies that have successfully supported learners in developing increased self-awareness and transferable learning skills. These teaching and learning strategies were recognised as part of a successful application to the 2008 AkoAotearoa Tertiary Teaching Excellence Awards. Since then I have been invited by AkoAotearoa to facilitate numerous workshops across New Zealand to share these strategies with tertiary educators. I believe that The Living Consensus could have a positive impact on a greater number of learners if the conceptual framework and associated strategies were shared with and facilitated by other adult educators. A research project that is currently underway aims to test this theory with a particular focus on youth transitioning from high school into adult working and learning environments.

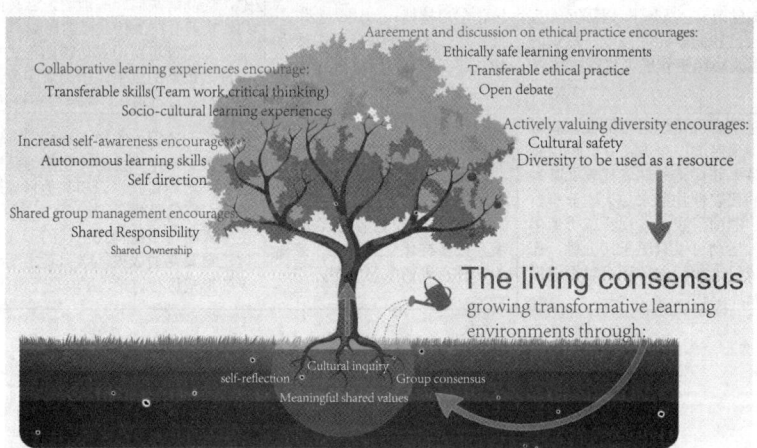

Figure 1 The Living Consensus Conceptual Framework

In response to recent government policy we are seeing more youth entering New Zealand's tertiary vocational learning institutions but to date little research has been conducted into teaching strategies for this group.

Many youth experience difficulty transitioning to these adult learning environments. The Living Consensus encompasses a number of well-known educational theories such as the work of Malcolm Knowles. His theory of Andragogy posits that adults have differing learning needs from those of children. His key assumptions about adult learners are that they are self-directed, have experience that can act as a resource, that their "readiness to learn" is closely linked to the roles they take socially and that they are "task-orientated" in their learning as opposed to "subject-orientated".

The Living Consensus aligns with Malcolm Knowles' assumptions about adult learners. The framework considers the difficulty that many youth experience when moving from a pedagogical learning environment to one which is based on Knowles theory of Andragogy. Selina Chan studied 27 participants who chose to learn a trade through apprenticeship in New Zealand many of whom were youth. The reasons given for youth to choose to train through apprenticeship included negative experiences and poor results achieved at school. Chan promotes the development of "metacognitive" and "learning to learn" skills to support the youth in their transition from school to work learning environments. These skills include critical thinking, reflecting, problem solving learning through inquiry and interaction with others. The Living Consensus framework provides a support structure that can be implemented to help learners develop these and other skills while providing positive and supportive learning experiences.

There are numerous learning theories that form the foundations of The Living Consensus framework. These theories can be categorised under four broader "Orientations to Learning": humanist, cognitivist, socio-cultural and behaviourist. Elements of each of these learning orientations are apparent in the living consensus.

Humanist learning theorists such as Carl Rogers tell us that adults have diverse life experiences, beliefs and world views that can enrich the learning environment. Rogers' work focuses on building learning relationships through facilitative practice, "realness", empathy and acceptance. "Facilitative practice" involves the use of both educational and counseling practices as Rogers believed that for successful learning experiences to occur the whole person needs to be considered. "Realness" refers to the authenticity of the facilitator whom Rogers suggests needs to "be themselves" without pretense in order to connect with learners and build successful learning relationships. Acceptance in this instance refers to the facilitator accepting and valuing the learner as an individual with unique ideas, experiences and a world view that can enhance the learning environment. Empathy becomes apparent when a facilitator gains a deep understanding of the students' experience of their learning journey.

The Living Consensus extends these ideas about learning relationships beyond that of the learner/facilitator connection to develop learning relationships amongst peers. In the researcher's experience, encouraging students to be authentic in their actions, value diversity and show empathy to those who walk alongside them on their learning journey contributes to an inclusive and transformative learning culture.

Socio-cultural learning theories emphasise the importance of both individual learning and peer learning relationships. These theories are based on the idea that adults can use their diversity of thinking, culture and experience to learn together through the observation of others and the social construction of knowledge. Lave and Wenger observe that communities of practice encourage the learners to fully immerse themselves in the learning to become an active participant of the group. Each community will develop its own socio-cultural practices that need to be observed and developed by each individual in order for them to fully engage.

The Living Consensus builds on this theory by supporting learners to develop socio-cultural practices that are unique to each cohort. The practices are based on the group's shared agreement on ethical practice and positive behaviours for their unique learning environment. Learners work throughout their programme to negotiate and adjust their consensus to adhere to their shared values. Alongside this work, an on-going investigation is carried out into the true meaning of each participant's values and how these values have been shaped.

These on-going experimentation and reflection processes that learners engage in as part of The Living Consensus are reflected in the cognitive learning orientation. Cognitive learning theories concern themselves with facilitating the "process of knowing" and a deep understanding of knowledge. Phil Race's cognitive learning theory "Ripples on a Pond" is based on experiential learning concepts that emphasise the importance of experience, practice, reflection and theorising. However, Race takes these ideas further positing that people move in and out of these stages throughout their learning experience and feedback from facilitators and peers is crucial to "making sense of" the learning. In his research Race made a number of discoveries about what made people feel good about their learning experiences. These were:

- gaining feedback from others;
- seeing others' reactions;
- receiving praise and compliments;
- learners being able to help other learners;
- learners noticing the effect of their learning on other people;
- seeing the results.

To integrate these discoveries Race includes peer teaching and peer assessment as stages in his learning theory and endorses the facilitation of group work. Teaching strategies that form part of the Living Consensus Framework are based on these ideas, breaking the cohort into sub-groups for various learning activities. The sub-groups facilitate learning, peer-assess other groups and reflect on their progress as a group. The groups are not only reflecting on their progress towards learning the subject, but also how they are operating as a group. Individuals are encouraged to reflect on their contribution to the group and the role they are taking within the group. These self-reflective practices are designed to increase self-awareness in learners in order to develop autonomous, self-regulating learning and working practices.

The fourth "Orientation to Learning" is behaviourism upon which many of the more traditional teaching practices are based. Behaviourist learning theories are based on the idea that learning and behaviours are both shaped by the environment, repetition and reinforcement (often through reward and punishment). Early studies that were conducted to prove behaviourist theories focused mainly on observable behaviour rather than cognitive thought processes or deeper understanding.

Although behaviourist theories have become less popular for many educators than cognitivist, humanistic and socio-cultural learning theories, components of these practices are still used in adult education today. When working within the framework of The Living Consensus learners decide as a cohort on the consequences for behaviours deemed unacceptable by their group consensus. The majority of the consequences set by groups are based on a reward and punishment model. Those who breach the agreed consensus are often subject to such a fate as having to make coffee for their peers at morning tea time or worse—provide morning tea for everyone. This practice that involves a form of punishment may seem draconian in today's andragogical learning environments however, each group of learners that I have facilitated using The Living Consensus model have expressed a desire for such consequences to be in place.

Perhaps this desire comes from conditioning gained by learning and working under behaviourist models? I have noticed through my practice that if The Living Consensus is facilitated to its full potential the motivation to be a positive participant in our newly formed shared learning culture becomes an intrinsic motivator that supersedes ether reward or punishment.

Yorks and Kasl encompass many of these learning theories in their more recent concept of "whole-person learning strategies". These strategies are based on "learning-within-relationship" and the links between group diversity and the need to develop "whole-person-learning" strategies in order to engage all learners in transformational learning processes. The Living Consensus has provided a framework for such learning strategies to be facilitated with successful results in my own teaching practice. The author's current research project seeks to ascertain if The Living Consensus framework and strategies can have the same engaging and transformative results for other teachers and their learners who are transitioning to the adult learning environment.

The Living Consensus is a framework that can be integrated within an existing programme of learning. The framework encourages the facilitator to look for "teachable moments" as opportunities to develop transferrable learning skills such as self-awareness, critical thinking, interpersonal skills, co-constructive practices and self-direction. Once the framework is in place these opportunities should arise more regularly and will become more apparent to the facilitators when the "Five Key Teaching and Learning Strategies" (Table 1) are being facilitated effectively.

The table below described how teachers can integrate the teaching strategies into their practice, what the anticipated benefits are for learners and the research goals of the project that the author is currently leading.

Table 1 Five Key Teaching and Learning Strategies

Teaching and learning strategy	Anticipated benefits	Research goals
Ethics agreement: An ethics agreement is facilitated through continuous reflection and discussion on what ethical practice is for each particular group of students within the context of their discipline and their learning organisation. The learners can reflect on this agreement on a weekly, fortnightly or monthly basis first as small groups then as a facilitated plenary.	This strategy aims to develop ethically safe learning cultures and encourages transferrable ethical practice in learners. Reflective practice, critical thinking and problem solving skills can be developed during the facilitation of this strategy.	To answer the question: What are facilitator and learner perceptions of the influence on an on-going ethics agreement discussion on the development of a transformative learning culture and transferrable ethical practice? Facilitators discuss outcomes of this activity with the researcher in semi structured interviews and learners discuss in focus groups meetings and complete a survey form.
Shared group management: is achieved through the use of the ethics agreement as mentioned above and further discussion on the consequences of adhering or not adhering to the agreement. This includes regular monitoring in the form of meetings that reflect on the effectiveness of the learning environment and the development of problem solving strategies (these meetings can be facilitated alongside the ethics agreement meetings)	Shared group management encourages shared responsibility and ownership of the learning environment. Critical thinking and problem solving skills can be developed through the implementation of this strategy and applied to future work and life-long learning situations.	To answer the question: What are facilitator and learner perceptions of the influence of shared group management on the development of a transformative learning culture and learners taking ownership and responsibility for their learning environment? Facilitators discuss outcomes of this activity with the researcher in semi structured interviews while learners discuss their perceptions in focus groups meetings and complete a survey form.
Self-reflective practice: is encouraged through regular learner reflection on their progress, the progress of the entire group and the progress of their smaller learning sub-groups on a regular basis. Reflection will be based on skill/knowledge development and the development of transferrable interpersonal and learning skills. Reflection can take place in self-reflective, sub-group meetings and in the ethics agreement meetings mentioned above.	Supporting learners to develop self-reflective practices increases self-awareness. Increased self-awareness may lead to autonomous working and learning skills and increased self-direction.	To answer the question: What are facilitator and learner perceptions of the influence of an on-going group, sub-group and self-reflective practices on the development of a transformative learning culture and self-awareness? Facilitators discuss outcomes of these activities with the researcher in semi structured interviews and learners discuss in focus groups meetings and complete a survey form.
Project based learning teams: are facilitated for learners working in small learning sub-groups. This work is project-based and students are asked to self and peer-assess their progress in terms of skill/knowledge development and their ability to work as a group.	These collaborative learning experiences aim to develop transferrable learning skills such as team work, critical thinking, problem-solving skills and co-constructive practices	To answer the question: What are facilitator and learner perceptions of the influence of collaborative learning experiences on the development of a transformative learning culture, critical thinking and problem-solving skills, team work and co-constructive practices? Facilitators discuss outcomes of these activities with the researcher in semi structured interviews and learners discuss in focus groups meetings and complete a survey form.
Cultural inquiry is used to investigate each individual learner's culture and world view. As part of this strategy each learner is invited to share an aspect of their culture by bringing and discussing an item that represents an aspect of their culture, sharing food, song, performance, video or similar. This practice can be limited to a 10 minute slot in each session or day and can be a revolving cycle depending on the structure of the course.	The practice of cultural inquiry increases self-awareness in learners and awareness of other world views. This strategy aims to build a culturally safe and inclusive learning environment where diversity is valued as a useful resource for learning.	To answer the question: What are facilitator and learner perceptions of the influence of cultural inquiry on the development of a culturally safe learning and inclusive environment, self-awareness and awareness of other world-views? Facilitators discuss outcomes of these activities with the researcher in semi structured interviews while learners discuss their perceptions in focus group meetings and complete a survey form.

团队合作

惠灵顿理工学院　Malcolm Doidge

引言

（你好，你好，大家好）

用毛利语寒暄过后，我想向大家介绍本次发言最重要的主题，即团队合作。

新西兰有着认同双元文化的基础，即土著部落的毛利文化和自19世纪至今新西兰移民后裔的文化。这是新西兰国家建立的双元文化框架。新西兰国家建立的愿望之一是两种文化能够共存，以造福所有新西兰人。这是一个民族的愿望。这门合作课程的目的是尽可能如实地向学生介绍新西兰相互合作的就业或工作环境。

研究的重点

合作是关于学生学习如何一起工作。新西兰的雇主想要的学生是在受聘后几乎能立即有效地在团队中工作以及独立工作。在文化设计领域，原生概念的研究将团队合作作为研究的中心。作为研究人员和教师，我们想要知道的是如何使用团队合作文化框架有效地设计学生合作学习方法。因此，本文将讨论团队合作作为一种教学方法的好处。

方法论

团队合作是各级创意技术本科课程的核心要求。教学中既采用合作项目，又注重培养学生独立学习的能力。在学生学习5级课程时引入合作方法是必要的和重要的第一步。向学生提供一个受特定文化框架约束的合作模式是迄今为止的一项重大发明。

本文将介绍使用苹果iPad技术如何帮助学生学习。这项技术的设计是专门用于促进团队成员之间的凝聚力。上课前，会发给每个小组一个iPad，并在一天课程结束后收回。学生使用 iPad 及其他从网上下载的免费数字应用程序。正是有了这些应用程序，学生才能够计划基于项目的学习。Evernote 笔记已被用于支持学生学习和建立一个给学生功课打分的比较公平的方法。学生将小组笔记在 Evernote 网站上发布，并邀请老师来看，只要有网络，小组所有成员和老师可以随时随地来看他们在做什么。正是有了这个应用程序，老师能够将小组中每个学生的功课与小组其他成员的功课区分开来。

教师给学生布置基于项目学习的学习摘要，并根据该摘要对小组的合作项目进行评估。最近的一个项目摘要是要求小组设计和制作一个棋盘游戏。

学生在设计这个项目时，能够使用各种技术，包括使用激光切割机、三维数字化模型、3D 打印和扫描、iPad 技术和数字图形技术。他们学习包装和印刷技术以及基本的工作室工作技能。小组项目设计中，学生必须选择一个现有的棋盘游戏，并在此基础上进行创新，比如国际象棋。

然后再选择 1960 年至 1990 年间新西兰电影或新西兰历史事件作为他们棋盘游戏设计的最终主题。

在大学一年级采取合作学习是发展成为目前基于项目的合作学习的关键的第一步。特别是前面所介绍的新西兰文化框架，它已经用于该合作课程，使学生能够决定个人在组内和组与组之间如何处事。我们以实践为主的研究主题是探讨如何使用文化框架来有效地促进合作学习，该框架目前分为三个相互依存的部分：

- Whanaugatanga（合作关系）；
- Manakitanga（培养关系）；
- Tikanga（指导原则）。

在过去，让学生参与合作项目一直是一个挑战。学生认为他们个人为小组项目所作的贡献没有得到认可，因为教师只给小组整个项目打分。在那时，个人在小组项目中所做的工作没有办法清楚地与其他小组成员的工作区分开来。学生的这种不满促使教师在一些简短合作项目的基础上开发了目前基于项目的学习方法。教学人员通过相互合作，自 2011 年以来的三年间已逐步完善了该课程。Evernote 软件的使用是能够将个人工作与小组中他人工作区分开来的关键。用 Evernote 软件创建一个小组工作簿，它可以让学生识别（加标签）小组工作薄中每个人的工作，学生还每周交作业参加小组评估。这些评估成为了师生互动的快照，最重要的是，在学习周学生还能评估小组内其他成员的工作表现。

这种方法是以证据为基础，并随着学生对团队合作理解的不断加深而逐步发展而来的。在开学的第一节课，教师寻求用学生自己制定的指导原则来培养学生间的合作关系。开学第一天，班上的所有小组在上课后一起制定文化框架。每个小组的学生都必须同意将该框架作为指导原则或行为规范。有些小组认为该框架还有可能用于调节小组内产生的矛盾冲突。

通过 Evernote，我们观察到小组合作关系的文化框架得到了学生和老师的共同支持。

对于学生来说，文化框架明确了小组工作的原则。比如，学生同意守时，准时参加会议以便不浪费小组其他成员的时间和精力。教师每天检查学生的出勤情况以监督准则的执行情况。滚动式出勤记录记录学生的一整天出勤率，包括上、下午。学生在下午课程结束时要向全班同学简要地介绍他们小组的项目情况。这使小组能衡量每个小组的工作进展，并因此反思自己小组项目的进度。

指导原则以及小组的执行情况，通过每周同学们的评估程序来加强。记录簿上将记载对小组其他成员做出评估的同学的名字。他们的名字被列在 4 个待评估的问题的上面。这 4 个问题的顺序为：

1. 参加小组会议了吗？
2. 对小组有突出贡献吗？
3. 致力于小组任务吗？
4. 分担大家的工作量了吗（whanaungatanga）？

评价等级为 1~4：

强烈不同意 =1；

不同意 =2；

同意 =3；

强烈同意 =4。

学生回答这 4 个问题最高可以得 16 分。也就是每个问题 4 分。每个问题得分累计相加得到总分。总分小于等于 10，则需要引起关注。

同学打分结果提示应当引起注意的任何小组，可以随时在网上查 Evernote 笔记，了解个人作业的上传频率或在每周评估结果反馈中可能反映出来的情绪低落或身处困境的信号。

Evernote 的使用可以使教师及时对学生的作业进行评估。使用 Evernote 在线笔记不需要打搅别人,这是 Evernote 在线笔记非常重要的优点。它使教师工作灵活,可以回答学生提出的一系列问题,而不必先将需要检查的作业从同学处收上来,然后再还回去。也就是说学生保留他们所有的研究材料,只要将材料上传到网上供老师和其他同学阅读即可。学生负责将做好的作业随时上传,包括个人作业和小组作业。这种透明度对教师和学生都有利。如有任何疑虑,可凭证据进行单独对话。特别需要提醒学生注意的事项可在网上指出供大家在线参考。学生然后可以提供没有发布在 Evernote 上的特定研究材料当证据。这样做,使学生觉得小组项目中自己个人所做的工作大家都看得见,可以与小组其他成员的工作区分开来,与此同时,个人完成的部分仍然可以和小组项目一起进行评估。

每个合作小组要安排自己小组成员的分工并负责组内的沟通。按文化框架规定一起工作的小组与没有原则约束的小组存在着一个不同点,那就是学生对小组的一种归属感、一种身份的象征。小组成员的个人表现会提高或损坏小组和组中每个成员的声誉。每个学生均应为会影响小组其他成员的个人行为负责。

其中的一个例子是学生发布在笔记上的信息。

"大家好,我很抱歉你们和我在一个组,我成了大家的累赘和麻烦,非常抱歉,B。"

回答"喂,没问题,我们都得经历这一步,两个人一起学习是一种乐趣。如果你愿意给我发短信,我们可以一起解决这个问题 LOL。"

大多数小组都会有问题。有些小组的问题教师可以通过 Evernote 上的笔记发现,这要归功于教师和小组都在使用的 iPad 的方便性能。因为它,教师才可以采取快速的、专业的方法来应对。

在上述的例子中,教师看到了信息,并与学院一起向学生伸出了援手。

教师向学生提供帮助时按程序也要遵守文化框架。它提醒学生要为小组负责并帮助缺乏自信的同学。帮助学习有困难的同学会让他们感觉自己是集体中的一员,可以提高他们的自信心。他们需要觉得更加自信能帮助别人和感觉到受尊重。时间一长,一个学生表现出来的耐心会帮助不太自信的其他小组成员充满集体责任感,增加小组的凝聚力。

结论

本合作课程的目的是提供一种尽可能贴近现实合作工作环境的一种体验。为了实现这个目标,一个文化设计指导原则给学生提供了一个小组内合作和小组间合作的工作框架。

对于学生来讲，这是一门创意技术领域的职业培训课程。然而，这种模式很有潜力可以广泛地用于其他领域。学生在合作工作过程中确实可以相互学习，一起学习如何与人合作，并带着压力完成项目。在犯错时，他们从错误中学习，还学习如何有成效地合作和相互支持。技术的应用在帮助学生参与小组合作项目时起着很重要的作用，它对学生和教师来讲既有用又透明。数字软件和iPad技术的应用与学生使用的大多数当代社会媒体一样，是大多数学生日常生活中不可缺少的一部分。然而，他们使用数字技术的能力，必须和使用其他大量可用的社会媒体和运行这些媒体的硬件的能力一样好。

作为体验式学习，合作课程还让学生参与一系列有利于教师评估学生合作项目的数字技术。这门课程的重要性，是在体验学习的基础上，让学生学习他们自认为与成为创意技术人员相关的技术，即2D、3D技术和跨学科领域的数字技术。

合作工作指南，从文化领域的角度来讲，与制定"大家共同遵守的"一般行为准则有关。培养相互尊重的关系和相互支持，可以减少一系列小组成员间和组与组之间的矛盾冲突。合作框架证明，通过小组成员间和组与组之间的相互合作，学生可以学到更多的东西。在文化框架的指导下，学生间的关系变得更有益，他们可以一起工作而不只是彼此存在却试图一个人去独立完成工作。

Mahi Tahi (Work Together)

Malcolm Doidge, Wellington Institute of Technology

Introduction

Tena Koutou, tena Koutou, tena koutou katoa (Greetings, greetings, greetings to you all)

With this greeting or mihi in Maori, I would like to introduce the most important idea of this presentation on collaboration. Mahi Tahi or "work together".

New Zealand has its foundation in a bi-cultural identity—the indigenous tribal Maori culture and, that of the descendants of subsequent immigrant cultures to New Zealand, from the 19th century to the present. This is the bi-cultural framework that New Zealand's national identity is founded on. One aspiration for nationhood in New Zealand is that, both cultures can work together, for the benefit of all New Zealanders. This is a national aspiration. The aim of this collaborative programme is to provide, for the students, an experience that is as close as possible to a collaborative employment or working environment in a New Zealand context.

Research Focus

Collaboration is about students learning how to work together. Employers in New Zealand want students who can be employed, almost immediately, to work effectively in teams as well as work individually. In cultural design, the study of indigenous concepts places Whanaungatanga, or working together, at the centre of study. Our area of inquiry, as researchers and teachers, is how the cultural framework of Whanaungatanga can be used to effectively structure student learning through collaboration. This paper will therefore consider the benefits of collaboration as a teaching methodology.

Methodology

Collaboration is a core requirement of the Bachelor of Creative Technologies at all levels. Collaborative projects are introduced in parallel with students' development towards independent study. Introducing students at level 5 to collaboration is a necessary and important induction process. Providing students with a model that has a specific cultural framework has been a key development.

This paper will consider how the use of Apple iPad technology supports student learning. This technology is specifically dedicated to facilitating cohesion within collaborative groups. Each collaborative group has an iPad assigned to it at the beginning of class. This technology is returned at the end of the day. Students use this technology in conjunction with a range of free digital applications (apps), downloaded from the internet. These apps are essential to students being able to plan project based learning. The Evernote app has been used to support student learning and develop a fairer marking response to student work contributions. Students post to their group notebook on the Evernote website and, having invited tutors to see the notebook as well, allow all students in a group and their tutors to see what they are doing, at any time and from any place with internet access. Tutors are also able to distinguish students individual efforts from those of other group members because of this app.

Students are given a project based learning brief. Their collaboration in groups will be assessed against this brief. The most recent iteration of this brief is one based on collaborative groups designing and making a board game.

Students are able to undertake a range of technologies in this project. These include using a laser cutter, 3D digital modeling, 3D printing and scanning, iPad technology and digital graphics technology. They learn packaging and printing skills and also basic workshop skills. Students must select, in their groups, an existing design for their board game to be based on. For example, chess.

A further selection is then made of either a New Zealand movie or a New Zealand historical context between 1960 and 1990 as a theme for the board games final design.

Introducing students to collaboration, in the first year of the degree, is a crucial first step that has evolved into the current, project based Collaborative Studies programme. The specifically New Zealand cultural framework, described above, has emerged to allow students to make decisions about how individuals conduct themselves, within groups and between groups. Our practice based research is an enquiry into how this cultural framework can be used to effectively facilitate student learning through collaboration. The framework currently has three interdependent parts:

- Whanaugatanga (collaborative relationships);
- Manakitanga (nurturing relationships);
- Tikanga (guidelines).

In the past, student engagement with collaboration was a challenge. Students didn't feel their individual contributions were recognised because groups only received a blanket assessment from tutors. At the time, evidence of individual contributions could not be clearly identified enough, to be distinguished from other group contributions to collaborative projects. This experience of students frustration led tutors to develop the current project based learning approach, developed over a number of iterations of collaborative briefs. Teaching staff, in an act of collegial collaboration, have gradually refined this programme over a three year period since 2011. The software Evernote is key to being able to distinguish individual contributions within a group. Evernote is used to create a group workbook. This software allows students to identify (tag) their individual contributions to the group notebook. Students also contribute weekly group evaluations. These evaluations become a snapshot of how students interact and most importantly, rate other members of their group over the study week.

This approach is evidence based and has evolved alongside a developing understanding by students of collaboration "Whanaugatanga". At the first class, tutors seek to foster cooperation through guidelines developed by students (Tikanga). All groups in the class on the first day contribute to Tikanga at the beginning of the session. Students in each group must agree on tikanga as guidelines or aspirational behavior. Some groups see these guidelines as having the potential to moderate any conflict that develops within the group.

We have observed that the cultural framework of group cooperation is supported by both the students' and tutors' use of Evernote technology.

For students, tikanga clarifies the guidelines towards making group contributions. For example, students agree to punctuality, meeting on time so as not to waste other group members' time and effort. Tutors keep a daily roll of class attendance to track adherence to this guideline. The roll documents attendance over a full day of study, both morning and afternoon. Students are asked to briefly present their research, as a group, to the class at the end of the afternoon. This allows groups to gauge the amount of progress in each group and allow reflection on their own revue sheet groups progress.

Guidelines, and a group's acknowledgement of them, is reinforced by the weekly peer evaluation process. The peer revue sheet will have the name of the student making the evaluation of other group members. These members are named and listed above four questions to be evaluated. These four questions are in the order:

1. Attends group meetings?
2. Contributes meaningfully to the group?
3. Engages in the group?
4. Shares the workload (whanaungatanga)?

The evaluation criteria are rated as a score on scale of 1 to 4 :

"strongly disagree" = 1;

"disagree" = 2;

"agree" = 3 ;

"strongly agree"= 4 .

The highest score a student can achieve is 16 over four questions. That is, a rating of 4 for each of the four questions.

For each question, scores given from 1-4 are added, in a column, to provide a total. Any score at 10 or below is a cause for concern.

For any group with peer revues indicating concern, Evernote notebooks can be checked online, at any time, for frequency in individual postings or any indicator of distress or hardship that might be reflected in the weekly peer revue return.

Evernote access allows tutors to make timely evaluations of student progress. Using Evernote's online notebooks, this process is non intrusive. This is a very important feature of online notebooks. It allows tutors to be flexible and responsive to students, over a range of issues, without having to recover from students, any physical work to be examined and then returned. This means students retain all their own research material while making it available to tutors and group members online. Students are responsible for posting progress on line, both individually and as a group. This transparency is of benefit to both tutors and students. Any concerns can be addressed with individuals, based on evidence. Areas of specific concern can be identified and referenced online. Students can then provide evidence of specific research material if not posted in Evernote. As a result, students feel that their individual contributions to their collaborative groups are visible and differentiated from other group members contributions. Yet this individual contributions can also be evaluated alongside their collaborative efforts.

Every group collaboration has a structure that members have to organize and also take responsibility for communicating within the group. Students working together in a cultural framework have a point of difference by comparison to groups who don't agree on guidelines (tikanga). This point of difference is one of encouraging a feeling of belonging to the group, a feeling of identity. The reputation of the group and individuals in the group is enhanced (or reduced) depending on the action of individual group members. Each student is responsible for their actions to the others in the group.

An example of this is this student posting from one notebook.

"Hey Team, I'm sorry that you are working with me. I have been a huge let down and such a hassle. Eternally sorry, B."

Reply: " Hey man, it's all good, we all got to pass and two people working together will be fun. If you want to text me we can get this done LOL."

Most groups experience problems. Some group's problems can be picked up by tutors in Evernote notebook postings. This is because of the ease of access made possible by the app on the iPad technology used by tutors and the groups. This enables tutors to react quickly and in a timely and professional way.

In this example, tutors saw the message and offered help in conjunction with institutional services.

The assistance given by tutors is also framed by Tikanga (guidelines) as part of this process. These remind students of their responsibility to the group and to help unconfident members. Attending to students who struggle to contribute helps them feel included and promotes confidence. They need to feel more confident to contribute and feel more respected. Over time the patience a student displays to less confident group members feeds "manakitanga" (a shared sense of responsibility) and strengthens the whole group.

Conclusion

The aim of this collaborative programme is to provid an experience that is as close as possible to a collaborative working environment. To facilitate this, a cultural design context provides students with a framework for cooperation in collaborative groups and between those groups.

For students, this is a vocational training environment, in a creative industries context. However, this model has potential for a much wider application. Students do learn from each other within this collaborative process and, they learn together how to cooperate and make a project happen under pressure. While they make mistakes and learn from them, students also learn how to collaborate productively and support each other. Technology plays an important part in facilitating student engagement with collaboration. This happens in a way that is both meaningful and transparent to teachers and students. Using digital apps and iPad technology, these technologies are aligned with most students' experience of contemporary social media. This is a seamless part of most of their lives. Their ability to engage with the digital processes however, has to be equal to their daily experience of other widely available social media and the hardware used to deliver it to them.

This collaborative programme also engages students in a range of digital technology skills, as experiential learning, that underpins tutors' assessment of students' collaborations. The importance of this project, based on their learning experience, is to engage students in learning what they perceive to be relevant skill sets for creative technologists. These are skills in 2D, 3D and digital areas with an interdisciplinary focus.

Collaborative guidelines, in a cultural context, are about developing more universal rules that "you all play by" (Tikanga). By nurturing respectful relationships (Manakitanga) and mutual support, there is a collective reference point for reducing conflict within groups and between groups. 'Whanaugatanga' affirms that we can learn so much more from working co-operatively, both within groups and between groups. With individuals guided by a cultural context, students share more meaningful

connections, by working together (Mahi Tahi), rather than simply existing around each other and trying to get on with the job, alone.

优秀教学法研讨
SYMPOSIUM: EXCELLENT VOCATIONAL TEACHING

让大专工程专业一年级学生参与教学过程的两种教学方法：翻转课堂式教学法和基于项目教学法

怀卡托理工学院　　Aidan Bigham

摘要：此次发言将探讨适合大专工程专业一年级学生的两种不同的课堂教学方法（工程基础和地质专业）。上述两门课程，均采用了以学生为中心的教学方法，目的是帮助学生记住所学内容和专业词汇以便能自然使用。每门课程均设计了学生可参与其中的教学活动以  及制造场景让学生能运用相关课堂所学知识并进行批判性评价。然后教师作为主导者，培养学生解决问题的自信心和能力。该教学方法的最终目的是培养学生能够随时随地学习的能力，把他们培养成为终身学习者。

关键词：翻转课堂式教学法；基于项目教学法；灵活教学法；混合教学法

工程基础为一门跨学科课程，是所有攻读工程专业（民用、机械和电力工程）学生的必修课。本课程是大专专业第一学期的课程，目的是帮助学生掌握工程基础知识以便日后能更好地学习其他专业课程，同时让学生有机会接触所有工程专业领域。该学科有许多预期的教学成果，在某些情形下成果之间几乎各不相干。学生通常认为这门学科学起来比较困难，原因有两个：一是缺乏数学基础，二是不能将抽象概念形象化以帮助理解。为了提高学生将概念形象化的能力和鼓励交叉学科间的相互合作，我设计了一个项目，让学生分成大组来完成。学生需要完成的项目是制作一辆车，然后让车载着货物（机械原理）独立行驶过一座桥（民用工程），在行进过程中，打开并穿越一个障碍臂（电动原理）。学生被分成混合学科工作小组（9~10个人一组），共同来完成这个项目。

作为小组项目，学生须进行有效沟通，书写报告和发表演讲。所有这些技能均为学生将来从事该行业要用到的技能。项目的所有部分均须按照学习成果的要求来完成。

该项目给学生提供了许多深入研究学习成果的机会，虽然有些成果可能和此项目无关。比如，人们可以测量线性运动（加速度、速度、距离）和车的行进速度。它不属于这个项目的范畴，但它是一节生动的课堂教学，帮助学生将他们所制造的物体的运动形象化。

学生的反馈结果说明他们对教学有较高的参与度。学生还指出他们与学习成果能更好地相互影响，使它们变得更容易理解。学生提出的唯一不足是学生小组人数太多，在下一次碰到这门课程时会将学生划分为更多的小组。

地质学（民用工程）教学过去采用传统的课题授课式教学方法。地质学涉猎领域广泛，专业词汇众多，因此，学生很难掌握课堂所传授的知识并将其在情境下加以运用。更何况需要利用每周有限的上课时间教授书本知识意味着几乎没有时间组织其他教学活动来帮助学生加强对所学知识的记忆或构建新知识。为了创造更多的学习机会，该课程经过重新设计改为采用翻转课堂教学法，将每一课题开发了可反复重复的在线教学活动（讲课、测验和论坛），辅以允许学生在一系列活动中相互合作的课上工作室活动。面对面授课要求学生使用一系列资源（课本和网络）进行主题研究并和其他同学分享自己的答案。教师作为主导者确保所有答案准确，如有知识遗漏，教师根据需要加以补充。这种混合教学方法，通过创造课堂情境，让学生有机会运用从在线教学中所学到的地质词汇，从而帮助学生学到更多的知识。对课堂教学的效果评估采取了定量数据方法。量性数据包括学生评估问卷调查，结果表明新开发的课程教学方法得到了学生的支持，在年底教学评估问卷调查活动中收到了大量的正面反馈意见。学生反馈中提到一些优点，例如：

学生可以在自己方便的时间在网上学习；

产生了一种责任感，学生要为自己的学习负责；

面对面上课更容易理解。

为了评估这种新的教学方法，我们将所收集的考试成绩与上一年的成绩进行了比较。内部考试结果显示成绩有所提高，但数据统计并不明显。外部考试结果显示学生成绩有很大提高，尤其令人兴奋的是成绩的后四分之一段提高得最多，由35%

提高到 54%。

在采取的两种教学方法中,学生自身要为自己的学习负责。在采取以学生为中心的不同教学方法时,教师扮演的是主导者的角色,管理和帮助学生在课程结束后顺利毕业。

Two Scenarios of Engaging First Year Engineering Students: The Inverted Classroom and Project Based Learning

Aidan Bigham, Waikato Institute of Technology

Abstract: This presentation explores two different classroom teaching environments (Engineering Fundamentals and Geology) for first year diploma engineering students. In both classroom environments a student centric approach is created, where the aim is to embed engineering content and terminology so it can be used naturally by the students. Each environment creates experiences in which the students can become involved within, as well as provides situations in which students can apply relevant course knowledge and critically appraise. The tutor then acts as a facilitator, scaffolding the students into capable and confident problem solvers. The ultimate aim of this approach is to create students who can learn anything at any time, hence creating lifelong learners.

Keywords: inverted classroom; project based learning; flexible learning; blended delivery

Engineering Fundamentals is a cross disciplinary paper which is compulsory for all diploma students (Civil, Mechanical and Electrical). This course is completed in the first semester of the diploma and its objective is to give all engineering students the engineering fundamental knowledge to succeed in future courses, while also exposing them to other engineering specialisations. The course has many learning outcomes, which in some cases have little relationships with each other. Students generally find this subject difficult for two reasons, either they lack some mathematical knowledge or because they can't visualise a concept to help understand it. To help improve the visualisation of concepts and to encourage cross disciplinary collaboration, a project was created to be completed in large teams. A scenario was given to the students which involved making a car that could carry a load (mechanical) to move unaided over a bridge (built by civil) and while travelling open a barrier arm so the car could pass through (electrical). Students were placed in consultancy groups of mixed disciplines (nine or ten per group) and worked together to solve the problem.

As part of the group work students were required to communicate effectively, write reports and give presentations. All of these skills are skills that students would be expected to use in industry. Students were also required to link all parts of the project to the learning outcomes of the course.

The project gave the class many opportunities to delve deeper into the learning outcomes that weren't necessarily part of the project. For example, linear motion was able to be measured (acceleration, velocity, distance) and the cars were raced. This was not part of the project, but it provided an engaging lesson to help visualise kinematics with objects that the students had created.

Student feedback showed higher engagement in the course. Students noted they had better interaction with the learning outcomes, which made them easier to understand. The only drawback mentioned was that the group sizes were too big, and more will be done to cater for this the next time this course is offered.

Geology (civil engineering) was previously taught in a traditional lecture environment. Geology is made up of a range of topics with a high volume of specific terminology, hence it was difficult for students to retain knowledge, and then to apply the new learning to contextualised (and examinable) situations. In addition, the need to use the limited time available each week to teach course content meant there was little time available for engaging class activities to help students reinforce knowledge or to construct new knowledge. To create more learning opportunities the course was redesigned into an inverted classroom. Repeatable online activities (lessons, quizzes and forum participation) were created to investigate each topic, complemented by in-class workshops where students worked collaboratively on a range of activities. The face-to-face sessions required students to research topics with the use of a range of resources (books and internet) and share their answers with other class members. The tutor acted as a facilitator ensuring all content was accurate and adding any missing knowledge as required. This mix was designed to increase retention of knowledge by creating situations in class where the students would use the geology terminology they had learnt online. Qualitative and quantitative data was gathered to test the effectiveness of the classroom. Quantitative data involved a student evaluation survey which showed the redeveloped course environment was supported by the students, with significant positive feedback in the end of year evaluation forms. Student responses included benefits such as:

- Having the ability to do the online lessons at a time that suited them;
- It created responsibility for their own learning;
- A better understanding of face-to-face class activities.

Quantitative data in the form of results were compared with the previous year to evaluate the new approach. Internal marks show an increase though not statistically significant. The external exam result showed a statistically significant (P test) increase in marks. In particular it was pleasing to see that the lower quartile exam mark showed the most movement; increasing from 35 % to 54 %.

In both classroom environments the onus is on the students to be responsible for their learning. By providing different types of student centric classrooms, the tutor would act as a facilitator; managing and helping the students achieve successful outcomes by the end of the course.

在高职学生顶岗实习中开展桥接教学的思考
——基于顶岗实习教学指导的反思

铜仁职业技术学院　谭子安

摘要：顶岗实习是高职学生将所学的理论知识和专业技术与实际工作"耦合"的实践过程，帮助学生将分散的知识能力信息"桥接"再构并组成自己的知识能力体系，是最终提高高职专业人才培养质量的有效方法。

关键词：顶岗实习；桥接教学法；教学质量

高等职业教育作为高等教育发展中的一个重要类型，其肩负的使命是培养面向生产、建设、服务和管理第一线需要的高素质技能型专门人才，在我国推进工业化、城镇化和新农村建设中具有不可替代的作用。不断提高高等职业教育的人才培养质量，有重要的现实意义。

"桥接"一词是通信科技领域使用的概念，其定义是基于公共的链路层协议将两个通信网络互连，并基于链路地址选择要传递的数据的过程。桥接教学是指基于知识信息的特点，依据其内在的逻辑联系和延展关系，将单个的、独立的知识点进行联结，并再构知识能力体系的过程。桥接教学作为一种方法用于高职学生顶岗实习阶段，旨在引导学生将分散的、独立的知识信息关联成统一的知识信息整体，帮助学生建构自己的知识能力体系，进而促进学生解决问题能力的提升，最终提高人才培养质量。

一、基于认知理论的高职学生顶岗实习中存在的问题分析

顶岗实习是高职专业人才培养中的重要环节，是学生将所学的基础理论知识和

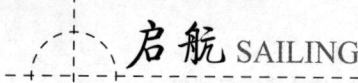

专业技术与实际工作"耦合"的实践过程，是毕业生走向社会和进入专业工作岗位前将知识信息再构和组成自己的知识体系的重要认知过程。但是，从近几年有关高职学生顶岗实习期间的教学和管理文献资料（包括指导学生顶岗实习的经验资料）来看，学生对顶岗实习的满意率不高，涉及的原因是多种多样的。就教学因素来说，主要有两类：一类是学生的个人因素，表现在学生在校学习、训练完成以后，虽已初步具备了从事某项专业工作所需的知识、技能和态度，但由于现行的以能力为主线的能力导向教学模式的缺陷，学生所学专业的学习模块、单项任务等单独存在，不能把众多的学习模块、单项任务等建构成自己的知识体系和行为能力体系，此时的学生是一个"表演型学生"，未进入"角色"；一类是校内教学与实践需求脱节，指导教师缺位。虽然近些年来各高职院校致力于工学结合课程建设，并取得了很多的成果，课程之间的逻辑关系对于大多数教师来说是了然于胸，但在实际教学中，很多教师注重按照事先的教学设计进行教学而忽略了课程之间的知识迁移的培养。教学过程虽然没有错误，甚至课堂教学很精彩，但由于知识能力点单一，不能应对客观实际情况的复杂多变，影响了专业综合能力的建构。加之一些高职院校虽安排了学生顶岗实习，但未安排相应的指导教师，顶岗实习形同"放羊"，学生不能在顶岗实习阶段得到应有帮助，知识能力再构和运用效果差。

在高度认识顶岗实习的重要性基础上，进一步重视顶岗实习中的教学活动开展，科学、认真地做好高职学生在顶岗实习期间的学习指导，是抓好顶岗实习中学生教学管理、提高学生顶岗实习满意率的重要举措，也是完善高职院校人才培养模式、最终提高人才培养质量的客观需要。

二、基于认知规律的顶岗实习中桥接教学探索

学生"所学非所用"或"用处不大"的认识从何而来并导致其对顶岗实习消极抵触呢？要分析这个问题，我们先从教育学和教育心理学等认知理论上进行探究。

1. 认知理论基础

现代教育学理论和教育心理学理论的研究成果，给我们揭示了认知的一般规律和认知过程。简单而言，人们对事物的认识都是从简单到复杂、从低级到高级、从特殊到一般、由表及里地感知事物，逐步建立牢固而清晰的表象，认识到客观事物规律的存在。

这种认知过程，归纳起来，可以分为以下三个环节或阶段：

首先是感知。教育心理学认为人类用心念来诠释自己器官所接收的信号就称为感知。感知是人们认识事物的初始阶段，如教师在教学活动中把知识、能力信息讲解给学生时，学生利用自己的感官开始感知。当然，这只是学生感知的一个方面。

其次是储存。学生将自己的感官所感受到的信息，经过自己的思维活动，融入自己的认知体系，变成自己的、特有的、可再次进行传播和加工的、牢固而清晰的信息。

最后是运用（创新）。学生根据自己的知识能力，将主观意识作用于客观事物的过程。分为两个方面：一是利用认知的事物的特性达到解决问题的目的，这是基础；一是根据自己的认知能力和事物的特性，谋划解决问题的新路径并最终解决问题，这就是创新。

2. 桥接教学在顶岗实习中的应用分析

顶岗实习位于学生认知过程中的运用（创新）阶段，是检验学生认知能力运用、衍射的实践过程，对学生的未来成长、发展有至关重要的作用。下面以市场营销专业顶岗实习中的桥接教学实例来说明。

市场营销专业的课程设计中，虽各高职院校各有不同，开设有自己职校特有的一些课程，但在行业通用能力课程和专业核心能力课程外开设管理学、经济学、统计学、财务管理、市场营销、经济法、消费者行为学、国际市场营销、市场调查、市场调查与预测、商务谈判等课程，基本满足了"培养系统地掌握经济学、管理学基本原理和熟悉市场营销、企业管理、经济、法律、财务管理等方面知识，具备独立从事营销业务、营销策划以及其他管理工作的高素质技能型专门人才"目标要求。人才培养的教学设计可以说是科学的。但在顶岗实习中，为什么学生对顶岗实习的认同度不高、实习满意率低呢？

追踪学生的顶岗实习活动，我们认为这与学生认知能力的运用、衍射能力低有关。一些学生没有专业意识，接待消费者时与普通店员的销售行为没有区别，只注重新品推荐、商品性能介绍，用"最好卖"或"卖得最多"来招徕顾客，把顶岗实习当成了"打工"，自然也就没有职业认同。针对此种情况，在教学指导中，我们通过桥接教学来指导学生的知识再构。

一是引导学生回忆课程的知识点。如在市场营销课程中，有市场细分的知识点和如何细分市场的能力点；那么在顶岗实习中，依据学生所在企业的商品该怎么细分市场？再如消费者的消费行为也是可以分类的，该怎么分呢？

二是指导学生将各课程的知识点衍射桥接。如销售流水账用统计的知识点分类整理后，可以是统计的数据分析的基础数据，也可以是市场调查的第一手资料、财务管理的原始台账数据。这些数据进而为管理学的经济活动分析、决策和财务分析提供参考。

三是促进学生认知能力体系再构。通过上述环节，使学生把单个的、独立的知识点、能力点变成一个整体并相互融合，"牵一发而动全身"，最终提高学生的创新能力。

桥接教学可以解决学生认知能力的运用、衍射能力低的问题，使学生的专业综合能力得到有效的训练和提高，职业观念进一步强化，顶岗实习效果逐渐显现，并可倒推课堂教学的教学技术改进。

三、桥接教学讨论

桥接教学是根据其对学生教学指导的功效并借用通信科技领域"桥接"一词的形象称谓。笔者虽对它进行了定义，但其科学性有待探讨。就其实用性而言，桥接教学还有以下特性：

1、桥接教学的基础是学生已掌握各模块单元的知识点和能力点。没有这些"支点"，就不可能"搭桥"。因此，强化学生各模块单元的知识学习和能力应用训练，是建"桥"的基础。

2、桥接教学教的不是内容，而是一种方法。桥接教学是引导学生将分散的、独立的知识信息关联成统一的知识信息整体，帮助学生建构自己的知识能力体系，进而促进学生解决问题的能力。

3、桥接教学的技巧特点是促进学生由"表演型"向"角色型"转变。学生不仅能完成老师教的"动作"，并能根据"角色"需要，完成"角色"的塑造。

四、结论

不断提高高职专业人才培养质量，是高职教育改革发展永恒的主题。基于教育活动的复杂性和职业教育的特殊性，教学方法的选择须以提高学生认知能力和运用能力为目的。桥接教学在高职学生顶岗实习阶段，能最好地发挥其作用，对提高高职人才培养质量有较好的效果。但桥接教学应用研究刚刚起步，需在其理论基础和科学性方面进一步探究并逐步完善。

Study on the Bridging Teaching Practice in the Post Internship of Higher Vocational College Students ——Reflection on Teaching Guidance About Post Internship

Tan Zi'an GanLi
Tongren Polytechnic College

Abstract: Post internship is a process in which higher vocational college students combine the theoretical knowledge and expertise they master in school with their practical work. Accordingly, this paper proposes that the bridging teaching practice in the post internship is of great significance in helping higher vocational college students combine discrete knowledge, abilities and information with each other, then reconstruct them and develop their own knowledge and capability system. This practice, thereby, is proved to be an effective approach to improve talents training quality of higher vocational education.

Keywords: post internship; bridging teaching approach; training quality

As an important type in higher education development, higher vocational education shoulders its mission to train high-quality skilled professionals for the forefront of production, construction, service and management, and plays an irreplaceable role in promoting industrialization, urbanization and new rural construction in our country. Continuously improving talents training quality of higher vocational education has important practical significance.

The term "bridging", originating from the field of communication technology, is defined as interconnecting the two communications network protocol based on the public link layer, and meanwhile, the process of selecting the data to transfer based on the link address. Bridging teaching refers to the process of linking single, independent knowledge points and then reconstructing knowledge and ability system according to their internal logic links and extended relationships based on the characteristics of knowledge and information. Bridging teaching, as a method used in the stage of the post internship of higher vocational college students, purports to guide the students to mingle discrete and independent knowledge and information into a unified whole. By doing so, we help students construct their own knowledge and ability system, thus promoting the students' problem-solving ability, and ultimately improving the quality of personnel training.

I. Analysis of the Problems Existing in Post Internship of Higher Vocational Students Based on Cognitive Theory

The post internship is a key link in the process of talents training of higher vocational education. It is not only the practical process in which students couple the theory and knowledge, and the expertise they master in school with their practical work, but also that in which the students restructure the knowledge and information and develop their own knowledge and ability system before they enter the society and took the professional position. In recent years, however, the students' satisfaction rate on post internship is not high in terms of the relevant teaching and management data during the post internship of higher vocational college students (including the information on studying experience of guiding students' post internship), which involves a variety of reasons. As far as factors concerning teaching are concerned, there are two categories: one is the students' personal factors. When students' studying and training are completed, although they are initially equipped with required knowledge, skills and attitudes for engaging in a profession, due to the fact that the current capability-oriented teaching model has shortages, the single study tasks and study modules related to students' majors stand alone. Students could not develop those numerous study modules and single tasks into their own knowledge system and behavior capability system. Therefore, he or she is simply a "performance-based student", and does not enter the "role". The other is ascribable to "out of touch with their teaching and practice requirements, and instructors' absence". Although in recent years, many higher vocational colleges are committed to combining learning with working curriculum development, and has made a lot of achievements, and the logical relationships between curriculum for most teachers are seemingly clear in their mind, in the actual teaching, many teachers focus on instructing in accordance with the prior teaching design and ignore the training of knowledge transfer between courses. Although there are no errors in the teaching process, and although classroom is very exciting, this practice, due to the singleness of knowledge and ability, can not help students face the complex objective factual circumstances and thus affected their professional comprehensive capacity building. Some higher vocational colleges, though arranged post internship for students, did not arrange appropriate instructors. In this case, such post internship is tantamount to "herding sheep". As a result, students can not get the necessary help during the internship stage and their ability to reconstruct and apply knowledge is very poor.

On the basis of high awareness of the importance of the post internship, further attentions should be paid to carrying out teaching activities in post internship. Scientific, earnest learning guidance are required during the post internship stage of higher vocational college students. This is an important measure taken to do a good job in students' teaching management during the post internship and improving students' satisfaction rate of the post internship. Above all, it is also the objective needs for perfecting the personnel training mode of higher vocational colleges, and ultimately improving the quality of personnel training.

II. Exploration of the Bridging Teaching in Post Internship Based on Cognitive Theory

1. Foundation of Cognitive Theory

Results of Modern educational theories and educational psychological researches reveal to us the general rules of cognition and cognitive processes. In short, people's understanding of things is a process of perceiving things from the simple to the complex, from the lower to higher, from the particular to the general, and from the outside to the inside, and gradually we establish a solid and clear image, and recognizes the law of objective reality.

In general, this cognitive process can be divided into the following three aspects or stages:

The first is perception. Educational psychology proposes that the process in which human being interpret with mind the received signals is called perception. Perception of things is the initial stage for people to understand things, e.g., ewhen teachers explain to the students the knowledge and capability information in the teaching activities, the students begin to use their senses to perceive them. Of course, this is only one aspect of students' perception of things.

Followed by storing. Students feel the information with their senses. Relying on their own thinking activities, they couple them into their cognitive system and turn them into their own, unique, solid and clear message which can be transmitted and processed again.

Finally, employment (innovation). According to their own knowledge and ability, students make subjective conscious acts on objective things, which consist of two sides: one is the basis, applying characteristics of cognitive things to achieve the purpose of solving the problem; the other is innovation, planning a new path to ultimately solve the problem, according to their cognitive abilities and characteristics of things.

2. Analysis of application of bridging teaching approach to post internship

Post internship exists in the using(innovation) stage of students' cognitive process. It is the practice process of testing the application and diffraction of students' cognitive ability and plays a crucial role in future growth and development of students. Below is the illustration of bridging teaching examples of marketing major post internship.

As to curriculum design of marketing major, different vocational colleges vary from each other. Vocational schools have set up some courses of their own vocational characteristics. They also set up such general ability and professional core ability courses in the industry as management studies, economics, statistics, financial management, marketing, law, consumer behavior, international marketing, market research, market research and forecasting and business negotiation, basically satisfying the objectives and requirements— "Training high-quality skilled talents that systematically master the basic principle of economics, management and are familiar with the marketing management economic laws, financial management knowledge, and have the independent work in the marketing business planning and other management work". Instructional design of talent training can be said to be scientific. Why do students' low recognition and satisfaction rate appear on post internship?

Tracking students' internship activities is believed to be related to students' low application and diffraction abilities of students' cognitive ability. Some students have no professional consciousness. They receive consumers without different sales behaviors from ordinary clerks, focusing only on product introduction and recommending new commodities,

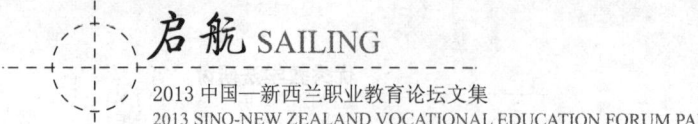

attracting customers with "the best seller" or "selling most" and think of the field work as a part-time job with no professional identity. In such cases, we guide the students' knowledge reconstruction through the bridging teaching instruction in the guidance of teaching.

Secondly, guiding students to diffract and bridge knowledge points of all courses. For example, after sorting the sales ledger with statistical knowledge, data can be the basis of statistical data analysis, and also can be the first-hand information of market research and the original accounting data of financial management. These data provide reference for economic activity analysis, financial analysis and decision of the management studies.

Thirdly, promoting the reconstruction of students' cognitive ability system. Through this link, we ought to enable students to merge the single, independent knowledge points and ability points into a whole, improve students' innovation ability.

Through bridging teaching instruction, the problem of students' low application and diffraction ability can be solved; students' professional comprehensive ability can be effectively trained and improved; the concept of career can be further strengthened; and the effect of post internship can gradually appear. The instruction also can promote the improvement of technology in classroom teaching.

III. Discussion on bridging teaching instruction

Bridging teaching instruction is an image name for "bridging" used in communication technology, based on students' teaching efficacy. Although it is defined, its scientific nature needs to be further explored. In terms of its usefulness, the bridging teaching instruction owns the following features:

Firstly, the basis of bridging teaching instruction is the knowledge and capacity points of each module unit students have mastered. Without these "fulcrums", it is impossible to "bridge". Strengthening the students' knowledge learning and capacity application training of each module unit is the basis of build "bridge".

Secondly, what we teach with bridging teaching instruction is not contents, but an approach. Bridging teaching instruction is to guide students to link such scattered, independent knowledge information into a unified knowledge information group, to help students construct their own knowledge and ability system, thus to contribute to students' ability to solve problems.

Thirdly, the characteristic of bridging teaching instruction is to help students change from "performers" to "roles". Students not only can complete the action the teacher taught, but also can complete the shaping of the role according to the requirements.

IV. Conclusion

Constantly improving the professional quality of personnel training is an eternal subject of the reform and development of higher vocational education. Based on the complexity of the education activity and the particularity of vocational education, teaching method should be chosen for the purpose of improving the students' cognitive ability and application ability. Making full use of bridging teaching instruction of the internship stage of higher vocational students has good effect on improving the quality of higher vocational talents training. The application research of bridging teaching instruction has just started, and needs to be further explored and improved in terms of its theoretical basis and scientific level.

强烈的欲望——以学生为中心的学习

奥塔哥理工学校　Peter Bilous

引言

什么产生火花？

我的教学生涯植根于在丛山中行走的激情。

• **热爱您教的课程**

激情最初引领我担当一名滑雪教练，然后使我逐渐涉足很多和高山旅行相关的其他领域。我的机械工程学位和8年

的从业实践让我对雪崩安全问题产生了强烈的兴趣，帮助我学习掌握相关的雪科学。

• **致力于将激情带给你的学生**

和人分享登山技能和经验的同时，看着同样的激情在他人身上快速燃烧是对我和最初激励我产生激情的雪山的最好奖赏。迄今我已经在奥塔哥理工学校执教不同水平的雪崩课程超过14年，且自2004年以来一直担任雪崩安全和雪上运动的课程经理。总而言之，我在北美、欧洲、亚洲和新西兰的山间教学已近30年。

我敢肯定，我的学生能感受到我对雪山的激情和安全分享这种激情所需的必要技能，我也同样肯定我的激情激发了学生的学习热情。

• **帮助学生早日确立学习动机和目标**

每次我给新生上课的第一天，我都会问学生他们来这里的动机是什么，他们的目标又是什么。

• **列出帮助学生达到目的步骤（以及全部课程）**

一旦确立学习目标，我会罗列出他们要实现这一目标所需要经历的过程——包括从头到尾每一步的课程是如何设计的。

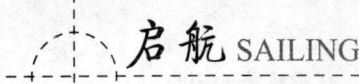

- **学习设计——收集木柴，点燃篝火**

作为一名滑雪者和登山者，在山地行走的挑战是效率和持久性。效率要求实际可行的技巧；持久性要求有效的风险管理。作为一名教练和滑雪向导，这些概念既适用于学生和顾客，也适用于你自己。回顾我所走过的旅程，我从我的导师、同事、学生、经历和大自然那里学到了很多。导师与我分享他们的激情、遇到的危险和成长的道路。同事借给我诚实、批判性的耳朵和阐明保持专业实践与时俱进的重要性。学生教我敞开心扉，听取他人意见，认识学习方式的多样性，并促使我开发多重教学策略。经验告诉我人为因素如何影响决策和每天总结、沟通和反思风险的重要性。大自然教我灵活多变，自发应对困难和机遇。我将我取得的很大部分成绩归功于我所提到的人和事，并利用一切机会将我在教学方式中所取得的经验教训和大家分享。

最终，我希望能给予处理激励、风险、沟通、个人的责任和决策的方法，并希望这种方法能应用到更广泛的领域中去，比如你所学的课程和生活本身。

具体来说，正如我在引言中提到的，我们首先从个人的激情中寻找动机和确定目标。接下来，我们学会如何学习，找出前进道路上的挑战和危险。很快，我们制定好战略，从整体上说明障碍和危险，包括人员、设备和环境（系统思维）的相互作用和影响。下一步，我们将我们所关心的问题告诉我们团队的成员，然后使用所有可能的手段将其通知整个（雪崩）团队。随着我们的行进，我们质疑和检验我们的想法，并根据现场情况修改我们的计划（选择较早确定的备选方案）。最后，学生和教师一起以积极的、建设性的态度反思当天的活动，加以改进以便下一次使用。教师最初引导这一进程，然后逐步过渡到让学生自己进行决策和反思，使学生在教师的监督下培养独立的决策能力和责任感。

使学生更容易想到的一个简单的登山理念是："在给定的条件下尽情享乐，并尽可能地做到安全和考虑周详，这样使你和其他人在将来能做得更好。"大多数报名参加学习雪崩安全的学生均提到这一点，但往往直到多年后才认识到上述建议的深远性。将这一理念与课堂和野外实地结合，让我想起了我的学生优先考虑的东西：边学习边玩，同时将注意力集中在一个共同的目标上——保证安全。

- **国际上最好的实践**

来这里学习的绝大多数学生均被课程的实用性和其在令人惊叹的高山环境中的运用所吸引。该课程的教学目的是培养导游、滑雪巡视员、户外活动指导和其他人员，使他们成为高度熟练的技术人员，帮助他们在山区环境中安全地工作和享受工作的乐趣。我个人的经验以及我与新西兰登山安全理事会（NZMSC）、加拿大雪崩协会（CAA）和美国雪崩研究和教育学院（AIARE）所建立的职业关系对我课程的开发帮助很大。这些关系不仅有助于保持甚至领先该行业国际教学标准，而且有助于在世界范围内提供所需的课程审计。

- 利益相关者的兴趣

在2007年，我需要重新开发雪崩第二阶段课程，开发一个使从业人员在他们的组织中发挥领导作用的课程。迄今，6年已经过去，业界对该课程的反馈仍然非常好。

从零开始，我组织了在这个行业内的利益相关者反思我们是如何学会（和继续学习）我们希望我们的毕业生要学习的技能的。雪崩有关行业的所有单位都派代表出席了会议；教练、滑雪场、道路建设养护、研究和教育界都有代表参加。同样重要的是，所有部门都参与了制定毕业生的合格标准和课程的教学目标。大家的意见和建议最终在课程设计中都得以体现。与这些利益相关者的充分协商对课程通过审批非常有帮助，也使课程极大地满足了利益相关者在实际工作中的需求。

- 辅导和目的明确的反馈

辅导的理念和反馈的好处已在雪崩领域及其以外的领域得到了很好的证明："有效的指导和辅导可以让经验不足的决策者积极参与建立自己的心理模型和决策技能。辅导在共同谋求新见解的过程中也促进双向学习。由于导师必须将决策问题和过程拆开并向学生阐明两者之间的关联，他们自己也会在这个教学过程中获得有关决策过程的有价值的深度见解。参与者表明指导老师需要付出的时间是值得关注的问题，但值得指出的是学生应该在自己的学习中发挥主导作用。""几个学习的例子包括观察、采访、研究雪崩专家以了解他们是如何成功地进行判断和决策的。反馈是做出正确的雪崩判断和决策的重要组成部分，因为没有有效的反馈，专家是不可能做出专业预测或判断的。"获取准确、及时、判断性的、描述过程细节的反馈是提高判断和决策能力的一个基本方法。

- 学生参与和团队决策

引导学生在课堂上学习理论知识是我最大的挑战之一。在案例分析和角色扮演中通过照片图像和视频片段使学生产生对山的联想是我为了填补两者之间差距使用的一个重要手段。我也相信，引导学生对理论知识在实际中的应用产生"为什么这样"

的疑问能加强学生有目的地参与。了解行动的原因有助于将各个步骤联系起来从而实现个人设定的目标和掌握所学的概念。建立一个希望所有参与者对决策过程提出自己的提议和重视他们的提议的学习环境能使学习和工作场所变化。

由此开发设计的课程,不仅尽可能多地安排学生进行现场体验式学习,而且有助于鼓励学生在课堂里自学,同时可以促进学生独立思考和团队合作。"团队学习的原则是通过对话方式提出问题,然后学生暂停他们自己的想法去悉心聆听和探索其他团队成员的思维模式。"让小组成员讨论个人行为模式对提高团队表现的重要性(个人能力),并鼓励大家提出自己的不同观点。

- 灵活的授课方式和批判性思维

雪崩课程采取的灵活授课方式允许一些学生在学习的同时继续工作。使用反思学习日志记录所学理论在工作场所的应用,鼓励学生进行批判性思维。而这种反思是学生在经历相关实践活动后所总结出来的经验。这种独立性学习、资源的有效利用和与同行/公众的沟通技巧正是利益相关者希望在雇员身上看到的,这些技能最终会使学生在野外环境工作中更安全。

- 反思性实践

在山上工作谋生有很大风险。随着时间的推移,你会懂得会有改变人的命运甚至夺走人生命的事件发生。幸运的是,我所经历的最大雪崩事件为前者,勉强避开了后者的噩运。

2006年我在工作中经历了一次很严重的雪崩事件。事件发生后,出于两个原因我仔细回顾了一下那天到底哪里出了问题。一个原因是我有点自私,关心自己的生死;另一个原因不像第一个那么自私。因为关乎生死的事件给我上了宝贵的一课,我强烈感到更多的听众——主要是我的同事和学生——可以从我的教训中获益。下图是将我部分埋掉了的雪崩,我当时在指导3个直升机滑雪的顾客。该雪崩大到足以埋

葬一辆卡车。它平均 70 厘米深，超过 200 米宽，约 100 米长——注意看看到山脊上的顾客。

我想用一个吸引人的方式来传递我想传达的严肃信息，所以想到了"Fork Stream"这一案例研究。它是一个小组活动，讨论用什么方式能传递"红旗"危险信号，及在那种情况下他们会做出什么样的决定。在第二部分，学生会发现他们决策的后果，什么人为因素会影响向导的决策能力以及会因此采取什么样的不同举措。

教学成果之一是学生明白了定期反思的重要性。在讨论结束时，很明显大家都知道了我是案例分析中的向导。这个事件帮我传递了一个重要信息，即每个人都会犯错，但你当时采取了什么措施以及事后你如何对待错误决定着逆境处理以及从逆境中学习的能力。案例研究引导学生采取团队的方式学习这一课程。个人亲身经历有助于弥补课堂教学和现实世界之间的差距，同时对学生产生感染力。案例研究向学生表明（提醒我）敞开心扉终身学习和个人成长的重要性。

"要改变学生的行为，唤起他们的情感反应是设计和传达信息的关键"。我对这点感觉是如此强烈，我已经将它写入了较高层次的雪崩学习课程（第 2 级），并已开始将它引入早期（第 1 级）课程。我们已经创建了一个教学氛围，那就是期望和鼓励所有学生在每天的野外实践结束后进行反思（以小组讨论的形式）。我们希望他们在出门前提出自己的预期计划，并与实际遇到的情况进行比较，然后解释差异产生的可能原因，并用批判性眼光看待自己处理风险的方式，说明他们当时作出了什么样的决定，及受了什么影响。最后，我们要求所有的参与者坦言他们从中学到了什么。

2008 年我在加拿大不列颠哥伦比亚省工作，作为在 Monashee 山雪地履带车滑雪的主向导，我采用了同样的原则：显著的成果是所有成员在离开教室时对当天活动相关的风险都有了充分认识，并对如何降低风险献计献策。这种风险意识和以解决问题为己任的态度极大地增强了他们在野外遇事积极应对（负责任的行为）的能力。这个过程的收获是所有团队成员学到了更好的预测技能，增加了日常风险的防范意识，并创造了一种氛围，使大家都不断致力于提高个人和团队的技能。而且很明显，由于大家的献计献策，团队提出了一系列解决问题的方案。

一个意想不到的成果是所有成员每天都有机会在一个相互支持的环境中诉说他们的忧虑，共同解决眼前的问题。队员没有必要把问题带回家去向他们的朋友或伴

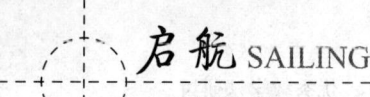

侣倾诉。这营造了更好的工作气氛,造就了心理健康的团队成员。所有这些成果都已被确认能减少亚当所描述的遭遇雪崩的风险。

采用这些策略的任何人都可以诚实地说他们以个人、专业和组织改善为目的,每天都批判性地研究当天的活动。这最终可以转变为安全性得到提高,事故与事件的发生几率减少。同样重要的是因为所有人(即学生或同事)都参与了风险识别,以及提出问题的解决办法,大家都更愿意服从和执行由此得出的决策和建议。

作为一个有效的学习工具,反思过程的优点在许多文献中均有记载:经常反思是将经验和知识转化为专业知识的根本,使我们从中能够获得新的见解,丰富我们的思维模式,以及明白突发事件产生的短暂影响在事发当时可能还没有被发现。

对过程进行反思可以学到新知识,并产生思维突变。

开发旨在帮助人们成为反思实践者的课程是"NDM(自然主义决策)研究的重点"。在行动中对自己的思维进行反思的能力是优秀专业人士与众不同的重要特征。

• 支持学习——共享温暖……

为了帮助我们的学员在学习期间取得成功,我提出了采用实际可行的指导方式协助提高工作场所技能的教学和提供灵活授课方式的理论支持系统。

指导老师和理论支持顾问由各行各业的专业人士组成。他们用自己的知识和经验帮助学生在学习中成长。指导过程的一个要求是必须从多方面征求意见反馈。鼓励学生尽可能使用多个来自不同行业和领域的导师,帮助他们从不同的角度看问题。也会为每个学生指定理论支持顾问,引导学生完成理论部分的学习。他们通常通过电子邮件和电话确定双方同意的反馈时限和交流方法,检查学生的作业和提供意见及学习方向以帮助学生顺利完成实践课程的学习。

• 评估学生的学习——每个学生都觉得舒适和温暖吗?

我评估的目标之一是向学生就其学习情况提供及时和相关的反馈。知道如何进一步改进学习过程和课程内容是另一个目标。等他们成为一个更好的学习者时,他们的学习动机和独立学习能力也将大大增强。

我是教学中使用形成性反馈的提倡者。根据我的经验,及时的、非正式的和经常的反馈是我们最成功的反馈模式。我认为前面提到反思是另一个建设性工具。因为我们确实想提高决策能力,学生不仅要考虑及分析每日的风险,还要考虑这些风险是否已得到团队有效管理或他们在当天有没有感觉到风险。如果有,他们需要解释为什么和我们能做些什么来更好地管理这些风险。然后我们问他们如果有的话什么人为因素可能已经影响了我们今天的决定？此外，我们在将来可以采用什么样的策略来更好地管理这些风险？最后要学生列出他们在这一天所学到的3件最重要的事。除了提供评估学生学习有价值的工具外，终结性和形成性评估使我的学生对我们教学的有效性提供了重要的反馈。反思评估结果提醒我们注意什么样的学生最好采用什么样的教学方法。其结果是，我也拓宽了我的教学方法使之适合更多的学习风格。同样重要的是修改那些已经被证明是最没有效果的教学方法。

- 评价教学——什么样的燃料能产生熊熊烈火？

评估教学结果是我用来衡量和改进我教学方法的一种方式。另一种方法是简单地问我的学生他们觉得哪种方法最有效。我不会直接去问，而是间接地通过监测他们的参与程度，通过问问题，发现他们的理解水平，并要求学生在每堂课结束时提供反馈，尤其是新课结束时。除了我们学校的正式反馈问卷调查，针对我的教学我利用类似的方式收集信息。在调查过程中，学生从讲师是否平易近人、是否能有效沟通、评估学生理解的能力以及营造积极的学习氛围等方面来评估讲师的教学方式和方法，同时要求学生提供改进意见。除了我们学校的正式反馈问卷调查，针对我的教学我也用类似的方式收集信息。

我认为所有的反馈意见都是我反思实践的一部分，如果是切实可行的相关理念，我会将其融入到教学中。这种反馈帮助我发现可以改进的地方、可以维持不变的地方和不需要花更多精力的地方。教学评估技巧、行动和真实的反馈结果相结合有助于改进课程和提高学生学习成绩。关闭反馈回路是指与当前学生讨论他们在目前学习的课程中所采纳的过去学生所提的建议。如果在课程的开始就收到反馈，往往可以做出积极的改变，使学生马上从中受益。

- 专业发展和领导能力——拨旺余火让火势蔓延……

持续提高专业水平是我特别推崇的一个刻意练习领域。我认为人们应该相信自己并不断提高自身的修养。我很幸运有奥塔哥理工学校作为我的主要雇主。学校不仅重视和支持这一做法，而且鼓励在这一领域中采取积极主动的措施。为了发挥我的作用，我坚持在教学的同时继续作为滑雪向导受雇于国内和国际的滑雪行业。在我从事的教学领域做一些实际野外工作有利于保持我的热情和检验我所传授给学生的理论和实践知识的正确性。结果证明，这方面的经验帮助我改进了在后续课程中的风险管理实践,并将其引入新西兰滑雪行业。参照海外使用的模式,我帮助启动了持续专业发展(CPD)分数系统作为新西兰所有雪崩教官评估的一部分。这个概念来自于我在加拿大雪崩协会(CAA)的工作经验。

我们采取了一些方法以保持教学与时俱进,和今天在座的各位目标一致:

• 参加教育或教学研讨会和参加工作室活动;

• 就你专业以外的领域发表意见,重点放在将知识运用到相关行业,如新西兰雪崩搜索和救援;

• 在行业时事快报上投稿;

• 在YouTube上传窍门和短片,特别是吸引年轻学习者的有效方法。

• 向你所在社区提供免费的入门讲习班或针对你觉得可能会从中学到一些技巧的特定群体,如新西兰自由滑雪协会(FSANZ),为他们12位最好的运动员参加世界竞赛举办为期2天的特殊训练班。课程按特定要求的水平向运动员传授减轻固有风险的最佳方法。

定期在专业行业工作不仅有助于保持知识技能的先进性,也可在学生和同事之间树立信誉。当你要把来自其他领域的新概念引入到你所在的行业或教学中去的时候,这一点尤为重要。最终,通过不断提高自己的个人和专业水平,可以激励他人像你一样;只有以身作则才能取得最佳效果。

• 结论——照料篝火

总而言之,我视我的生活和我从事的教学为不断持续的工作,一个不断学习的过程。这个过程很像是一盆火,需要定期加柴才可使火焰更旺。我常常这样想,我所做的改进可使我的学生直接受益,他们将来也会发出和我一样的光和热。从我的学生、同事以及我自己的错误中我学到了很多,我真的很高兴能点燃他们对所学知识的激情。感谢你们的宝贵时间和有机会与你们分享这些想法和意见。愿你们的火焰燃烧得更旺盛。

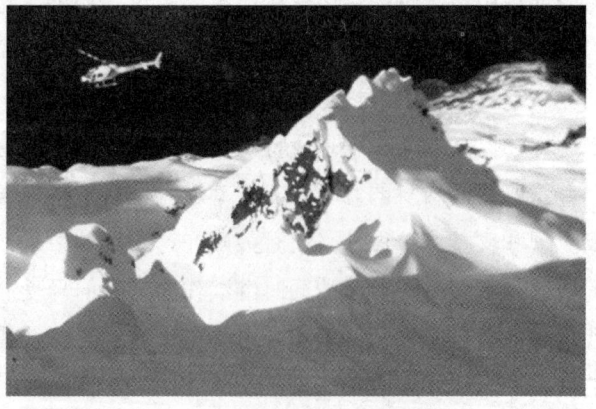

Burning Desire—Student Centered Learning

Peter Bilous, Otago Polytechnic

Introduction

What creates the spark?

My teaching career was seeded from a passion for moving through the mountains.

- Be Passionate About Your Subject

That passion initially led me to teaching skiing, then evolved to many other aspects of alpine travel. A Mechanical Engineering degree and eight years in professional practice heightened my interest of avalanche safety concerns and aided my grasp of the associated snow science.

- Be Equally Committed to Sharing That Passion With Your Students

The reward of sharing mountain skills and experiences while watching the passion grow in others soon became as fulfilling as the environment which initially inspired me. I have now been teaching avalanche curriculum for more than 14 years for Otago Polytechnic in various capacities and have been the Programme Manager for Avalanche Safety and Snowsport Instruction since 2004. All told, I have been teaching in the mountains for nearly three decades in North America, Europe, Asia and New Zealand.

I'm certain my students sense my passion for the environment and required skills necessary to share it safely. I am equally certain that those students are motivated to learn as a result.

- Establish Their Motivation or Goals Early

On the 1st day of each course I teach, I ask my students what their motivation is for being there—what are their goals?

• Outline the Steps (and Course Curriculum) That Will Help Them Get There

Once goals have been established, I outline the steps they will need to reach those goals—including how the course curriculum has been designed to cover each step along the way.

• Learning Design—Gathering the Wood... and Igniting the Fire

As a skier and climber, the challenge of mountain movement is efficiency and longevity. Efficiency demands practiced solid technique; longevity requires effective risk management. As an instructor and ski guide, these concepts apply to students and clients, as well as yourself. Along the path, I have learned from my mentors, colleagues, students, experiences and nature. Mentors shared their passion, perils and development pathway. Colleagues lent an honest, critical ear and illustrated the importance of professional practice currency. Students taught me the value of an open mind, listening, recognizing diverse learning styles and spurred me to develop multiple teaching strategies. Experience taught me how human factors affect decision making and the importance of defining, communicating and reflecting on daily risk. The environment taught me flexibility, spontaneity, hardship and opportunity. I owe much to these people and factors and use every chance to share the lessons learnt in my teaching approach and methodology.

Ultimately, I hope to impart an approach to motivation, risk, communication, personal responsibility and decision making that can be applied to a wider context, like courses of yours and life itself.

Specifically, as I mentioned in the introduction, we begin by developing motivation from personal passion and defining goals. Next, we learn how to learn, identifying the challenges and hazards along the way. We soon develop strategies to address these obstacles and dangers together holistically; that includes the interaction and impact of people, equipment and the environment (systems thinking). From here, we communicate our concerns amongst our group and to a wider (avalanche) community using all available technology. We question and test our thoughts as we travel, changing our plans (to earlier identified options) as conditions dictate. Lastly, both students and instructors reflect on the day's activities, both positively and constructively; to improve the process for the next time. Tutors initially lead this process and progressively shift decisions and reflection to the students to foster decision making independence and responsibility while under the instructor's watch.

A simpler mountain philosophy that students often relate easier to is: "Have as much fun as possible, given the conditions, and do it safely and considerately enough so you and others can do it well into the future". Most of the students who enroll to study avalanche safety identify with this without considering the far-reaching applications mentioned above, often until years later. Integrating this philosophy into the classroom and field reminds me of something prioritized by my students: Have fun while learning, whilst maintaining focus on a common goal—our safety.

- International Best Practice

The vast majority of learners that enter my classrooms are drawn to the practical aspect of the programme and its application in a stunning alpine environment. The programme outcomes are to train guides, ski patrollers, outdoor instructors and others to become highly skilled technicians and help them enjoy and work in the mountain environment safely. My own experience and the professional relationships fostered with New Zealand Mountain Safety Council (NZMSC), the Canadian Avalanche Association (CAA) and The American Institute for Avalanche Research and Education

(AIARE) has played an important role in developing the programmes. These relationships not only help maintain and even lead international educational standards, but also provide much needed moderation on a global scale.

• Stakeholder's Interest

In 2007 an opportunity arose to redevelop the Stage 2 Avalanche programme, a programme intended for practitioners to assume a leading role within their organization. Now, six years on, industry feedback remains extremely positive.

Starting with a clean slate, I drew together a team of industry stakeholders to reflect on how we had learned (and continue to learn) the skills that we wanted our graduates to possess. All aspects of the avalanche sector were represented—guiding, ski fields, roading, research and education. Equally important, all sectors engaged and contributed to the process of defining the graduate profile and learning outcomes. The groups concerns and contributions were ultimately reflected in the course design. The thorough consultation of those stakeholders immensely aided the acceptance of the programme and the curriculum to meet their objectives in the workplace.

• Mentoring and Focused Feedback

The mentoring concepts and feedback benefits are well supported within the avalanche realm and beyond: "Effective mentoring and coaching actively engages less-experienced decision-makers in building their mental models and decision skills. Mentoring also fosters two-way learning in a mutual search for new insight. Since the mentor must decouple the decision problem and process, and articulate the components to the protégé, they also receive valuable insight into the decision process. Participants articulated a concern for the time commitment required to be a mentor, however it is important to note that the protégé should take a leadership role in their own learning."

"Several (learning) examples include observing, interviewing, and/or studying avalanche experts in order to understand how they successfully arrived at judgment and decision action. Feedback is a critical component of sound avalanche judgment and decision-making, since without effective feedback it may be impossible to achieve expert predictive or diagnostic abilities." "Obtaining feedback that is accurate, timely, diagnostic, and process-focused is a fundamental method to enhance judgment and decision expertise."

- Learner Engagement and Group Decision Making

Actively engaging learners with the theoretical aspects in a classroom setting is one of my greatest challenges. Frequent visual connection with the mountains through photos images and video footage applied to case studies and role playing are an important means I use to bridge the gap between the two. I also believe empowering students with the "why" of theoretical grounding and the practical application underpins purposeful engagement. Understanding the reason for actions helps link the steps to achieve personally set goals and creates ownership of the concepts. Establishing an environment where all are expected to contribute to the decision making process, and their contributions valued, leads to more meaningful study, and workplace, while promoting independent thought and team benefits.

The programmes, as a result, are not only designed to maximize experiential opportunities in the field, but help motivate students' own learning in the classroom. "The discipline of team learning is based upon reflective inquiry using dialogue, where people suspend their views and enter into deep listening to explore mental models of other team members." "Focus group participants discussed the importance of personally modeling the behaviors that foster team performance (personal mastery), and encouraging the sharing of different points of view."

• Flexible Delivery and Critical Thinking

The flexible delivery opportunities incorporated in the avalanche programmes have allowed some students to continue to work while studying when it best suits them. Incorporating reflective learning journals to record workplace applications of the theory presented encourages critical thinking. Again, this is expressed at a practical and relevant level. It is this level of independence, effective resource use and peer/public communication skills that the stakeholders demand in the workplace and ultimately make the students safer in the field.

• Reflective Practice

Earning a living by working in the mountains carries significant risks. One learns over time that there are life changing events and life ending events. Luckily, my most significant avalanche incident was the former, narrowly averting the statistical notoriety of the latter.

In 2006, while working in industry, I had a significant avalanche involvement. As part of that experience, I had a critical look at what went wrong on that day for two reasons. One is a bit selfish and centers about my own longevity/mortality, the other, less so. As I learned hard but valuable lessons, I felt very strongly that a larger audience should benefit—mainly my colleagues and students. The image you see below is the avalanche that partially buried me while I was heli-ski guiding 3 clients. It was big enough to bury a truck. It averaged 70cm deep, was over 200m wide and about 100m long—note the clients visible on the ridge.

I wanted an engaging way to deliver the sobering messages that I needed to convey, so I came up with the "Fork Stream" case study. This is done in groups and discusses what signs created "red flags" for them and what decision they would have made on the day. In part 2, they discover the consequence of their decisions, what human factors may have affected the guide's decision making capabilities and what they might do differently.

One of its key outcomes is that the student understands the value of reflective practice on a regular basis. Upon the conclusion of the exercise, it becomes apparent the guide in the case study is me. This helps me convey the point that everybody makes mistakes—it's what you do about it at the time and into the future that defines your ability to manage and learn from adversity. The case study guides them through this process using a team approach. Personal involvement helps close the gap between the classroom and the real world while appealing to the emotions of my students. The case study shows the students (and reminds me) the importance of, and being open to, lifelong learning and personal growth.

"Evoking an emotional response in students is essential to designing and delivering a message that is targeted to altering behavior" . I feel so strongly about this that I have written it into the curriculum of avalanche studies at the higher (Stage 2) level and have begun to introduce it at the earlier (Stage 1) level. We have created an atmosphere on the course where all are empowered and expected to reflect (in a group discussion format) daily after field sessions. We want them to comment on what they anticipated prior to going out in the field, compare it to what actually was encountered, explain possible reasons for inconsistencies, critically look at the way the risk was managed, what decisions they made and what may have influenced them. Lastly, we want all to acknowledge what was learnt.

While working in British Columbia, Canada in 2008 I employed these same principles as Chief Guide of a Cat-Skiing operation in the Monashee Mountains: The significant outcome is that all members left the room fully aware of the risks associated with the day and had contributed to the means of minimizing them. This awareness and ownership of solution greatly enhances the chance that they will act accordingly (responsibly) in the field. Outcomes of this process were the development of better forecasting skills by all team members, increased situation awareness of the daily risk and creating an environment where all are striving to constantly improve personally and operationally. It also becomes obvious that a team approach here provides an array of solutions that they contributed to.

An unexpected outcome was that all members had a daily opportunity to vent their concerns in a supportive environment that can jointly resolve the issues at hand. It wasn't necessary for any team members to go home and "dump" on their friend or partner. This makes for a much better atmosphere to work in and a mentally healthier team member. All these outcomes have been identified to reduce the risks of avalanche involvements as described by Adams.

Anyone that employs these strategies can honestly say that every day they critically examine the day's activities with the goal of personal, professional and organizational improvement. This ultimately translates to improved safety and less accidents and incidents. Equally important is to note that because all were involved in identifying issues of concern (i.e. students or colleagues); including their resolution, all are much more willing to "buy into" the resulting policies and recommendations that result.

The benefits of the reflection process as an effective learning tool are well documented:

"Frequent reflection is fundamental to transforming experience and knowledge events into expertise, enables us to derive new insights, richer mental models, and an understanding of causal influences that may not have been identified at the time".

"Reflection on processes generates learning and may stimulate a breakthough in thinking".

"Developing programs aimed at helping people become reflective practitioners is a key focus of NDM (Naturalistic Decision Making) research".

"The ability to reflect on one's thinking while acting is a key characteristic that distinguishes the exceptional professional".

• Support for Learning—Sharing the Warmth …

To aid our learners achieve success while studying, I mentioned the practical mentoring incorporated to assist the workplace up-skilling component and theory support systems for the flexibly delivered portions. The Mentors and Theory Support Advisors are made up of a range of professionals from a variety of industry sectors and operations. They draw on their knowledge and experience to assist students' growth during the programme. A requirement of the mentoring process is that feedback must be solicited from more than one source. Students are encouraged to use of as many mentors as possible from an array of operations and industry sectors to provide a wider prospective.

Theory support advisors are also assigned to each student to guide them through the theory portion of the learning. They normally communicate via email and phone to establish mutually agreeable feedback timeframes and communication methods, review work and provide comment and direction to enhance understanding and success on the practical aspects of the course.

• Gauging Student Learning—Is Everyone Comfortable and Warm?

I aim for assessment to provide students with timely, relevant feedback on their progress as a learner. Knowing how to further improve on the learning process, as well as course content, is another goal. As they become a better learner, their motivation to learn and ability to do this independently is greatly enhanced.

I am a great believer of using formative feedback on our courses. From my experience, immediate, informal and often has been our most successful feedback formula. I consider the reflective thought previously mentioned as another formative tool. Since we are really trying to develop decision making, students not only consider and comment on the daily hazards, but also consider whether these risks were managed by the group effectively or if they ever felt at risk that day? If so, they need to explain why and what can we do to better manage those risks. Then we ask them what human factors, if any, may have influenced our decisions today? Also, what strategies might we employ to better manage this in the future? Lastly they are to list the 3 most important things they learned on the day. Along with providing a valuable tool for evaluating student learning, both summative and formative assessment provides my team great feedback on our teaching effectiveness. Reflecting on assessment results draws attention to what works best for which students. Resultantly, I have broadened my teaching skills to reach more learning styles. Equally important is altering what has shown to be least effective practice.

- Evaluating the Teaching—Which Fuel Creates the Best Blaze?

Assessment results are one way I use to evaluate and modify my teaching methods. Another way is to simply ask my students what works best. I do this informally by monitoring their engagement level, asking questions, searching for their level of understanding and asking for their feedback at the end of lessons, particularly new lessons. Besides my institution's formal feedback surveys, I utilize similar feedback specific to my teaching. During this process, students evaluate the individual lecturers teaching practices and methods from whether the lecturer is approachable and communicates effectively to the lecturer's ability to assess the students understanding and the creation of a positive learning environment. Students are also asked to consider improvements that could be incorporated.

I consider all comments as part of my reflective practice and incorporate relevant ideas into the learning where practical and appropriate. This feedback helps me define the areas we can improve upon, areas where we should maintain what we are currently doing and areas that perhaps need less emphasis. The combination of teaching evaluation techniques, action and results from these solicited responses help the programme and our students constantly improve. Closing the feedback loop means discussing with current students how past students suggestions have been incorporated into their current programme. If the feedback is received early in the programme, it is often possible to make positive changes that they can immediately benefit from.

- **Professional Development and Leadership—Stoking the Embers and Spreading the Flame …**

Continuing professional development is an area of engaging in deliberate practice that I am particularly committed to. I think that that one has to believe in themselves and look to personally better themselves continually. I feel fortunate to have Otago Polytechnic as an employer who not only values and supports this approach, but encourages pro-active initiative in this area. To enhance my effectiveness, I continue to work in industry, domestically and internationally as a ski guide while teaching. Working in the field I teach helps maintain my enthusiasm and test the theoretical and practical aspects delivered to students. As evidenced from the outcomes, this experience strongly influences the improved risk management practices used on subsequent courses and introduced to my industry in New Zealand. Looking at models used overseas, I helped initiate a Continuing Professional Development (CPD) points system as part of the validation process for all avalanche instructors in New Zealand. The concept was adopted from my working internationally with the Canadian Avalanche Association (CAA).

Some of the means that we employ to stay current are much like your presence here:

• Education or teaching seminars and workshop attendance;

• Speaking outside your specific area of expertise focusing on aligning transferable concepts, e.g. New Zealand Avalanche Search and Rescue;

• Contributing to industry newsletters;

• Uploading tips and footage on You Tube, particularly effective means to reach young learners;

• Contribute to your local community by providing free entry level workshops or even targeting specific groups that you feel might benefit from some tips, e.g. Free Ski Association of New Zealand (FSANZ) through a 2 day specifically designed course for 12 of their top athletes competing on the world circuit. The work delivered a message about the best means of mitigating the inherent risks, catered for their specific level.

Regularly working in industry not only maintains currency in practice, it builds credibility with students and colleagues. This is particularly important when you are introducing new concepts to either industry or education that may have originated in the other sector. Ultimately, by personally and professionally bettering yourself continually, you encourage others to do the same; leading by example best achieves these results.

Conclusion—Tending the Fire

In summary, I view life and my involvement in teaching as a constant work in progress and a learning process. That process is much like a fire that requires regular tending to burn brightly. I like to think that the improvements made directly benefit my learners and they will also glow to the same extent. I learn a lot from my students, colleagues and my own mistakes and really enjoy igniting others' passion for their subject. Thank you for your time and this opportunity to share these thoughts and ideas with you. May your flames burn bright.

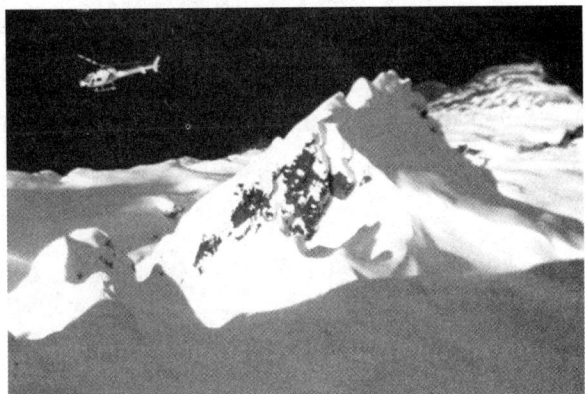

模拟学习体验及在情境化学习中解决问题

丰盛湾理工学院　Sam Honey

"告诉我，我会忘记；教给我，我可能记住；让我参与，我才能学会。"

传统的教学方法是以教师为主；教师采取自己喜欢的教材，以自己喜欢的方式进行教学，有时与实际知识需求相比，课程灵活性非常差。这种情况通常出现在教师以讲课的方式传授知识。如果不出意外的话，学生只要在课堂上对
老师所讲的内容照抄以便课后学习，然后在闭卷书面考试中再原封不动地当作自己所学到的知识加以复述即可。尽管这种教学方式对背诵过去的事实和照搬信息比较有效，但却几乎不提供学生参与教学的机会。因此，它很少鼓励学生自己思考和使用有创意的学习方法来加深对知识的理解。

教师作为教学的主导者

孔夫子在大约2500年以前说过，如果让学生参与学习过程，教给他们知识在实际中的应用，学生才能学会。让学生参与，意味着学生会将自己的生活经验、想法及实际运用带进学习过程并与他人分享。以学生为中心的教学方法要求教师作为课堂教学的主导者，而不是知识的喷泉。我的演讲主要给大家举例说明在传统的职业教育理论课堂教学中，如何轻松地让学生在模拟现实生活场景中运用所学知识，以及如何在安全环境下运用自己的知识。以我的教学为例，（年轻人都想成为执法人员，通常指警察）但在现实生活中他们不能穿警装进行实践——如果冒充警察会被逮捕。因此，我需要给他们提供其他模拟实践方法以帮助学生掌握所学知识和实际运用。

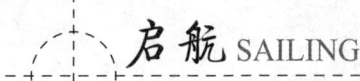

在这里我只给大家介绍一节教学场景课程来说明我是如何使用情景化教学的，在教学过程中，学生运用各种以学生为中心的教学方法，比如课堂小组讨论，通过使用英特网和参考该领域的专家论坛进行调研活动，研究案例，观看视频剪辑以及讨论媒体上刊登的各种新闻等，学习"必备知识"。学生然后将所学知识运用于经常举行的各种实践活动，如模拟角色扮演。这样给学生提供机会证明他们在实践中能够运用所学知识和临场发挥，以培养学生的自信。

举例说明模拟学习场景可以在传统的四壁围成的教室里进行

在这个例子中，班上的学生是整个活动的组织者，教师只负责主导过程以及提出一些适当的问题和观点供学生参考。通过教学，学生需要了解警察在实际工作中的各种职责以及警察如何与社区合作降低犯罪率。班上的学生举行一次模拟社区会议。将学生分为不同小组，每组 6~10 人，着重讲述他们所生活的城市社区所面临的 3~4 个实际问题，他们首先详细说明问题，然后指出警察须采取什么行动与社区配合才能减少这些问题。他们在地图上标出该社区的地理区域，找出该区域所存在的问题以及可用的警力与资源。接下来决定谁来扮演在解决上述问题时警察的不同角色。然后他们为召开社区会议进行准备，搜集开会时与社区讨论的相关资料。他们不需要讨论或书面汇报会议情况，而是要用表演的形式展示开会过程，期间社区人员可以向他们提问。每个小组均有机会在社区会议上发言。

这是一个在课堂教学中组织模拟场景教学的例子，如果教学内容和时间允许，也可在其他场所组织类似的模拟教学，那样也许会更逼真。至少，根据小组数量多少，这样的活动包括学生的准备时间在内，可以在 3 小时内完成。我将这个例子用作该教学主题的最终结论，但也可对其加以修改用于教学的各个阶段，也可只角色表演教学的指定内容而不必囊括整个主题。20 分钟的简短角色表演，只演出整个过程的一部分，尤其是在时间不足的情况下，一样可以达到预期效果。

职业教育情景化教学方法应用的其他例子

人类有限的想象力限制了各种可能性。虽然在计划过程中必须考虑时间和资源，但模拟场景可以以任何规模在任何时间进行。记住，坐着听讲不是最有效的学习方法。模拟场景的重点是让学生可在现实生活中运用所学知识。其他实际应用例子可能为：

• 用于电子产品。学生不需要在课堂上向老师和其他同学介绍有关电子设备的知识，相反，可以将它变为一个实际的电子展向出席模拟交易会的"潜在投资者"或"买家"(因为他们是现实生活中的实际买家而不是老师)介绍自己的电子产品。他们可以边展示边介绍,并回答客户提出的问题。

• 用于焊接。通过一个实际项目,让学生们传授与其他学生不同的焊接方法,并解释自己在做什么以及如何将其应用于更大的项目。产品也许可以销售或作为礼物送人。

• 用于市场营销。让学生们在一个模拟产品展销会上向"潜在企业家"展示自己的营销想法,或在模拟营销创新会展上设立展台参展,其他学生可现场参观展览并提问。如果可行的话,邀请真正的企业家参加。

• 用于科学领域。让学生布置实验设备,现场向同行学生演示实际操作,或在内部网发布,重点是让学生负责实际操作并有机会口头回答问题。

• 用于木工行业。让学生向有意向的建筑业主/房主提供建筑咨询,解释他们使用的建筑方法和为什么选择这些方法,或带领潜在的房屋买家看房,并解释该建筑所使用的建筑技术以及为什么使用这些技术。

为什么模拟学习场景有效

模拟学习场景有效是因为:

• 能鼓励学生非常自信地在教室这个安全的环境里展示所学的理论知识。

• 能激励学生将来创新地运用知识,而不是简单地回顾。

• 它要求学生使用研究技能、小组合作技能,培养学生在工作场所发言时的自信心。

所学的知识通过实践记忆深刻,这样学生们更容易记住整个工作程序及如何在现实生活中运用所学知识。

• 因为了解整个程序,学生能够将所学的零零碎碎的知识融会贯通,更易于建立自信心。

• 模拟体验教学适用于由入门课程到学位课程的所有职业教育课程(通过更加详细的案例)。

• 教师可利用角色扮演培养学生自信心,还可在学生注意力不集中时使用它,将它作为一种动觉式学习方法。

一开始教师需要花时间准备,思考和计划在模拟场景教学中最有效的场景,一旦完成,它很容易在一系列教学主题中得到运用。教师还可实事求是地评估学生对知识运用的理解,找出可能需要重新讲解的学习内容。

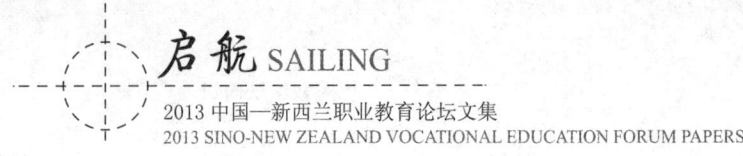

Simulated Learning Experiences and Using Problem Solving in Contextualised Learning

Sam Honey, Bay of Plenty Polytechnic

Tell me and I'll forget; show me and I may remember; involve me and I'll understand.

Traditional pedagogies are teacher focused; learning is delivered through teacher preferred resources, in the teacher's preferred way sometimes to a very inflexible curriculum of what knowledge is required. Most commonly this occurs in the form of lecturing information to students who, if all goes to plan, dutifully copy the words of their teacher so that they can "study" them and report them back as assumed knowledge and understanding, in a written closed book test. Whilst this style of teaching may have worked well for reciting past facts and regurgitating information, it does little to involve the student in the learning. Therefore it does very little in encouraging students to use their own intelligence and creative learning processes to enhance their knowledge and understanding.

The Teacher as a Learning Facilitator

As Confucius said approximately two and a half thousand years ago, if we involve students in their learning, and show them the real life application of their knowledge, they will understand. Involving students means to let them bring their own experiences and ideas and real life applications to their knowledge building and share these with others. Student centred teaching requires the teacher to be a facilitator of learning opportunities, rather than the fountain of all knowledge. My presentation focuses on examples of how traditional vocational theory type classes can easily use simulated real-life learning experiences for students to practice their understanding, and apply their knowledge in a safe environment. In my students' case (young people intending to become law enforcement officers, usually police) they are not able to don police uniforms to practice their skills in the real world—they would be arrested for impersonating police officers! Therefore I need to provide them with alternative real-life simulated activities to help embed their knowledge and practice.

Here I explain just one teaching scenario to highlight my own use of contextualised learning; however, the ideas can be applied to a wide variety of vocational theory lessons, as an alternative to writing information down and showing understanding in written form. As a part of this process students learn "must know" material in a variety of student centred ways in the classroom such as group discussion, peer research activities using internet and experts in the field, examining case studies and video clips, and discussing current events through media articles. They then apply their understanding of the material through frequent practical application opportunities such as role play simulations. This gives them the opportunity to show that they can apply their knowledge, think on the spot and build confidence in their practice.

Example Application of a Simulation Learning Activity That can Be Done in a Traditional Four-Walled Classroom

In this example the class of students are the organisers of the whole activity—the teacher facilitates the process only and offers questions or points to consider where appropriate. In my class, students need to understand in a practical sense, the various roles of NZ police and how police interact with the community to reduce crime. The students hold a mock (simulated) community meeting with their class. In separate groups of between 6 and 10 students each, they highlight 3–4 real life issues faced by a real community in their city, they detail these issues and then indicate all of the police roles needed to be able to interact with the community to minimise those issues. They use visual maps to outline the community area. They research the problems in that area and the realistic availability of police staff and resources. They decide who will "be" the officer for each police role involved in dealing with the issues. They then prepare a "community" meeting and research the information they would need to be able to discuss with the "community". Instead of reporting this back in writing or discussion, they actually act out the meeting in progress, with "community members" able to ask them questions. Each group has the opportunity to address the "community".

Whilst this particular example is a simulated environment in the classroom, simulations can also be held in other available venues which may be more "real life" depending on your topic and time available. At a minimum though, depending on the amount of groups to present, this activity, including students' preparation, can be completed in three hours. It is used in this example as a conclusion to the topic, but can be modified to be used at any stage of a topic, and can be a specified part of the topic rather than the summary of the whole. Shorter 20 minute role pay scenarios, capturing one stage of a process only, can be just as effective, especially where there is less time available.

Examples of Other Vocational Applications of Contextualised Scenarios

The possibilities are really limited only by the imagination. Although time and resources are definitely taken into account in the planning, simulations can be of any size and timeframe. Remember that sitting and listening is not the most effective way to learn. The key with scenario simulations is that the students can practice applying their understanding in real world experiences. Examples of other applications could be:

• For electronics, instead of students presenting their understanding of a piece of equipment to the teacher and students at their desks, turn it into an actual presentation of the equipment to "potential investors" or "buyers" who are at a mock trade fair (as these are the customers in real life, not the teacher…). They demonstrate and explain at the same time and have to respond to questions from the "customer".

• For welding, have students teach other students how to weld in different ways through a project, and explain what they are doing and how it can apply to a bigger idea. Perhaps the products can be sold or used as gifts?

• For business marketing, have students present a marketing idea to "potential business owners" in a mock product expo, or a mock marketing innovation expo. Students set up stalls and presentations; other students walk around to view the live presentations and ask questions. Invite real business owners if possible!

• For science, set up the experiment and demonstrate live to fellow students, or podcast it through an intranet site. The key is that the students control delivery and have the opportunity to respond verbally to questions.

• For carpentry, have students undertake a building consultation with a "prospective building/house owner". Let them explain the methods they are using and why they have chosen those ways, or take potential building buyers through a building and explain the techniques used and why.

Why Simulated Learning Environments are Effective

Simulated learning activities are effective because

• They encourage students to confidently demonstrate their understanding of "theory", in the safe peer environment of their classroom.

• It encourages student creativity in how knowledge can be applied in the future, not only retrospectively.

- It requires students to utilise research skills, team work skills and develop their confidence in addressing other people in a work environment.
- The knowledge gained is embedded in a practical way and this makes it easier for them to remember how processes work and how they will apply their knowledge in a real-life situation.
- It builds confidence in the student (and teacher) that they understand the whole process and can link the pieces of learning together.
- They can be applied across the whole spectrum of qualification levels in vocational education from introductory courses through to degrees (with much more detailed cases).
- When the teacher builds confidence in the use of role plays, they can also use them at any time student attention wanes and as a kinaesthetic form of learning.

Preparation time is needed for the teacher initially to think out and plan the most effective scenarios to use in simulation, but once this has been done, the processes are easily applied to a variety of topics studied. The teacher can also honestly assess the students' progress in understanding the application of their knowledge, and identify areas that may need going over.

行业中基于工作过程的教学，通向成功的体系、策略和实践

新西兰教育研究协会　Karen Vaughan

学习和工作：两者在工作过程中相辅相成

众所周知，工作场所可以是一个很好的学习环境。在工作场所可以学到课堂里很难学到的东西——学习的真实性。在工作场所学习意味着学习者必须接触到真实的工作环境、真实的客人、真实的工作期限以及承担真正的后果。

这是我们在对知识和学习进行思考时在想法上发生的一个很重要的转变。不同知识的学习和学习形式已经不再是单纯地选择是在学院学习（理论知识）还是在工作场所学习（实践知识）。我们知道不同知识、技能的学习和性格的培养需要不同的学习环境。人们在学校已经学不到将来工作和生活所需的全部技能了。很多工作场所需要的知识、技能和性格的培养不能只通过在校学习或者通过工作本身来进行。然而我们也知道，特定的工作知识和技能不能在教育机构，如一个职业学院中学到。我们越来越多地意识到，工作场所学习应该被正式列入正规教育，且工作场所在向学习者提供有计划的学习实践方面应发挥更重要的作用。

本演讲的中心内容是关于工作场所学习及在工作中学习。它可以作为一个广泛的教育课程的一部分，如那些与职业教育相关的课程。同时，它也可以作为一个独立的"在职学习"课程。新西兰教育研究理事会通过一些在新西兰开设的课程，已经着手研究在职学习的效果。这些项目包括：

与建筑施工行业培训组织合作开发了一套系统，用于评估在职学习或者行业环境下的学习；

在老年护理行业、园艺行业和旅游行业研究了一些很好的在职学习的实例；

研究调查了在一般的医学实践（家庭医生）和木工领域里学徒和学习者是如何将理论和实践相结合的；

审阅了世界上关于在职业场所学习的研究结果。

通过这些项目，我们发现了一些适合雇主和雇员双方利益的有效在职学习的共性和意见分歧。在这个演讲里我不能对成功的在职学习的所有方面进行介绍。不过我选出了一些最令人感兴趣和最重要的方面来向大家说明，经过精心计划工作场所是如何成为好的学习环境的。其中也不乏挑战，它们和课堂教学所遇到的挑战不一样，但是它们为每个学习者、雇主以及整个行业所带来的好处却意义深远。

机构赋予学习优先权

第一个重要原则是关于机构如何理解并赋予学习优先权的。最好的工作场所是不会任凭员工们的学习顺其自然的。他们并不是仅仅把有关学习的内容写在文件里。他们会让学习实际可行并随处可见。同时，他们也确保至少指派一名人员负责促进员工们在工作场所的学习。

我们对一个社区组织进行了研究，该组织向老年人、无家可归者、残疾人士或需要家庭帮助的人士提供服务。该组织有一个管理人员负责监督员工招聘、员工培养和就业培训。该管理人员的职责很广，这意味着她对学习者和客人的需求都有着深刻的了解。她可以确保那些设计的培训课程能满足上述双方的需求。我们也对一个葡萄园进行了研究，该葡萄园的经理通过让大家看到自己的日常学习来表明该公司努力促进学习。

支持框架和职工手册

第二个重要原则是企业要有关于公司经营活动和管理机构的职工手册，为工人/学习者们提供支持框架或临时帮助，然后逐步放手。放手后，学习者们可以去学习所需的知识、技能、性格（态度、判断力、辨别力、理解力）培养以及更加独立的解决问题和运用批判性思维的能力。

在我们进行调研的那些工作场所中，我们看到了不同的支持框架的实例。学习者决不会被"硬推"到他们的工作岗位上，而是给他们一定的时间去适应。通常情况下，他们都会和一个能够指导他们的同事结成一组。学习者有机会去熟悉工作程序，学习该问些什么问题、向谁问和什么时候问。

在家庭护理机构，新来的护工要跟随一个有经验的护工工作一周。该机构还建立了一个联络网，让每个护工都能够和总公司的个案工作者保持密切联系。这一点非常重要，因为该项工作都是独立进行的。每个工作人员都有自己的工作，独自去客人家探访，而客人们通常也都是一个人独居。该联络网将一些非常独立的个体工作者组成了一个团体。

评估支持学习

另一个重要原则是如何对学习进行评估。在新西兰，很多行业都有自己的行业培训机构（ITO）来监管资格和行业标准。我们和建筑行业培训机构（BCITO）合作，研究并协助他们开发了一个体系来对木工学徒的学习进行评估。建筑行业培训机构组建了一个"评估团队"：雇主（培训方）、培训顾问（建筑行业培训机构的评估员）、学徒（学习者）和审计员（向培训顾问提供咨询服务的建筑行业培训机构的顾问）。他们分别有各自的职责，但作为一个团队一起工作，就像一个弦乐四重奏乐团。

评估活动围绕着学习者展开，并在学习者熟悉的环境中进行。这可以让学习者证明他知道什么，在实际工作中做过什么。培训顾问和学徒一起巡视建筑工地，实地观察工作和讨论工作。

学徒们需要收集并出示他们学习的证据。评估工作并不要求学习者们完成一整套类似作业本式的作业，他们可以用自己喜欢的任何形式来完成自己的工作记录。一些学生做了包含照片和图画的剪贴簿，另一些学生则采取网上写博客的形式来进行记录。这是一个以学生为中心的学习，它只要能有助于学习者来对自己的工作进行思考就行，而不需要在作业本上打勾来选择答案。

通过定期邀请培训顾问参加工作室活动，建筑行业培训机构制定了一套评估标准。这些顾问们研究学徒的工作，讨论他们的学习材料，然后决定如何对学生的能力进行评价。有时候他们辩论得很激烈，但是所有人都习惯了一起工作以便进行知识创新。迄今为止，他们的工作前景很乐观。评估包括对知识和技能更为严谨的评估；评估者能更自信更自发地做出评估决定；评估已经成为雇主、评估师和学徒三方共同的责任；学徒们的学习积极性有了提高。

关于工作场所学习机构方面存在的问题

工作场所或企业如何理解自己作为学习机构的职责（而并不仅是追求利润、提供产品和服务的中心）至关重要。这是一个好的职场学习的基础。根据我们的分析，这些机构的主要职责为：

  与追求的企业文化和企业需求相一致；

  为学习提供充足的资源；

  致力于促进每个人的学习；

  为有意义的学习提供充足的时间；

  鼓励创新和谨慎的风险防范；

  提供在日常工作中学习的机会；

  使学习受到认可和得到回报。

工作场所学习面临的教学问题

  我们的分析也指出了明确的学习和教学方法及策略的重要性。它们主要包括：

  体察学习者的学习节奏和以前的经验；

  学习者和辅导者对目标和进程具有相同的理解；

  学习者和目标及进程有利益关系；

  在合适的环境中学习；

  灵活地运用一系列教学方式；

  学习者可以在实践中运用和展示新知识；

  提供反馈意见以指导下一步的学习。

  根据我们的理解，工作场所的学习不仅仅是学习公司的组织结构，而是学习各个工作场所的工作实践。上述两个方面密不可分。

  例如，如果不考虑工作场所的需求（一个机构方面的问题），只体察学习者的学习节奏和知识水平（一个教学方面的问题）是不会成为有意义的学习的。同样，除非所开设的课程与学习者的工作有关，课程设计有特色、吸引人、技术性强，否则公司支持每个员工学习的承诺根本没有任何意义。

  上述两个方面也存在着紧密的联系。例如，一个公司可能会投资优质的教学资源，但是除非给学习者足够的时间来利用它，否则他们的学习潜力也会受到影响。学习节奏也很重要，如果学习者不经过实践和听取反馈意见，只是一味地试图去学习所有内容的话，那么他们对知识会掌握得不牢固，而且会很快忘记所学内容。虽然快速完成学历课程可能会提高一个机构的声誉，但它并不是一个来衡量人们真正学会了什么，学到了什么和会做什么的令人信服的标准。

上述的两个问题间存在一个平衡。工作场所的条件和结构有助于决定教学的特点和质量（例如，学习者能坚持与否不仅仅取决于学习者自身的性格，还可以通过工作场所的支持例如辅导来得到加强）。

挑战：机会、合适的环境、反思

学习效果的好坏取决于积极运用知识、培养能力和实践机会的多少。而机会又取决于是否有合适的环境，即实现或实施的可能性。我们所面临的挑战是学习所需的合适环境在学习机构中会分配不均。医院里经常如此，新来的人往往发现很难加入实际操作人员队伍。

另一个挑战是学习者可能会犯错误而雇主可能会因此限制他们的学习机会。反思性实践可以帮助解决这个问题。为了能够让学习者从错误中学习，机构必须要创建一个安全的环境，不能采取惩罚行为，并给学习者机会讨论所发生的事故。研究表明，这种措施可以十分有效地防止同样错误的再次发生，并在工作场所创造一种团队感。

另一个挑战是商业模式可能会限制学习机会。如果一个建筑商只用预制桁架来建屋顶，那么他的学徒就不可能学会用屋脊和屋面排水沟来构建框架。一些国家的医院经常救治许多枪伤患者，可是在新西兰这样的事件却很少发生，所以新西兰掌握治疗枪伤技术的医生很少。在这种情况下，可以安排大家短时间地调换一下工作岗位。它可以让人们有机会去体验不同的工作、不同的工作环境和人事关系。它还可以促进雇主更加重视学习需求从而提前做计划。它可以激励学习者对自己的学习负责，为自己争取学习机会和展示自己的积极性。这些正是雇主真正看重的素质。

根据特定的环境来调整原则

工作场所学习是一个提高知识、学习技能、培养性格以及建立实践小组的一个很好的方式。但是工作场所学习的真实性同时也让学习变得很困难，因为工作场所既是一个学习的场所也是一个生产的场所。在很多情况下，与其要将企业进行重新调整以便为在职学习者提供更多的机会，不如把他们送去参加一个培训课程或送到学院学习来得更简单。然而人们不可能在学校学到所有的知识。学习并不是一个简单直接的过程。它实际上需要给学习者提供参与实践的机会，使学习目的性更强。这样学习者才能提高自己的能力和判断力，来决定如何在实践中发挥自己的才能。

Learning On-the-job for Industry: Systems, Strategies and Practices for Success

Karen Vaughan, New Zealand Educational Research Association

Learning and Work: A Partnership in Progress

It is becoming common knowledge that workplaces can be a rich environment for learning. They can offer something that classrooms struggle to offer—authenticity of learning. Learning in the workplace means that learners must deal with real situations, real customers, real deadlines and real consequences.

This is an important shift in how we think about knowledge and learning. The alignment of different knowledges and forms of learning with either institutions (for "the theory") or workplaces (for "the practical") is no longer sustainable. We know that different knowledges, skills, and dispositions require development in different settings. School can no longer completely prepare people for work and life. Much of the knowledge, skills, and dispositions needed for the workplace cannot only be learned there or through the work itself. However, we also know that work-specific knowledge and "know-how" cannot be learned in an institution such as a vocational college. What we realise more and more is that workplace learning needs to be included in formal education programmes and that workplaces need to play a greater role in providing structured learning experiences for learners.

This presentation is about the learning that occurs in workplaces and through work. It can be part of a broader educational programme, such as that connected with vocational colleges. It might also stand alone as "learning on-the-job". NZCER has studied effective learning in the workplace through a number of projects conducted around New Zealand. Our projects include:

• working with the Building and Construction Industry Training Organisation to develop a system for assessment of learning on-the-job or in industry settings;

• studying examples of good workplace learning in the aged care industry, horticulture industry, and tourism industry;

• investigating how theory and practice are integrated by apprentices and learners in the fields of general practice medicine (family doctors) and carpentry;

• reviewing workplace learning research from around the world.

These projects have given us the opportunity to pinpoint the common principles and dimensions of effective workplace learning for both employers and employees. I cannot cover every possible aspect of successful workplace learning in this talk. However, I have picked out some of the most interesting and important ones that demonstrate how workplaces can be good learning environments if they are carefully structured to be. There are many challenges involved, and these are different from the challenges of a classroom, but the rewards can be substantial—for individual learners, for employers, and for whole industries.

The Organisation Prioritises Learning

The first important principle is about the way the organisation understands and priorities learning. The best workplaces do not leave learning to chance. They do not just write about learning in documents. They make learning practical and visible within the business. They also ensure there is always at least one person who is dedicated to promoting learning in their workplace.

We studied a community organisation that provided services for people who are older, homeless, disabled or requiring family support. The organisation had a management overseeing recruitment, induction, staff development and training programmes. The broadness of her role meant she got a deep understanding of the learners and the clients' needs. She was able to ensure that programmes were designed to meet both groups of needs. We also studied a vineyard where the training manager constantly demonstrated his company's commitment to learning by making his own learning visible everyday.

Scaffolding and Structured Orientation

The second important principle is about having structured orientation to the business and sytems that provide scaffolding or temporary support for workers/learners which is then gradually dismantled. As it is dismantled, it allows the development of the know-how, skills, and disposition (attitudes, judgement, discretion, understanding) needed and more independent problem-solving and critical thinking.

In workplaces we have studied, we saw different examples of scaffolding. Learners were never just "dropped" into their roles. They were given time to settle in. They are often paired with a colleague who can guide them. The learner has a chance to learn work processes and what questions to ask, who to ask them of, and when to ask.

In the homecare organisation, new careworkers would follow an experienced careworker for a week. The organisation also created a network that kept individual careworkers in close contact with caseworkers back in the main office. This was invaluable because the work can be very isolating. Each careworker is on their own, visiting a client who is in their own home and usually living alone. The network created a community out of something that looked very individualised.

Assessment Supports the Learning

Another important principle relates to how learning is assessed. Many

优秀教学法研讨
SYMPOSIUM: EXCELLENT VOCATIONAL TEACHING

New Zealand industries have an Industry Training Organisation (ITO) to oversee qualifications and industry standards. We worked with the Building and Construction Industry Training Organisation (BCITO) to study and help develop the system for assessing carpentry apprentices' learning. The BCITO created an "assessment team": employer (trainer), Training Advisor (the BCITO assessor), apprentice (learner), and moderator (the BCITO advisor to the Training Advisor). They have different roles but work as a team—like a string quartet.

The assessment process is built around the learner and takes place in a context that is familiar to the learner. This allows him to show what he knows and has actually done. The Training Advisor and apprentice walk around the building site together, looking at and discussing the work.

The apprentices need to gather and show evidence of their learning. Instead of making them do this in one set form like a workbook, they can create their own portfolios in any form they like. Some make scrapbooks with photographs and drawings, others write blogs online. It is learner-centred and it helps the learner reflect on their work instead of just ticking boxes in a workbook.

The BCITO created a community of assessment practice by bringing their Training Advisors together for regular workshops. The Advisors study examples of apprentice work and discuss the evidence and how they make judgements about competence. There are fierce debates sometimes but everyone is getting used to working together to create new knowledge. The results so far are very promising. They include more seamless assessment of knowledge and skills; more confident and spontaneous assessment decisions by assessors; that assessment has become a shared responsibility among employer, assessor, and apprentice; and that apprentices' motivation to learn have been improved .

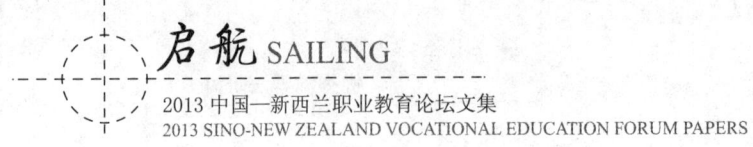

Organisational Dimensions of On-the-job Learning

The way the workplace or business understands its role as a learning organisation (not only a centre for profit and product or service delivery) is critical. This is the foundation for good workplace learning. According to our analysis, the main dimensions are:

• alignment with desired culture and business needs;

• strategic directions reflected in aims and processes;

• learning adequately resourced;

• commitment shown to everyone's learning;

• sufficient time for meaningful learning;

• innovation & thoughtful risks encouraged;

• opportunities to learn in everyday work;

• learning recognised and rewarded.

Pedagogical Dimensions of On-the-job Learning

Our analysis has also highlighted the importance of clear learning and teaching approaches and strategies. The main dimensions are:

• sensitivity to learners' pace and previous experiences;

• learners and mentors sharing understandings about goals and processes;

• learners having a stake in goals and processes;

• learning occuring in context;

• a flexible range of approaches is used;

• chances for learners to practice and demonstrate new learning;

• feedback given to guide future learning.

What we're seeing is that workplace learning is not just about the structures of each organisation but about the practices in each workplace. There are critical interdependencies between the sets.

For example, showing sensitivity to the learners' pace and level (a pedagogical dimension) on its own is unlikely to produce relevant learning without an alignment to the needs of the workplace (an organisational dimension). Similarly, there is little point in a company being committed to everyone's learning (organisational), unless the learning that is on offer is relevant to the learners, well designed and engaging, and technically relevant (pedagogical).

There are also critical interdependencies within each set. For example, a company might invest in high-quality learning resources, but unless time is protected for learners to engage with the materials, the learning potential is limited. The pace of learning is also important—trying to "cover" learning objectives without practice and feedback leads to "fragile" learning and to forgetting. While fast completion of qualifications may enhance the reputation of an organisation, this is not a convincing measure of what people truly understand, or know or are able to do.

There's a balancing act between the two sets of dimensions. Workplace conditions and structures help determine the character (and quality) of the teaching and learning that occurs (for example, learner persistence is not just an individual characteristic; it can be strengthened by workplace practices like mentoring).

Challenges: Access, Affordances, Reflection

Learning is only as good as the opportunity to actively apply knowledge, develop competencies and participate. Opportunities are only as good as their affordances—that is, their possibility for realisation or action. The challenge is that affordances to learn can be distributed across organisations in unequal ways. Hospitals are often like this. Newcomers find it difficult to gain entry into communities of practice.

Another challenge is that learners can make mistakes and employers can limit their opportunities to learn. Reflective practices can help with this. In order to learn from mistakes, the organisation needs to create a safe environment, without punishment, and allow people to discuss what has happened. Research shows this to be very effective at preventing the same mistakes from occurring again and in creating a sense of community in the workplace.

Another challenge is that a business model can limit opportunities to learn. If a builder only uses pre-fabricated trusses for roofs, the apprentice will never learn to build framing with hips and valleys. In some countries, medical clinics deal with a lot of gunshot wounds. In New Zealand this is rare so few doctors develop the skills to deal with them. In this case, people can arrange to swap workplaces for short periods of time. It gives people a chance to experience different work, workplace conditions, and relationships. It also encourages employers to pay more attention to learning needs and to plan ahead for it. It encourages learners to take charge of their learning and ask for opportunities and show initiative qualities that employers really value.

Adapt Principles to Specific Settings

Learning on-the-job is a wonderful way to develop knowledge, skills, dispositions, and communities of practice. However, the authenticity of learning on-the-job is also what makes it hard to do. This is because the workplace is both for learning and for production. In many ways, it is easier to send people to a course or an institution than to re-organise things in ways that expand opportunities to learn while on-the-job. However, nobody can get all their knowledge from a course in an institution. Learning is not totally linear. It is really a case of structuring people's participation and making the learning intentional so that learners can develop competence and judgement about how to practice that competence.

乐学引起兴趣，好学达成目标
——寓教于乐互动式教学方法探讨

内蒙古电子信息职业技术学院　郑志丽

摘要：基于高职学生学情及课程特点分析的基础上，选择寓教于乐互动式教学方法，并探讨在课程中的实施与效果分析，最终促成学生相关职业能力的提升，达成教学目标。

关键词：寓教于乐；互动教学；方法探讨

教学方法的选择是完成教学任务、达到教学目标的重要途径和有效手段，要因学生的学情、学科的特点、目标的高低而异。

根据近年来的教学经验，结合高职培养目标和高职学生的特点，在公共关系课程的教学中，应用寓教于乐互动式教学方法，提高学生的学习兴趣，培养学生自主学习、实际操作的能力，通过此教学法的应用和探索，我们取得了一定的教学效果。

一、寓教于乐互动式教学方法的提出

孔子认为，作为教学过程的一方——学生的学习活动，本身就应该是快乐之事。在《论语》里，就有记载："学而时习之，不亦乐乎？" "知之者，不如好之者，好之者，不如乐之者。"他认为，学生对学习的积极情绪体验，能促进学生的学习活动，提升学习效果。

寓教于乐在中小学阶段作为教育思想探讨得较多，那么对于高职学生而言，年龄上已是成人，已处于大学教育阶段，在学习上应该具有自我学习的能力和习惯，但实际情况并非如此。从文献资料以及本人实际的教学实施中可以发现：高职学生看似高考成绩不理想，无奈选择进入高职院校学习，其实根本的原因是这些学生在学习方面存在着诸如学习认知能力不高、学习方法（认知策略、知识的迁移、记忆策略）缺乏、学习习惯不良、学习兴趣不高等一些问题。面对这样的学生群体，首要的是唤起他们的学习兴趣，激发他们的学习动力，使他们成为学习的主体，通过互动式教学方法的实施，变"要我学"为"我乐学"和"我要学"，进而达到培养目标。

互动式教学方法是教师"教"和学生"学"两个过程互相作用的整体性动态过程。具体表现为教师的主导施教和学生的主体认识相辅相成的课堂活动过程，即"教"和"学"之间相互联系、相互促进、有序发展的整体性活动。通过调节师生关系及其相互作用，形成和谐的师生互动、生生互动、学习个体与教学中介的互动，强化人与环境的影响，以产生教学共振，达到提高教学效果。

二、寓教于乐互动式教学方法的实施

本文以本人所承担的公共关系课程为载体，探讨寓教于乐互动式教学方法的实施。

互动式教学方法中主要尝试和实施了案例教学法、角色扮演法、情景模拟法、社会实践法。

（一）案例教学法

案例教学的中心环节是课堂呈现。在课堂上用基于问题的学习法（PBL），首先教师提出问题（问题的设计应以公关实践中的复杂情境为核心，难度要适中。如"QQ大战360危机公关的成效如何"案例）；其次学生分析问题（学生分成每组3~5人的若干研究小组，针对问题组内讨论，确定小组发言人陈述本组观点，小组间引入竞争机制，组间可以自由辩论）；再次，师生评价问题。学生们通过充分研究讨论对该问题已有较多认识，在该阶段中教师可适时予以总结概括，回归公关理论。与此同时，教师还应引导学生回顾在解决问题过程中的收获，并反思尚存的不足，这些活动也包含了学习者评价自己以及合作伙伴在解决问题过程中的表现。

（二）角色扮演法

角色扮演法通过设定社会情境中的不同角色扮演，增加学生对社会大量感性体验的实践教学方法，既能够增加学生对情景的体验，调动学习积极性，又能够提高学生的实际能力，增强教学效果。

如在公关礼仪教学中，讲中餐礼仪，由老师与一名学生进行情境模拟，其他学生从观看进餐的过程中提出礼仪问题,通过错误礼仪动作的解说进行礼仪正确示范,在示范过后,分队安排任务,由各队分别扮演不同情境下的礼仪活动,比如第一组表演就餐入座,第二组表演点餐,第三组表演用餐中餐具的摆放,第四组表演餐巾的使用,第五组表演米饭面食的食用方法,第六组表演用餐完毕如何离开。通过全流程的表演让学生在做中出错,通过做找到问题,之后纠正以做到正确的礼仪。

我国教育家叶圣陶先生曾说过:"教师之为教,不在全盘授予,而在相机诱导,必令学生运其才智,勤其练习,领悟之源广开,纯熟之功弥深,乃为善教者也。"通过角色扮演学生成为行动者,其认知的主体作用被强化,主观能动性能得到最大化的发挥。

(三)情景模拟法

在教学中将现实中的情境模拟到教室中可以让学生更贴切地学习,将"书本公关"转变为"实践公关"。在模拟情境中帮助学生对案例事件进行还原和演示,并通过理论学习加入对情境的想象,使案例事件变得贴近学生的思维范围,通过老师的引导让学生在表演中体会问题、解决问题,在潜移默化中培养公关意识。

比如让学生组队进行百吉纳马奶酒营销活动策划方案,第一阶段,设计策划阶段,给产品选定销售对象,为其设计广告语,并选定广告宣传场所。第二阶段,准备实施阶段,策划路演内容,进行人员活动分工及设施安排。第三阶段,将销售现场安排在教室内,由学生布置会场,悬挂宣传横幅,以其他学生为顾客进行现场销售,在规定时间内表演策划内容。第四阶段,对各队表现进行评定,找出策划优缺点,讨论各队在各环节出现的问题,并互相提出改进的意见。

在创设的具体场景中,学生在浓烈的参与氛围中,倾情投入,表现欲望得到充分满足,同时也增强了学生对公关工作的感性认识,使教学内容更贴近社会实际。

(四)实战教学法

在教学过程中,致力于寻求接近社会实际状况的学习情境,给学生以真实的社会环境、真实的工作项目,学生通过完成真实的工作任务掌握知识的教学方法即实战教学法。其特点在于:学生面对的环境接近企业实际运营状况或者说就是企业的实际的运营状况,因此,更能提高学生掌握实际技能的能力。同时,实战教学法直接指出学生努力的目标。目标富有挑战性,能激发学生的学习热情、增强学习的积极性和主动性。

实战教学方法的实施首先以专业社团的形式设立公关实体，联系"实践单位"，寻找实战项目。在寻找实战项目时，优先选择、挖掘校内的可利用的项目资源，如学校拟举行的大型的文娱、社会活动等，有选择性地及时介入，如财经管理系成立了"大学生创业实战基地"时，抓住"大学生创业实战基地"开业的时机，由参加公共关系实训的学生负责为其策划和举行盛大的开业暨剪彩仪式。通过此次实训，同学们的感受与课堂中的实例讲解和模拟的训练完全不同，所有的体验都是真实的，任何一个环节不到位都会导致实战目的的落空或实战效果的降低。学生们融入真实的事件中去，正如同学们所说，"不是在完成作业，而是在做一件有意义的事情。"

又如在学习公共关系工作过程时设计了四个项目：

项目之一是公关调查，在讲述调查的方法、程序及调查报告的撰写的基础上，将学生分成若干小组，以"关于某某企业社会形象的调查"或"某某产品消费者满意程调查"等为题目；采取问卷调查或访谈法等方式，调查完毕撰写调查报告。

项目之二公关策划，各公关小组根据上述调查发现的问题，进行公关策划，以解决存在的问题或隐患，并将公关策划方案提交企业，请企业的有关人员对该策划方案做出评判。

项目之三是公关实施，老师在征求企业的同意的前提下，可选取具有可行性的方案，组织学生去实施。

项目之四是活动评估，请同学们讲讲心得体会，交流经验，撰写公共关系活动评估报告，对整个活动进行总结。

每一阶段结束或整体任务结束的时候，组织组内成员之间相互打分，分数计入实战成绩。

学生通过真实的项目，激起了学习和实践的兴趣，非常乐意完成各项目，最终将理论知识转化成技能和经验。

三、寓教于乐互动式教学方法的全程评估

采用全程评估的方法评定学习效果，即过程性综合评定和终结性考试相结合。

过程性综合评定：分为四大类评定，第一类是课堂团队讨论，在规定时间内团队发言，根据表现评定 A、B、C、D、E 五个等级，每个等级是 20 分，分别有评定标准。第二类是实训作业，以团队合作完成为主，有 PPT、调查报告等形式。第三类是角色扮演，根据章节内容有广告表演、即兴演讲、礼仪展示等。第四类是实践活动（情景

模拟、实战项目），由学生自拍视频，通过视频材料体现活动内容，以评定结果。

终结性考试：采用现场定策划主题，现场团队定时完成任务，分为两个阶段。第一阶段是策划设计，要求交策划方案。第二阶段是现场答辩，由老师针对策划方案中的内容进行现场提问，通过学生的回答来评定活动的可行性。在第二阶段，除答辩队之外的所有学生都是评委，老师评分占60%，学生总评占40%。这样的评分过程，既调动了学生参与的积极性，也极大地提高了学生独立设计、开拓创新的能力。

公关教学寓教于乐的互动式教学方法将枯燥乏味的讲台变成酣畅表演的舞台，将学生从台下的观众角色变为领衔主演和团队协作的友情出演，使公关魅力在师生互动中得以淋漓尽致的展现。通过师生互动、生生互动的教学共振，使学者快乐，教者快乐，教学相长，何乐而不为呢！

Interest Aroused in Enjoyment, Teaching Objectives Achieved in Curiousness
—Discussion on the Interactive Teaching Method of Edutainment

Zheng Zhili, Inner Mongolia Electronic Vocational Technical College

Abstract: The interactive teaching method of edutainment is applied based on the analysis of higher vocational college students' learning situation and course features. Its implementation and effect in classes are also discussed to finally enhance students' relevant vocational capacity and achieve the teaching objectivity.

Keywords: edutainment; interactive teaching; method discussion

Choosing an effective teaching method is an important and efficient way to realize teaching task and teaching objective which should be made according to students' learning situation, course features and degree of learning objective.

The interactive teaching method of edutainment is applied in public relation classes, based on the teaching experience in recent years and combined with the training objective and features of higher vocational college students, in order to arouse their learning interest and train their capacity of independent study and actual operation. Some degree of teaching effect has been achieved through the application and exploration of this teaching method.

I. Proposal of the Interactive Teaching Method of Edutainment

Confucius holds that as a party of teaching process, students' study activities shall be a happy thing. His ideas are recorded in *The Analects of Confucius* such as "Is it not pleasant to learn with a constant perseverance and application?" "He who knows the truth is not equal to him who loves it, and he who loves it is not equal to him who delights in it." In his mind, students' positive emotional experience can promote their study and strengthen learning effect.

Edutainment is discussed much in middle and primary school as an educational thought. Those higher vocational college students in their adulthood and university education stage are considered to be capable of self-learning. However, this was not the case in real situation. It has been found in document and the author's practical teaching that though it seems that the reason why higher vocational college students choose vocational colleges helplessly is their poor college entrance examination achievement, the fundamental reason is their low learning cognitive ability, lack of learning methods (cognitive strategies, transfer of learning and memory strategies), poor study habit and interest, etc. The first thing we should do in face of this student group is to arouse their learning interest and stimulate their learning motivation to turn them into the master of learning and turn the "force-to-learn" teaching method into "enjoy-learning" and "want-to-learn" through interactive teaching method, thus to achieve the training objective.

The interactive teaching method is an integrated dynamic process of interwork of teachers' teaching and students learning. In practice, it shows as complementary class process of teachers' leading teaching and students' cognition, i.e., the integrated process of interrelation, mutual promotion and orderly development of "teaching" and "learning". Through adjusting relationship and interaction between teachers and students, a teaching method can be achieved with harmonious teacher-student interaction, student-student interaction and interaction between learning individual and teaching meditation, which can strengthen influence of human and environment in order to produce teaching assonance and promote teaching effect.

II. Implementation of the Interactive Teaching Method of Edutainment

This speech discusses the implementation of the interactive teaching method of edutainment based on the subject Public Relations assumed by the author.

The interactive teaching method mainly tries and implements case method of instruction, role playing method, situational simulation exercise and social practice method.

(I) Case Method of Instruction

The central part of this method is representation in class. PBL (problem-based-learning) is applied in class. Firstly, teachers propose a problem (the problem should be designed with the complex conditions of the public relations practice as the core and moderate difficulty. For instance, how is the efficiency of QQ battles with 360 crisis public relations?); then students analyze the problem (students are divided into several research groups, three to five students in each and discuss the problem within their own group. Then they let their representative to state their opinion. Competitive

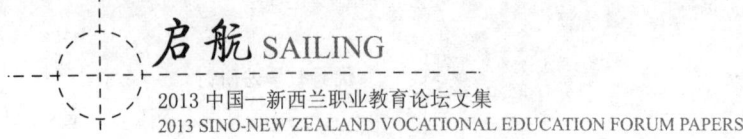

mechanism is applied between groups and free debate is allowed between groups). At last, teachers and students evaluate the problem. Since students have known much about the problem after full study and discussion, teacher can draw the problem back to public relations by making summary prompt. Meanwhile, the teacher should also lead students to review their achievement and weaknesses in problem solving process. These activities also include learner's evaluation of performance of their partners and themselves in learning process.

(II) Role Playing Method

Role playing method is a teaching method which can increase students' social emotional experience through playing different roles in social context. This method not only can add context experience to students but also motivate their learning initiative, promote their practical operation ability and enhance the teaching effect.

Take the teaching of etiquette for public relations as an example. In the teaching of etiquette in Chinese meal, the teacher makes situation simulation together with a student and other students present problems during the simulation. Correct etiquette is demonstrated by analyzing the false one. After the demonstration, students are divided into different groups to do etiquette in different situation respectively. For example, the first group performs seating in repast; the second group performs ordering; the third performs placing tableware; the fourth performs using napkin; the fifth performs eating rice and cooked wheaten food and the sixth group performs how to leave the table after finishing the meal. Through the performance of full etiquette students find errors during this process and correct them.

Ye Shengtao, a famous Chinese educationist, once said, "Teachers should not teach by duck-stuffing but should lead students to learn in proper way. Thus students will make full use of their capacity in their assiduous study and then understand knowledge profoundly and use them proficiently. This is the brilliant teaching method". Students become the doer in role play. Their cognitive effect is strengthened and subjective initiative is given full play.

(III) Situational Simulation Exercise

Simulation of real situation in class can make students have a more vivid experience when learning knowledge in textbook, turning "public relations in textbook" into "public relations in practice". Situational simulation exercise can restore and demonstrate the case to students and the theory students learned helps them to imagine the situation and makes it closer to their thinking scope. Students get consciousness of public relations in the performance by proposing and resolving problems through teacher's guidance.

For instance, let students write planning scheme for marketing campaign of Best kino kumiss in groups. Stage One—design and planning. Let them choose target customers for the product, design slogan and determine the advertising place. Stage Two—preparing implementation. Let them make a plan for road show and division of work and make facilities arrangement. Stage Three, let students arrange sales site in class and hang the promotional banners and sell the product to other students who play the role of customers. Stage Four, the teacher makes an evaluation of each group and finds advantages and disadvantages of their strategies and then let them discuss their problem in each stages and present ideas for improvement.

In the simulation of real situation, students take an active part in it. Their desire for performance is fully satisfied and their perceptual knowledge of public relations is strengthened which makes teaching content closer to the practice.

(IV) Practical Teaching Method

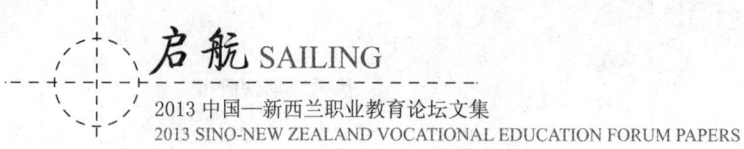

Practical teaching method is a method dedicating to find a learning situation close to real social situation in teaching process, offering students genuine social environment and work program and making them acquire the knowledge by accomplishing real work task. Its characteristics is that the situation that students face is close to the actual operation conditions of enterprises or in other words it is the actual operation conditions, thus it can improve their capacity of mastering practical skills. Meanwhile, practical teaching method points out objective for students directly which is challengeable and stimulates their learning enthusiasm and initiative.

Practical teaching method is implemented by setting PR entity firstly in the form of professional association and then contacting "practice unit" and finding practical program. Available resources within college should be fully considered and made used of, such as large-scaled recreational and social activities to be held in school, and interfere promptly and selectively. For example, when school of financial management establishes "College Students' Entrepreneurial Practice Base", students participating in the practical training can seize this chance and make arrangement and planning for opening and ribbon-cutting ceremony. Students know the entire difference between example explanation and the simulative exercise. Their experience is genuine, thus any failure during the process will make the practical training void and weaken its effect. Students are engaged in real conditions and just as what they say, "we are not just finishing our homework but doing something meaningful".

Here is another example: four programs are made in the process of learning public relations.

The first program is PR research. After teaching students research method, procedures and survey report writing, the teacher divides them into several groups. Let them finish research titled "research on social image of XX Group" or "research on customer satisfaction of product XX" by applying questionnaire or interview and write survey report.

The second program is PR planning. PR groups make PR planning according to the above research to solve present or potential problems and then submit the plan to the enterprise and ask them to make an evaluation.

The third program is PR implementation. The teacher can select a feasible plan to organize students to implement under the permitting of that enterprise.

The fourth program is activity evaluation. Let students exchange their feelings and experience and write PR activity evaluation report to make a summery of the whole activity.

At the end of each stage or task, let student give score to other members in their own group and include the score in the final practical result.

Real program stimulates students' learning and practical interest and makes them take active part in finishing those programs and transforms theory and knowledge into skill and experience finally.

III. Whole Evaluation of the Interactive Teaching Method of Edutainment

To apply whole evaluation method to assess learning effect is to combine comprehensive process evaluation with summative test.

Comprehensive process evaluation can be classified into four categories. The first category is group discussion in class. Each group states in given time and is evaluated in five grades—A, B, C, D, E, twenty points of each grade and each has its evaluation standard. The second category is practical training task mainly depending on group cooperation in forms of PPT, research report, etc. The third category is role play. According to the content of that chapter, various forms can be chosen such as advertising performance, impromptu address, etiquette demonstration, etc. The fourth category is practical activities (scenario simulation and practical program). Students are asked to take video of their activity for eventual evaluation.

Summative test: planning theme is determined on site and student groups finish their task in given time. There are two stages. The first stage is planning design. In this stage students are required to submit planning scheme. The second stage is to make site defense. In this stage the teacher presents questions according to students' planning scheme and evaluates its feasibility through their reply. Except for students making defense, all the other students are judges whose evaluation account for 40 percentages in the final evaluation and the teacher's evaluation account for 60 percentages. It can not only arouse students' initiative of participation but also improve their ability to make planning scheme independently and their capacity of innovation.

The interactive teaching method of edutainment in PR turns boring class into brilliant stage for students' performance and students from audience into protagonists or friendship performance in group cooperation. The charm of PR is fully exposed in teacher-student interaction. Why not apply this teaching method since it can make teaching consonance in teacher-student and student-student interaction and let both of them enjoy teaching process?

由"是的，厨师长"到"为什么，厨师长"的教学策略转换

奥塔哥理工学院　Adrian Woodhouse

在与传统的烹饪艺术教育彻底告别后，奥塔哥理工学院在2012年推出了"设计为主导"的烹饪艺术本科专业（BCA）课程。该课程取代了传统的师傅/学徒制基于能力培养的教学框架，代之以学生为主导的探索、实验和体验式的教学模式。这种烹饪艺术教育领域的创新方法改变了教师和学生的角色。在这个新的框架模式下，教师的主要作用是主导和促进学生学习知识和知识传播的进程。

在学习烹饪艺术本科课程时，学生利用创意设计方法参与项目简介设计。这次通过项目设计进行的教学尝试取得了意想不到的成功，它通过"关联性"原则，深刻地观察学生对所学知识的理解程度。关联性是一种学习策略，允许学生将他们的已有经验与烹饪世界相联系，然后在整个设计过程中将二者融为一体。这个强有力的教学导管激发了学生的学习自觉性，提高了学生的参与程度和理解程度。

随着项目的开展，目前有意将关联性策略纳入项目开发及相关的考核指南。作为反思实践者，很显然教学是一个动态的过程，它将随着"受教者"和"烹饪艺术"世界的发展和协同效应的实现而不断发展。传授今天的书本知识已不再重要，重要的是传授明天的生存之道。

烹饪艺术本科专业的发展背景

烹饪艺术本科专业是本着采用创意方法进行烹饪设计的理念创立的，它为新西兰首创，也可能是世界首创。课程结构设置方法独特，是为了使学生可以拥有一个

充满创意、学习方式灵活和相互协作的学习环境以及提倡和支持为发展烹饪艺术进行创业思维和批判性思维的文化氛围。

在一个 59% 的新餐饮店在开业的前 3 年面临倒闭的行业，服务行业和学术界都在呼吁要扶植一个新的烹饪艺术实践者在这种恶劣的商业环境中能够生存和蓬勃发展。

正因为如此，该课程的主要教学成果之一是进一步保证用其他的技能武装学生协助他们顺利迈入 21 世纪。这些技能包括创意思维和团队协作。同时，在 3 年的课程学习中引导每位学生去发现和明确自己的烹饪艺术价值和信仰，并由此将他们分配在烹饪艺术领域常用的最合适的实践小组。

学习环境

在烹饪艺术本科专业，讲师的职责由知识和内容的主宰转变为知识收集、加工的主导者，并反过来再学习。

根据社会文化和社会建构主义理论框架进行教学。这种教学采取以学习者为中心的原则、体验式的学习方法和反思实践活动，并将它们贯穿于日常教学和考核活动中。尤其是课程遵循四个建构主义教育理念。它们是：

协作——与他人一起学习和向他人学习；

会话——运用反思式对话和创意式学习策略；

情境——强调工作场所和终身学习，重视文化和个人多样性；

知识建构——运用深度学习方法，通过体验积累知识。

西方传统的烹饪教育只注重培养学生实用的烹饪技能，而烹饪艺术本科课程则侧重培养学生的基本菜肴摆盘技能，以及如何根据就餐环境和商业风格进行相应调整。因此，学生所参与的设计项目既是一种学习，也是一种考核，二者密不可分。

正如 Earl 所言，烹饪艺术本科课程有别于西方传统烹饪教育理念，它认为评估是一个学习的过程。

传统的烹饪教育将总结性评估视为判断学习者能力和知识水平的权威判断方法。通过纵观整个学习过程，烹饪艺术本科专业的教学团队承认学习者绝大部分的知识是在项目设计过程中学到的。

讲故事式"连通性"学习

许多国家一直重视讲故事,将其视为学习过程的一部分,近年来,实践学家和研究人员都主张高等学校应将讲故事策略纳入教学。此主张的重要原因之一是因为讲故事包容和重视文化差异,是人际交往的焦点。

从开学第一年的第一个项目开始,讲师鼓励烹饪艺术本科专业的学生通过菜式的构思和发明,找到自己真实的心声,讲述自己的故事。这方面的一个例子是一个简单的柠檬挞甜点,这是一道源自法国的经典甜点(参见图1)。自古以来,讲师会示范这道甜点的做法,然后要求学生模仿直到讲师认为满意为止。如今,通过讲故事策略,学生学会了面点和奶油制作的基本技能,通过启发,要求学生设计一道讲述自己故事的甜点(参见图2)。

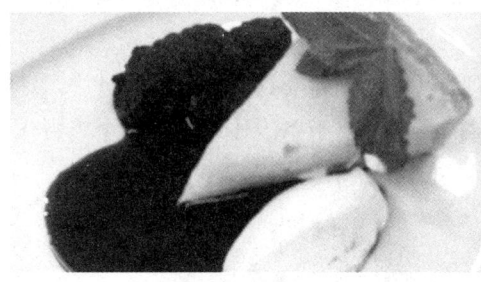 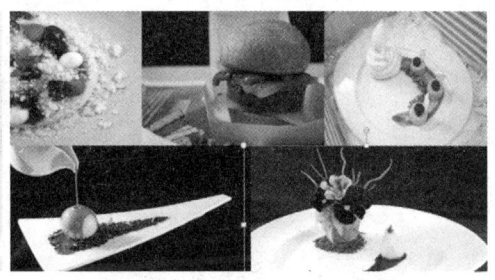

图1 柠檬挞　　　　　　　　图2 由学生设计的讲故事的甜品

学生学习案例

下面的图片来自于 BCA 一个二年级的学生,它是一个如何在学习和评估过程中将"连通性"和讲故事联系起来的学习案例。这些图片来自于一个叫梁泽菲的中国学生之手,她热爱艺术、摄影和探索中国烹饪技能和文化。从课程的一开始,我们就鼓励泽菲将她的兴趣融入项目设计中,目的是证明她如何在烹饪艺术世界里能够为自己的价值观找到一席之地。

第一年的一个项目要求学生设计一个菜式,它要包含野生觅食元素,并讲述奥塔哥一个地方的故事。觅食和地方特色是西方世界烹饪艺术的两大主要发展方向。

图3是本地称为海港牙的一张照片。泽菲选择将她的艺术兴趣与这个项目联系起来设计一个菜式(图4),用野猪肉做成传统的中国饺子。

图3 奥塔哥的艺术装置,港口牙　　　图4 野猪肉做成的中国饺子

在二年级的一个名为烹饪比赛的课程中,泽菲需要设计一道鸡肉菜肴,并根据世界厨师协会(WACAS)的烹饪规则要求来完成。图5是最终设计菜式,它的设计灵感来自中国传统的庆祝活动和庆祝方法。在这个设计中,我们再次看到了泽菲对文化遗产的兴趣和艺术性设计以及菜肴的实用性。随后,泽菲持续在比赛中胜出。

为了采用当代前卫风格的烹饪方法,学生被要求探索和发明一个菜式,这个菜式既要使用分子烹饪技术,又要能激发人们的怀旧情怀。在这个菜式的设计中,泽菲使用了真空低温烹调法和充气酱汁,此菜的灵感来自于中国传统上将一个鸡蛋作为生日礼物以预祝身体强健事业繁荣兴旺。图6中的菜肴为最终菜式。

图5 三杯咸味鸡肉沙拉　　　图6 由分子激发的生日礼物

另一个二年级项目设计要求学生设计一款适合在农贸市场销售的产品。这就要求学生了解农贸市场的消费者——谁是我们烹饪艺术世界的消费者?该项目要求泽菲设计一款产品,它要符合农贸市场消费者要求产品健康且为本地优质食品的消费观,同时还要讲述一个真实的故事。泽菲与同学一起,设计出一款中国传统的汤饺,由新西兰天然食材做成,作为目前市场上出售的油炸饺子的健康替代品。参见图7的最终产品。

优秀教学法研讨
SYMPOSIUM: EXCELLENT VOCATIONAL TEACHING

图7　新西兰羊肉薄荷汤饺

案例研究的最后一个例子是设计一个小型商业计划及支持这个计划的样本菜谱。本课程要求学生结合本地消费行为去探索目前的餐饮潮流来构思一个独特的创业计划书。在这个项目中，泽菲根据拼盘、价格合理和健康食品这三个当前的餐饮潮流，设计了一个取名为"老友"（见图8）的商业计划。老友给人们提供了一个轻松、实惠的就餐体验，传统的中式菜肴采取又大众又健康的方法烧制。

结论

虽然我介绍的是一个中国学生的故事，但她的故事并不是个别现象。我可以同样讲述一个当地新西兰人、毛利人的故事或来自太平洋岛屿学生的故事。

通过采用"连通性"的学习方法，学生在学习和课堂表现方面取得了重大成果。

第一个成果是，在高涨的学习积极性的带动下，学生的参与度得到很大提高。这些都是学生成为知识收集和加工的主体并反过来学习的直接成果。

通过知识探索和加工，学生对所学内容和价值以及如何将它们融入烹饪艺术舞台有了更深入的了解。最后，教育价值来

图8　"老友"可视化的业务概念

自学习者和职业教育的相互连接，真正的、真实的学习和终身学习正是发生在这些"连接"的时刻。

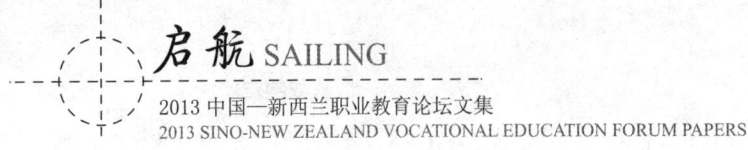

Learning Strategies for Transforming From a "Yes Chef" to a "Why Chef" Learning Environment

Adrian Woodhouse, Otago Polytechnic

In a radical break away from traditional culinary arts education, in 2012 Otago Polytechnic launched its "design-led", Bachelor of Culinary Arts (BCA) programme. The program has replaced the conventional Master/Apprentice competency based framework with a learning model which embraces student led exploration, experimentation and experience. This innovative approach to culinary arts education has altered the roles of the educator and the learner. As educators in this new framework, the primary role is to mentor and facilitate the process of student knowledge acquisition and dissemination.

On the BCA programme students engage in project briefs utilising the creative methodologies of design. The unforeseen success of this inquiry based project learning has been the observation of a deeper student understanding through the principle of "connectedness". Connectedness is a learning strategy which allows the student to connect their known world with that of culinary arts and integrate them both throughout the design process. This powerful pedagogical conduit inspires intrinsic motivation, heightened levels of student engagement and deep learning.

As the program unfolds, connectedness strategies are now intentionally incorporated into the project development and associated assessment guidelines. As reflective practitioners it is apparent that this is a dynamic process that will be ongoing as the worlds of the "learner" and "culinary arts" evolve and synergies are realised. No longer is it appropriate to teach the content of today but the survival strategies for tomorrow.

Background to the BCA Programme

The BCA curriculum is founded on the creative methodologies of culinary design and is the first of its type in New Zealand and possibly the only one of its type in the world. The programme is structured in such a way that allows students to learn in a creative, flexible and collaborative environment whilst within a culture that promotes and supports culinary-driven entrepreneurial thinking and critical thinking.

In an industry where 59% of new hospitality businesses will fail within the first three years there have been calls from both the hospitality industry and academia to foster a new culinary practioner to withstand and flourish in this harsh commercial environment.

As such, one of the key outcomes of the programme is to future proof the student by equipping them with additional skills to support them well into the 21st Century. These skills include creative ways of thinking and collaborative working processes. Alongside this, each student is guided over the three year programme to identify and articulate their culinary values and beliefs and where these might be best positioned within the various communities of practice that exist within the domains of culinary arts.

Learning Environment

In the BCA learning environment the lecturer's role is transformed form that of the master of content and knowledge to that of the facilitator of knowledge gathering, processing and in turn learning.

The learning environment operates within a socio-cultural and social constructivist framework. This approach has learner-centric principles, experiential learning approaches and reflective activities embedded within its everyday teaching and assessment activities. In particular, the programme adheres to four of the tenets of the constructivist pedagogy. These are:

• collaboration—learning with and from others;

• conversation—using reflective dialogue and creative learning strategies;

• context—emphasising workplace and lifelong learning that values cultural and personal diversity; and,

• construction of knowledge—making meaning from experience using deep learning approaches.

While western culinary education traditionally focuses on the competency of practical cookery skills only, the Bachelor of Culinary Arts is focused on students gaining an understanding of fundamental dish techniques and how these can be adapted and manipulated in relation to the various hospitality environments and their related commercial idiosyncrasies. As such students engage in design projects which operate in an interlinked way through their dual inclusion of learning and assessment as one.

Drawing on the work of Earl, the BCA programme deviates from traditional Western culinary education, with its view that assessment is part of the learning process.

Conventional culinary education views summative assessment as a quality judgment of the learner's abilities and knowledge. Through adopting a holistic view to the learning process, the teaching team on the BCA acknowledges that learners do most of their learning when they work on their design projects.

"Connectedness" —Learning Approach Through Storytelling

While many cultures have always valued storytelling telling as part of the learning process, in recent years practitioners and researchers have advocated for a storytelling strategy to be adopted in higher education. One of the key reasons for its inclusion is because storytelling accommodates and values cultural differences and lies at the heart of human interaction.

From the very first project on year one the BCA students are encouraged to find an authentic voice and tell their own stories through the dishes they conceive and create. An example of this would be a simple lemon tart dessert which is derived from the classical French repertoire (see Figure 1). Traditionally this dish would be demonstrated by the lecturer and the students would replicate the dish until the lecturer had determined that competency was achieved. Utilising the storytelling approach the student adapts the fundamental skills of pastry and egg custard and, through inspiration, designs a dish that tells their own story (see Figure 2).

Figure 1 A Lemon Tart

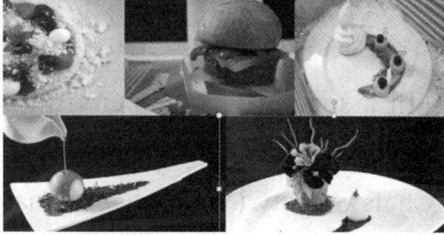
Figure 2 Storytelling Desserts Designed by Students

A Student Case Study

The following images are from a second year BCA student and can be considered as a case study of how "connectedness" storytelling is integrated within the learning and assessment process. The images are from a Chinese student called Zefei Liang who has a passion for art, photography and exploring Chinese cooking and culture. From the beginning of the programme, Zefei has been encouraged to incorporate these interests into her projects with the intention of her identifying how her value sets can find a place within the culinary arts community.

One of the projects in the first year of the programme requires students to design a dish that contains wild foraged ingredients that tells the story of a place in Otago. Foraging and local identity are two major movements in culinary arts within the western world.

Figure 3 is a picture of a local installation called the Harbour teeth. Zefei chose to connect her interest in art with this project and design a dish (Figure 4) which includes wild boar prepared into traditional Chinese dumplings.

Figure 3 Otago Art Installation, Harbour Teeth   Figure 4 Wild Boar Prepared as Chinese Dumplings

In a second year paper titled Culinary Competitions, Zefei was required to design a chicken dish and deliver it under the World Association of Chefs Society (WACAS) culinary guidelines. Figure 5 is of the final dish which takes reference from traditional Chinese celebrations and techniques. Again in this project we see Zefei interests in cultural hertitage and art included design and the service of the dishes. Subsequently Zefei went on to win the competition.

Figure 5 Three Cup Chicken with Salty Chicken Salad   Figure 6 A Molecular Inspired Birthday Present

As part of engaging in contemporary avant garde practice, students are asked to explore and create a dish which incorporates molecular gastronomy techniques and nostalgic triggers. For this project Zefei designed a dish which utilizes the molecular techniques of sous vide and aerated sauces to create a dish which takes reference from the Chinese tradition of gifting an egg for prosperity on your birthday. The final dish can be viewed in Figure 6.

Another year two project requires students to design a product suitable for sale at a farmers market. This requires the student to understand the world of the farmers market consumers— who are our consumers in the world of culinary arts? This project required Zefei to design a product that aligns with the farmers market consumers values of healthy, local premium quality food with an authentic story. Working collaboratively with fellow students, Zefei's design outcome was a traditional Chinese soup dumpling made with natural New Zealand ingredients and a healthier alternative to the current fried offering. See the Figure 7 for the final outcome.

Figure 7 Chinese Soup Dumplings of New Zealand Lamb and Mint

The final example in this case study is the development of a small business concept and a supporting sample menu. This paper asks students

Figure 8 Visualisation of the Business Concept Lo Yau

to explore current dining trends along with local consumer behaviors to conceive a unique entrepreneurial business endeavor. In this project, Zefei integrated the current dining trends of shared platters; affordability and healthy food to develop a business concept titled Lo Yau (see Figure 8). Lo Yau offers a fun and affordable dining experience which takes traditional Chinese dishes and produces them in a way that is both communal and healthy.

Conclusions

While the above case study is that of one Chinese student, it is not alone. The same story could have been told of a rural New Zealand, Maori or Pacific Island student.

By employing a "Connectedness" learning approach, the programme has noticed some significant outcomes in their students learning and related classroom behaviours.

The first of these outcomes is that there are heightened levels of student engagement supported with increased levels of intrinsic motivation. These are the direct outcomes of the students taking ownership of their knowledge gathering and processing and in turn learning.

As a result of this students exploration and processing, students are gaining a deeper understanding of both the content and value perspective and how these are integration into the culinary arts arena.

And finally the pedagogical value comes from the connection of learners and vocational worlds; it is in these moments of "connection" that the real, authentic and learning for life occurs.

在沙特阿拉伯朱拜勒工业学院建立的优质教育发展中心

怀卡托理工学院　John Clayton

在经济全球化的当今世界，教育界、工业界和政府机构均已认识到毕业生的可就业技能、知识水平及个人能力是保证行业在全球竞争力的关键。为了保持并最终提高受教者的可就业技能，教育机构已经下定决心要进行教育改革。

作为沙特阿拉伯王国（KSA）最具影响力的学院，为了提高教育成果，朱拜勒工业学院（JTI）与新西兰理工学院联合，对目前沙特阿拉伯王国采用的知识考核为主的课程教学及传统的教学方式进行了一次综合考察。考察期间，朱拜勒工业学院认识到应将教育重点转移，注重受教者可就业知识和能力的培养。在发现新西兰理工学院已经成功地采用了以学生为中心、注重能力培养的教学方法后，他们找到怀卡托学院，要求他们帮助在朱拜勒工业学院建立一个优质教育发展中心（QEDC），率先采用以能力培养为主的教学方法。QEDC的发展包含四个阶段——设计、建立、实施和评估。本文将简要介绍每个阶段所开展的活动。

设计：这个阶段的工作重点为设计，推广和建立所提议的中心。共分为四个工作流程。

• 设计理念：优质教育发展中心为一个独立的整体机构中心，负责提供课程大纲的开发及教师培训，中心的工作人员对中心这两个工作职能应有全面的了解。

• 职能：中心有四个工作职能——优质教师培训，前沿课程开发，电子教材与印刷教材及资源制作和教学研究。

• 场所：优质教育发展中心（QEDC）必须有所需的专用设施、靠近朱拜勒工业学院（JTI）校园中心及校方利益相关者。因此，建议中心应设在新批准修建的图书馆内。

•能力：为保证中心有效运转，必须对中心工作人员就他们即将从事的工作进行全面培训。培训涉及管理、课程设计和开发以及成人教育原理。

中心的建立：这个阶段向选拔出来的朱拜勒工业学院的教学人员，详细介绍了以能力培养为主的教学原理，及其在教师培训及教学大纲开发中的应用。此外，为课程开发人员和培训者提供的培训包含了专门的课程模块。这种培训共有三个部分：

•基础教学：为工作人员介绍了以能力培养为主的课程大纲的开发原理、以能力培养为主的教学原理、考核方法和审计机制、教学设计、在线学习入门、高级课程大纲设计及撰写以能力培养为主的教学成果、课堂及工作室教学和课堂管理。

•成人教学证书：朱拜勒工业学院工作人员接受了怀卡托理工学院（Wintec）工作人员提供的为期两周的集中全职培训，目的是巩固他们在第 1 部分培训课程中所学的知识。课程结束后对他们进行了评估，并给他们颁发了结业证书。

•CAPSTONE 综合培训：重点培训回到朱拜勒工业学院及优质教育发展中心后需完成将要承担的相关任务的所有朱拜勒工作人员。任务包括在朱拜勒工业学院创建开发以能力培养为主的四门课程的大纲文件和模板，以及开发培训培训人员的教学资源和入门课程。

实施：这个阶段从朱拜勒工业学院工作人员从新西兰返回沙特阿拉伯后开始实施。该阶段分两步进行：首先，将目前开设的一年级以成绩为主的课程系统的转化为以能力为主的课程。其次，所有技术课程的老师接受以学生为中心的学习和自主学习的理论基础知识培训。培训分为三部分。

•培训手册：以优质教育发展中心的工作人员为主，怀卡托理工学院为辅，为朱拜勒工业学院出版了培训手册。该手册分为两部分。第一部分解释了以能力培养为主的教学基本原理及朱拜勒工业学院改革的理论依据。第二部分提供了将要开设的培训课程的课程简介以及课程设计、考核方法和教案开发需要的模板。

•为期一周的培训课程：该培训课程包括 20 节独立讲座，面向所有朱拜勒工业学院技术培训教师，共有 14 个单元。向工作人员介绍以能力培养为主的课程大纲的开发原理、以能力培养为主的教学原理、考核和审计机制、教学设计、在线学习入门、高级课程设计及撰写以能力培养为主的教学成果、课堂及工作室教学和课堂管理。

课程修订：培训结束后，工作人员使用通用模板开始对他们所从事的教学课程进行修改。模板内容包括考核内容和教学方法。每个工作人员在修改工作中均得到了优质教育发展中心的一对一支持。

评价阶段：这个阶段重点评估优质教育发展中心的建立对教学方法和朱拜勒工业学院所开设的课程带来的影响。选择对两个领域进行评估：第一，审核和评估课程修订过程；第二，评估教学培训效果及学生成绩。采取采访、文件评估和观察的方式收集数据。

• 课程大纲审核：大多数受访者对优质教育发展中心的工作人员提供的支持表示感谢，认为在对大纲做出修改以适应以能力培养为主的教学过程中因为有了模板而使工作得到了简化。在文件评估中注意到在课程模块的排序和选择上还有待改进。然而，对课程大纲已经做出了重大修改，已经着手进行持续的修订工作。

• 教与学：调查表明，在朱拜勒工业学院工作人员对介绍以能力培养为主的培训课程的满意度越来越高。对优质教育发展中心在培训方面所提供的支持，也给予了非常积极的反馈。然而，鉴于新的教学方法才刚刚采用，还不能对其所带来的影响做出全面评估。这项评估将在实施一周年后进行。

结论与建议：优质教育发展中心项目非常成功。该中心现已在朱拜勒工业学院全部建成，现由经验丰富且胜任的管理者来管理。中心取得的主要成果：

• 为中心制订了一个"具有远见、目标明确且战略化"的规划；

• 成功地完成了以能力为主的课程大纲修订；

• 所有朱拜勒工业学院技术教学人员参加了为期一周的培训课程，准备实施新的课程大纲；

为确保中心的持续成功发展，朱拜勒工业学院需要确保：

• 学院需要储备足够的经过培训、持有证书且经验丰富的教学人员在中心工作，既可全职又可兼职；

• 继续提供介绍以学生为中心的教学方法的工作室；

• 学院应设置一个量身定制的正式教师学历证书课程以满足朱拜勒理工学院的特殊需求；

• 该中心已迁入了专为其建造的永久建筑。

The Establishment of a Quality Education Development Centre in Jubail Technical Institute: Kingdom of Saudi Arabia

John Clayton, Waikato Institute of Technology

In this pervasive global economy educational providers, industry bodies and government agencies have recognised the level of work-ready skills, knowledge and competence of graduating learners is the key to remaining globally competitive. To maintain, and ultimately improve, the work-readiness of learner's educational institutions are demonstrating a commitment to educational renewal.

As part of a national drive within the Kingdom of Saudi Arabia (KSA) to improve educational outcomes, Jubail Technical Institute (JTI), in con-junction with New Zealand Institutes of Technology, undertook a comprehensive review of the achievement based curriculum currently delivered and their traditional teaching practices. During this review JTI recognised their approach to educational provision should be re-focused on, and be defined by, the successful demonstrations of work-ready skills knowledge and competence of each learner. Recognising New Zealand Institutes of Technology had successfully adopted learner centric competency-based educational practices they approached Wintec to help in the establishment of a Quality and Educational Development Centre (QEDC) at JTI to lead the adoption of competency-based educational practices. This development of QEDC followed a four-phased framework, design, establish, implement and evaluate. This paper will briefly explain activities undertaken in each phase.

DESIGN: This phase focused on the conceptualisation, promotion and establishment of the proposed centre. It considered four work streams:

- CONCEPTUALISATION: The QEDC centre was conceptualised as a single integrated centre providing both curriculum development and instructor training, and that the staff of the centre have a thorough knowledge of both of these functions.
- FUNCTIONALITY: The centre was comprised of four integrated functions; high quality instructor training, state of the art curriculum development, digital and paper-based educational media and resource production and pedagogical research.
- LOCATION: It was considered essential that the QEDC was located in purpose-designed facility close to the heart of the JTI campus and their stakeholders. It was recommended that the QEDC be located in a newly commissioned library.
- CAPABILITY: For the centre to be effective it was considered important that staff received detailed training in the roles they were to undertake. This would involve management, curriculum design and development and the principles of adult education.

ESTABLISHMENT: This phase was structured to provide selected JTI staff with a thorough grounding in the principles of competency-based teaching and learning and the application of these principles in instructor training and curriculum development. In addition, the training programme provided specialist modules for the curriculum development staff and the master trainers. There were three parts to this training:

- FOUNDATIONS OF TEACHING AND LEARNING: This part of the training introduced staff to the principles of competency-based curriculum development, principles of competency-based learning and teaching, assessment and moderation, instructional design, introduction to e-learning, advanced curriculum design, writing competency-based learning outcomes, classroom and workshop teaching and classroom management.

• **CERTIFICATE IN ADULT TEACHING**: JTI staff undertook a concentrated two week full time programme with other staff from Wintec. This was designed to consolidate the knowledge they gained from Part 1 of the training programme. This course was assessed and JTI staff were awarded with a formal Certificate on completion.

• **CAPSTONE TRAINING**: This part focused on all JTI staff completing authentic tasks related to activities they would undertake on their return to JTI and QEDC. Tasks included, creating competency based curriculum documents and templates for the four curriculum development in departments in JTI and the development of resources for train the trainer and induction courses.

IMPLEMENTATION: This phase commenced when the JTI staff returned to Saudi Arabia from New Zealand. Two work streams were established: firstly, a systematic conversion of the current curricula offered in year one from achievement to competency-based was undertaken. Secondly, all technical tutors undertook training the theoretical foundations of student cantered learning (SCL) and Self Directed Learning (SDL). There were three parts to this phase.

• **TRAINING MANUAL**: This focused on QEDC staff, supported by Wintec, publishing a training manual for all JTI staff. The manual was divided into two sections. Section one explained the fundamentals of competency based education and underlying rationale for JTI to change to competency-based delivery. Section two provided an outline of the training modules to be offered and the templates to be used in the development of curricula, assessments and lesson plans.

• **ONE WEEK TRAINING COURSE**: The one week training course, comprising of twenty discrete sessions, was offered to all technical training tutors at JTI in blocks of fourteen. The sessions introduced staff to the principles of competency-based curriculum development, principles of competency-based learning and teaching, assessment and moderation, instructional design, introduction to e-learning, advanced curriculum design, writing competency-based learning outcomes, classroom and workshop teaching and classroom management.

• CURRICULUM REVISION: On completion of the training staff began a review of the curricula they delivered using a common template. The template was structured to include assessment tasks and teaching and learning approaches. Staff were individually supported in this review by QEDC.

EVALUATION: This phase was focused on evaluating the impact of the establishment of QEDC on teaching and learning practices and the curriculum delivered at JTI. Two areas of evaluation were identified: first, the review and evaluation of the process of curriculum revision; second, evaluation of the effectiveness of the training offered in teaching and learning and student achievement. Data was gathered through interviews, review of documents and observation.

• CURRICULUM REVIEW: Most of those interviewed appreciated the support received by QEDC staff and considered the changes needed to create the new competency-based curriculum were simplified with the provision of the template, although it did take some time to do this thoroughly. In reviewing the documentation it was noted changes still needed to be made in the sequencing and selection of modules. However, significant changes had been made and an on-going process of revision was in place.

• TEACHING AND LEARNING: The interviews indicated there was a consistently high level of satisfaction from staff for the training programme that introduced competency-based training to JTI. There was also very

positive feedback about the support provided by QEDC staff for those leading the sessions. However, given the teaching and learning practices had only recently been introduced, no full evaluation of the impact of these changes could be made. This will be undertaken at the end of a full year of implementation.

CONCLUSIONS AND RECOMMENDATIONS: The establishment of the Quality and Educational Development Centre project has been very successful. The centre is now well established within JTI and is run by experienced and highly capable practitioners. Key outputs have been:

• A vision, mission and strategic plan for the centre have been developed.

• Extensive curriculum revision to a competency-based format has been completed successfully.

All JTI technical instructors participated in an initial one-week training programme to prepare them for the introduction of the new curriculum.

To ensure the continued success and development of the centre, JTI needs to ensure:

• That there is an appropriate pool of trained, certificated and experienced academic staff available to work in the centre on a full time and/or part time basis;

• On-going workshops, with a focus on student centred learning, be continued to be offered;

• JTI investigate the award of a formal instructor qualification tailored to meet the particular needs of JTI;

• The centre is moved into permanent purpose built facilities.

四、教学现场
Open Class

观摩课：传感器与过程控制

杜晓妮

正式上课前，各组学生将预习作业写在展示板上。老师在各组间巡查，和学生讨论部分问题。

上课。

杜晓妮老师：上一个单元学习了光电传感器，了解了光电传感器的基本知识，并且我们利用实训台做了相应的应用程序的设计。本单元我们将用4个课时的时间，来学习霍尔传感器。首先我和大家一起来认识一下霍尔传感器。我们希望通过这堂课的学习，同学们能了解霍尔传感器的工作原理，能解释霍尔效应，这是非常重要的一个基本的要求。另外，我们以实训设备为载体，希望同学们通过对应用程序的设计具体地了解在实际生产设备中，霍尔传感器是如何工作的。下面，请大家一起看一段视频，看的时候，请大家注意如何理解霍尔效应，并且了解在视频所示的工作系统中霍尔传感器的工作原理是怎样。视频结束后会请同学回答问题。请认真观看，认真思考。

播放视频。电子点火系统的工作过程、工作原理以及霍尔传感器在此系统中的工作方式。

杜晓妮老师：视频结束了，大家刚才看得非常认真。通过这个视频，大家听到了对霍尔效应的解释，以及霍尔效应发生的载体——霍尔元件。下面请一个同学说一下他所理解的霍尔效应是怎样的。

各组同学积极准备回答问题。

杜晓妮老师：刚才在播放视频过程中，离我最近的这个组中，刘大蛟同学观看得非常认真，那么请刘大蛟同学来分享一下他所理解的霍尔效应吧。

刘大蛟同学走到他们组的展板前，利用他画好的霍尔效应原理图进行解释：我理解的霍尔效应是这样的，就是在通有电流的一个金属板上，加一匀强磁场，如果匀强磁场的方向和电流的方向是垂直的，那么就会在这个金属板与匀强磁场都垂直的方向上产生一个电势差,这个电势差就叫作霍尔电动势,这种现象就叫作霍尔效应。

杜晓妮老师:看来确实是课下做准备了,非常好,请坐。产生霍尔效应的元件就是霍尔元件,刚才视频中也提到,霍尔元件可以是金属的,也可以是半导体的,但是金属的霍尔效应不明显,所以一般情况下都用半导体来做霍尔元件。这是第一个问题。大家注意的是,首先,霍尔效应的示意图是怎么画的,如何用文字解释霍尔效应,还要知道霍尔元件的基本组成,这就是第二个问题,霍尔传感器有哪些类型?请大家根据课前预习来分享一下信息。

各组同学积极准备回答问题。

杜晓妮老师:好,6组的刘儒琛同学来说一下这个问题吧。

刘儒琛同学走到他们组的展板前,利用他画好的霍尔传感器的特性曲线图来回答这个问题:霍尔传感器分为线性型霍尔传感器和开关型霍尔传感器,线性型霍尔传感器由霍尔元件及其他基本元件组成,(指着线性型霍尔传感器的特性曲线图说)这是它的电压和磁场的关系曲线;开关型霍尔传感器主要有差分放大器、斯密特触发器以及霍尔元件组成,(指着开关型霍尔传感器的特性曲线图说)这是它的电压和磁场的变化关系曲线图,线性型霍尔传感器的输出量是模拟量,开关型霍尔传感器的输出量是数字量。

杜晓妮老师:非常好!请坐!首先,刘儒琛同学准备了有哪些类型的霍尔传感器,将两种类型的霍尔传感器的特性曲线图也准备好了——开关型和线性型。其次,他还准备了每种类型的霍尔传感器的组成部分也就是基本电路有哪些,这部分会在下半堂课的内容中通过系统地对传感器特性的分析去学习。第三,刘儒琛同学也说出,这两种类型的霍尔传感器分别能够检测怎样的信号。通过这两个同学的回答,我们知道了关于霍尔传感器的基本知识。那么,基本认识有了。下面,以具体的实训台为载体,我们怎样进行应用程序的设计呢?这首先需要我们了解实训台,要知道霍尔传感器在实训台上具体的位置,及其能够完成怎样的功能检测。请看,这是H2实训台,我们请同学回答一下今天的第三个问题,霍尔传感器在H2移动控制实训台上的应用情况是怎样的?

各组同学积极准备回答问题。

杜晓妮老师:我们请巩向环同学吧。

巩向环同学走向投影幕,用教杆指着相应的部位回答道:H2型台一共有3个霍尔传感器，其分别位于垂直气缸和气爪气缸，分别是用来对垂直气缸的复位检测、垂直气缸的至位检测、气爪气缸的检测，分别用 I0.7、I1.0 和 I1.1 来表示。

杜晓妮老师：啊！他的准备很充分！请坐！刚才我们已经知道了，霍尔传感器可以检测开关量和模拟量。H2 台上，霍尔传感器就是用来进行开关信号的检测，大家看，这是垂直气缸和气爪气缸，霍尔传感器主要用于气缸的。注意，我们在学习上个单元的光电传感器部分时发现，同学们对于输入输出的编号容易混淆，Q 代表的是 PLC 上相对于垂直气缸的输出，而开关在控制系统中是作为输入信号的。所以，大家一定注意这两种信号的区分。要检测垂直气缸的复位的话，就需要用到复位检测霍尔传感器，它对应的输入点是 I0.7，不知大家课下做应用程序设计时，是不是会用反了？它的至位检测端是 I1.0，这是对于气缸的。还有一个气爪呀，它需要打开和关闭，如何检测呢？是用 I1.1 来完成的。这就是 H2 台的应用情况。我发现有几个组的展板上的作业是关于 H2 台的程序设计，等下我们会请他们来讲一下他们程序设计的想法。下面，请大家看一下，这是 H3 台，它的霍尔传感器的应用情况又是怎样的呢？

各组同学积极准备回答问题。

杜晓妮老师：请丁亚伦来说一下吧。

丁亚伦同学走向投影幕，用教杆指着相应的部位回答道：在 H3 台上有 5 个霍尔传感器，它们分别位于单动气缸的两侧，它们的功能主要是单动气缸的复位检测与单动气缸的至位检测，复位检测与 PLC 的 I1.0 相连，至位检测与 PLC 的 I1.1 相连。另外 3 个霍尔传感器位于双动气缸的两侧和中间，功能也是负责双动气缸的复位和至位，双动气缸的复位检测霍尔传感器与 PLC 的 I0.5 相连，气缸 1 的至位检测霍尔传感器与 PLC 的 I0.6 相连，气缸 2 的至位检测霍尔传感器与 PLC 的 I0.7 相连。

杜晓妮老师：你说的都很对，但是请你现在再给大家具体地指一指双动气缸的复位位置在哪里。

丁亚伦同学用教杆正确指示出 H3 台上双动气缸的复位霍尔传感器所在的位置，并说：在这里。

杜晓妮老师：是的，在这里。有没有同学注意到他刚才指的位置？（此时，有同学指出丁亚伦同学刚才指示的位置有误。）是啊，既然已经知道这个位置，那么在给同学们讲的时候要指清楚、说清楚。好吗？谢谢你，丁亚伦，请坐。

H3 台和 H2 台上，霍尔传感器的应用情况是一样的，那就是，在气动装置中作为开关,检测气缸的复位和至位。要对双动气缸和单动气缸的输出进行程序设计,就首先要清楚,它们的输入是怎样的,还不清楚的,请抓紧时间记录一下,因为等一下要进行应用程序的设计了,如果输入输出点不正确的话,程序在实训台上是无法正常运行的。

以上,通过对H2、H3两个实训台上霍尔传感器的应用情况的了解,我们知道了,霍尔传感器都是作为开关使用的,所以此时,霍尔传感器就可以叫做"霍尔开关",在我们刚才看到的视频中,霍尔传感器在电子打火系统中也是作为开关量的检测装置。叶片通过磁场时,屏蔽掉了信号,所以就关断了电路;叶片离开磁场时,就接通了电路,这样一开一关实现整个系统的运行。这是对H3台的了解。

课前大家已经把作业写在展板上了,下面,我们了解一下各个组的程序设计情况是怎样的。注意:在讲程序设计作业时,一定要说清楚该程序完成怎样的功能以及该程序的运行过程是怎样的。

各组同学积极准备回答问题。

杜晓妮老师: 我们随机找一个就近的组吧。(2组的宋鹏同学跃跃欲试)那么就请2组的宋鹏同学来讲一下吧。

宋鹏同学走向他们组的展板,先改正了几个输入信号的编号,然后讲到:我们组是根据H2移动台利用霍尔传感器的至位复位信号控制垂直气缸上下伸缩的往返运动。整个程序是这样的:按下启动按钮,至位信号接通,复位信号断开,垂直气缸伸缩,至位信号断开,复位信号接通,垂直气缸收回。整个过程中,按下停止按钮,垂直气缸就会停止运行。

杜晓妮老师: 很好,听了刚才的内容,宋鹏同学马上意识到,设备上垂直气缸是Q0.4,而他课前写的垂直气缸编号为Q0.5。Q0.5是气爪,他混淆了两个不同的执行装置,如果真上实训台上运行该程序的话,会发现,气缸是没有动作的。所以他一上来的时候,先将Q0.5改为Q0.4。这里也要提醒同学们,进行程序设计前,大家一定要清楚设备上的线号关系。

另外,I1.4是启动按钮。接下去一个条件是至位信号I1.0,而垂直气缸的初始状态在哪里?(同学们集体回答:复位位置。)对啊,复位位置的线号是I0.7,如果是初始状态也就是复位状态的话,I0.7对应的常开触点是接通的,常闭触点是断开的。与之相反,至位位置的常开应该是……(部分同学回答:是断开的。)是啊,断开的，那么这条路能接通吗？（同学们回答：不能。）不能接通，是不是气缸也不能得电啊？那么，有什么办法解决吗？宋鹏，补充一下吧。

宋鹏同学将编号进行了修改。

杜晓妮老师：同学们看看，他是怎么改的？把I1.0和I0.7，也就是至位检测和复位检测调换了一下，这样肯定是没问题啦。如果不调换编号，有没有同学有办法把这个程序的问题继续修改一下？

杨进平同学站起来，走到展板前，用笔一边改，一边说道：可以把I1.0换成常闭触点，把I0.7换成常开触点。（然后杨进平同学回到座位。）

杜晓妮老师：解释一下杨进平的方法，他在启动电路中仍用I1.0，由于I1.0是至位检测，此时不得点，常闭触点就是闭合的，所以，用常闭触点；反之，停止电路中的I0.7复位检测是接通的，所以，用常开触点，那么，气缸就可得电了。霍尔传感器此时发挥作用。

杜晓妮老师转向展板旁的宋鹏：你们的程序到此可以了吗？

宋鹏同学：可以了。

杜晓妮老师：宋鹏他们组用的是启动——保持——停止的编程方法，利用霍尔传感器，实现单动气缸的至位、复位的运动控制。

杜晓妮老师转向展板旁的宋鹏：很好，请坐。

杜晓妮老师：其他组的同学们比较一下自己的程序跟他们的有什么不同。

各组同学积极准备回答问题。

杜晓妮老师：大家看，3组的程序非常不一样，就请3组的同学来说一下他们的程序设计的方法吧。

杨进平同学站起来。

杜晓妮老师：好，请杨进平同学来说说吧。

杨进平同学走到他们组的展板旁，说道：这是我们组设计的关于垂直气缸往返运动的程序。为了不造成点动，我们用了一个辅助继电器M0.0，初始状态时，气缸在复位位置，I0.7常开触点是接通的，按下启动按钮I1.4，M0.0得电并保持状态，那么，气缸Q0.4就至位，之后，至位开关I1.0接通，Q0.4就复位，这就是垂直气缸的往返运动。按下停止按钮I1.5，气缸回到初始位置。

杜晓妮老师：你们的程序中，气缸的运动是单次还是往复的？

杨进平同学：往复的。

杜晓妮老师：可以实现往复运动？

杨进平同学：在 H2 台上可以形成气缸的往复运动。

杜晓妮老师：好。也是 H2 实训台，也是垂直气缸的程序设计，应用了霍尔传感器。杨进平请坐。

杨进平同学回位坐好。

杜晓妮老师：大家看，这两个程序的功能都是一样的，对象也是一样的，方法不同，宋鹏组是起保停电路，杨进平组直接用至位复位指令输出。杨进平组的程序中，他们希望得到往复运动，这个程序我们也给大家做了一个，等下会一起分享、分析。我们继续来看其他组的程序设计吧。

各组同学积极准备回答问题。

杜晓妮老师：四组的同学给我讲一下他们的程序吧。

丁学飞同学站起来走向他们组的展板。

杜晓妮老师：好，丁学飞同学说一下他们的程序。

丁学飞同学来到他们组的展板旁，指示着程序说到：这是我们 4 组设计的一个关于 H2 型台霍尔传感器应用的小程序。按下启动按钮 I1.4，我们定义了一个辅助继电器 M0.0，它得电并保持得电状态，第二个逻辑行中 M0.0 接通，复位开关 I0.7 得电，就对气缸进行至位控制，当至位开关 I1.0 得电接通，又使气缸复位。这样往复运动，如此循环。

杜晓妮老师：一直循环下去？什么时候停止呀？

丁学飞同学仔细地看了看程序，说：没有设计停止。

杜晓妮老师：没有设计停止，这个气缸会非常辛苦地一直在至位复位、至位复位……

丁学飞同学开始修改。

杜晓妮老师：我们看到丁学飞要想办法让气缸停止了。

丁学飞同学修改程序。

丁学飞同学修改好后，说：我是这样改的，当按下停止按钮 I1.5 执行 R 指令，复位 M0.0，那么第二个逻辑行的公共控制信号断电，这样就全部断电，气缸就可以停止了。

杜晓妮老师：可以了？大家明白丁学飞的意思了吗？他的方法很简单，也是用至位复位指令输出的形式，实现对辅助继电器M0.0的控制，从而控制霍尔传感器信号的接通、断开，最终使垂直气缸能够运行和停止。

在刚才杨进平讲的程序和丁学飞讲的程序中，大家听到了都有让气缸的启动（运行）和停止，方法不一样，杨进平用的是I1.5断开，使M0.0至位信号失电，丁学飞用的是I1.5接通来复位M0.0，不同的方法，都能实现气缸的往返运动并使它停止。

刚才看的都是H2台的。现在，5组有一个H3台的程序，我们一起来看看吧。

罗帅同学走向他们组的展板。

杜晓妮老师：好，有请罗帅。

罗帅同学走到他们组的展板旁，说到：我们组设计的是H3台单动气缸的运行程序。当按下启动按钮I1.3以后，若检测到I1.0，则Q0.6接通，气缸伸出去，当它运行到至位位置以后，至位开关I1.1常闭触点断开，Q0.6缩回，回到复位位置。这个程序可以使气缸进行往返运动。

杜晓妮老师：单动气缸进行往返运动……什么时候停止呢？

罗帅同学看了看程序，说：我们组也没有加上这个控制。

杜晓妮老师：没有加。那I1.4是做什么的？

罗帅同学：I1.4？

杜晓妮老师和其他同学一起说：I1.4就是……停止按钮，所以，有停止控制信号了。好，这样就可以了。罗帅请坐。

罗帅同学回位坐好。

杜晓妮老师：对于H3台，他们组用霍尔传感器I1.0和I1.1，对单动气缸实现至位和复位。方法与刚刚H2台的方法是一样的。

我们马上要上实训台进行程序的调试与运行了，在这之前，请大家再修改一下自己的程序，保证能够成功运行。

下面，请大家看一个例子。（投影幕上展示）这个程序是H2台的应用程序，目的是使Q0.4垂直气缸可以做往返运动。在例子中，借助辅助继电器M0.0，使用启动按钮I1.4实现对Q0.4的启动，I0.7是复位开关，I0.2是什么？（杨进平起来回答：H2台上小车工件检测传感器。）是的，那么这个传感器是什么类型的传感器？（部分同学回答：光电传感器。）是啊，这就是上个单元我们学习的光电传感器，这个

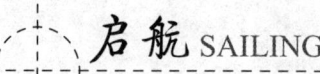

条件大家可以用，也可以不用，这是对上个单元内容的延续和复习。这样，电路接通，使垂直气缸可以出去，I1.0 至位开关得电，则缩回，这样，该程序就实现了气缸的往返运动的控制。

下面，大家看一下这个程序的运行视频。

播放视频。

杜晓妮老师：这就是刚才的程序在 H2 实训台上的运行过程。刚才提醒过大家，程序设计时，所有相关的内容一定要完整，包括梯形图、语句表，并且一定要把程序的功能用一句话表达出来，并说明程序的具体运行过程。

杜晓妮老师结合视频和丁学飞组的程序，指出杨进平组设计的程序中出现的技术问题，以及相关问题的解决方法。

总结部分。

杜晓妮老师：这节课和大家一起初步认识了霍尔传感器，知道了其控制原理、类型，并通过课下作业的讨论，知道了霍尔传感器在实际设备中怎样运行。

这部分内容就到这里，大家把材料整理一下。我们要进入下一阶段的学习了。

各组同学将"小组学习评价表"等资料粘贴到展示板上。

杜晓妮老师：下节课我们要做的工作是：1. 上机来调试、运行程序，2. 通过具体的电路分析来了解霍尔传感器的基本特性，3. 了解霍尔传感器在实际生产生活中的应用情况。

这节课就到这里。下课。

班长：起立。

全班同学：老师再见。

杜晓妮老师：同学们再见。请坐。

下课。

Transducer and Process Control

Du Xiaoni

Before the class, the students of each group showed their preview assignment on the display board, with the teacher discussing some questions with the students when moving around.

The class began.

Ms. Du Xiaoni: "We have studied the last chapter of photoelectric sensor, knowing its basic knowledge and did some design for application program accordingly. In this unit, we are going to study Hall sensor in 4 credit hours. Firstly, let's get to know Hall sensor which could help us know its working principle and Hall Effect, which is a basic requirement. And we will get to know how Hall sensor works in the real production. Now let's watch a video to help us understand Hall Effect and the work principle of Hall sensor. After the video I'd like to ask some of you to answer related questions."

Play video: the working process and working principle of electronic ignition system, and Hall sensor's working manner.

Ms. Du Xioani: "We have gotten the introduction for Hall Effect and the carrier of Hall Effect through this video, now I'd like to ask one student to share his understandings."

Each group of students preparing to answer.

Ms. Du Xiaoni: "I'd like to ask Liu Dajiao to share his view on Hall Effect."

The student Liu Dajiao came up to the board and explained by his drawn Hall Effect schematic diagram. "In my understanding", he said, "Hall Effect is on an electric metal board, plus a uniform magnetic field. If the two directions are vertical, there is a potential difference. The difference is called Hall electrodynamic force, and this phenomenon is called Hall Effect."

Ms. Du Xiaoni: "Well done, please be seated. The cause element of Hall Effect is Hall Element, just as we have seen in the video, the Hall Element could be mental, or semiconductor, but the effect of mental element is not

271

apparent, so we use semiconductor normally. This is the first question, Hall Effect. Please notice how we drew the schematic diagram and how to explain Hall Effect literally. And we are expected to know basic component of Hall Element, which is the second question—how many kinds of Hall Element are there? Now please share your information about this question."

Each group of students preparing to answer.

Ms. Du Xiaoni:" OK. Now let's welcome Liu Ruchen from group 6 to share his view."

Student Liu Ruchen came up to his board, explained by his Hall sensor graph. "There are two kinds of Hall sensor, linear-type and switch-type. The linear-type is composed of Hall element and some basic elements," Liu said, pointing to the linear-type Hall element graph, "and this is the relation curve of voltage and magnetic field." "Switch-type Hall element is composed of differential amplifier, Schmitt trigger and Hall element, " Liu said, pointing to the switch-type Hall element graph, "this is the relation curve of voltage and magnetic field. The linear-type Hall element's output quantity is analog quantity, the Switch-type Hall element's output quantity is digital quantity. That is our answer."

Ms. Du Xiaoni: "Very good. Please be seated. Firstly, Liu Ruchen prepared two kinds of Hall Sensors and their different graphs, linear-type and switch-type. Secondly, he also prepared the components of different Hall sensor, the basic electric circuit, which will be studied in the latter part of our class through the analysis of sensor characteristics. Thirdly, Liu further expressed how to test the signal of different kind of sensors, so that we could learn the basic knowledge of Hall sensor. Then based on the basic learning, how could we design the application program? So we should learn the training platform, get to know the location of Hall sensor and what function test could achieve. Now may I have your attention for this

H2 training platform, and get ready to answer my third question, what is the application of Hall sensor on H2 Mobility Control platform? "

Each group of students preparing to answer.

Ms. Du Xiaoni: " Let's welcome Gong Xianghuan to share his view."

Student Gong Xianghuan walked to the screen, pointing to the according position and said, "there are 3 Hall sensors on the H2 platform, located at vertical cylinder and gripper cylinder, to test the reset and location of vertical cylinder, test the gripper cylinder, which could be signed by I0.7, I1.0 and I1.1."

Ms. Du Xiaoni: "Great, well prepared. Please be seated. We have learned the Hall sensor could test the switch status and analog quantity, on the H2 platform, Hall sensor could be used to test the switch signal, everybody. They are vertical cylinder and gripper cylinder. Hall sensor is mainly used by cylinder. Please be noticed, when we studied the last unit of photoelectric sensor, some students easily confound the input and output serial number; Q stood for PLC output of vertical cylinder, whereas the switch is used for input signal in the controlling system. So we could tell the difference between the two kinds of signal. If we want to test the reset of vertical cylinder, the reset test of Hall sensor could be employed, while input should be I0.7, I wonder if any of your design of the application program after class could be reverse. Its test position is I1.0; it is for cylinder. And we know there is also a gripper, which need to be turned on and off, to be tested, by I1.1. This is the application of H2 platform. I have noticed the assignment of a couple of groups refer to H2 platform program designing, I will ask them to share their ideas of designing. And next, this is H3 platform. How does its Hall sensor work?"

Each group of students preparing to answer.

Ms. Du Xiaoni: "Next let's welcome Ding Yalun to give us an

introduction."

Student Ding Yalun walked to the screen, pointing to the according position and said, " There are 5 Hall sensors on H3 platform, located on the two sides of single-acting cylinder. Their main functions are the reset test and position test of single-acting cylinder. Reset test is connected with PLC I1.0; position test is connected with PLC I1.1. The other three Hall sensors located on the two sides and the middle of double-acting cylinder—their main functions are the reset test and position test of double-acting cylinder. Reset test is connected with PLC I0.5; cylinder 1 position test is connected with PLC I0.6; cylinder 2 position test is connected with PLC I0.7."

Ms. Du Xiaoni: "Yes, you are right, but now could you point at the reset location of double-cylinder? "

Student Ding pointed the reset location of H3 platform double-cylinder correctly and said, "It is here."

Ms. Du Xiaoni: "Yes, it is. Did anyone of you notice the location he pointed at? (Then someone pointed out Ding Yalun's incorrect pointing.) Well, now that you are clear about this location, please point and illustrate clearly. Thank you. Ding Yalun, please be seated.

"It is the same in application for Hall sensor on platform H3 and H2. That is, working as a switch in the pneumatic actuator to test the reset and location of cylinder. Programming should be designed for the output of double-acting cylinder and single-acting cylinder. So we are required to be clear about the input; if not, please write it down now, or the program would not work properly on the platform due to the incorrect input and output point.

"Now through the learning of the application of Hall sensor on H2 and H3 platform, we have learned that Hall sensor works as switch, so we could call Hall sensor 'Hall Switch'. Just as shown in the video we have watched,

Hall sensor also works as detector in the electronic lighter system. When the vane goes through magnetic field, the signal could be screened and the electric circuit could be cut off. With the vane off magnetic field, the electric circuit is connected. So the whole system works properly through off and on. That is what we have learned on H3 platform.

"Now that you have written down your assignment on the display board before the class, let's check each group's program designing works. When you illustrate your assignment, please make clear the function of the program and how to run this program."

Each group of students are preparing to answer.

Ms. Du Xiaoni: "Let's choose a nearer group at random. (Student Song Peng itched to try) Then let's welcome Song Peng."

Student Song Peng approached to their board, modified some series of numbers of input signal and then said, "Our group takes H2 movable platform which uses Hall sensor's reset and location signal control the up and down movement of vertical cylinders. The whole program is: press down the start button, connect signal appear, reset signal cut, vertical cylinder stretch out and draw back, connect signal cut, reset signal connected, vertical cylinder draw back. In the whole process, if we press down the stop button, the vertical cylinder could stop.

Ms. Du Xiaoni: "Very good. After our study, Song Peng realized immediately that on the equipment the vertical cylinder is Q0.4, while the number he wrote before the class for vertical cylinder was Q0.5. Q0.5 is pneumatic claw. He confounded two different operating devices. If it was operated on the platform, you would find the cylinder doesn't work. So that he modified Q0.5 to Q0.4 as soon as he came to the platform. And I'd like to mention to all of you, please make clear the relationship of the line type before design program.

"Besides, I1.4 is a start button. The requirement to press the button is location signal I1.0, but where is the initial state of vertical cylinder? (All of the students answered: reset location) Yes, the line number for reset is I0.7, if the initial state is the reset state. The normally open contact I0.7 should be connected, and the normally closed contact should be cut. And on the contrary, the location position should be—(some students answered, cut off). Yes, it is cut off, but could it be connected? (Students answered, no). No connection, and the cylinder could not get through the electricity either. Then could we have more good ideas? Song Peng, please try to make some changes."

Student Song changed the numbers.

Ms. Du Xiaoni: "Now let's see how he changed it. Exchange I1.0 and I0.7, which are the location test and reset test. Definitely no problem. If we didn't change the number, could you change this program?"

Student Yang Jinping came to his feet, walk to the board, modifying while saying, "we could change I1.0 to normally-closed contact, and change I0.7 to normally-open contact."(Yang went back to his seat.)

Ms. Du Xiaoni: "I'd like to make a further explanation on Yang's method. He used I1.0 when started electric circuit, because I1.0 is location test, so there was no contact. Since the normally-closed contact is closed, he used it. When he stopped the I0.7 of electric circuit, on the other hand, the reset test is connected. So when we use normally-open contact, the cylinder gets electricity and hall sensor works."

Ms. Du Xiaoni turned to Song Peng who stood by the board, "now could your program work?"

Student Song Peng: " Yes."

Ms. Du Xiaoni: "Song Peng's group employ the programming method of start-maintain-stop, using Hall sensor to achieve single-acting cylinder's control of location and reset."

Ms. Du Xiaoni turned to Song Peng, "Well done. Please be seated."

Student Song Peng went back to his seat.

Ms. Du Xiaoni: "The other group of students, please compare your own program with theirs'."

Each group of students preparing to answer.

Ms. Du Xiaoni: "Everybody, please look at the program of Group 3. Their program is quite different. Now let's welcome the student from Group 3 to give us an explanation on their program."

Student Yang Jinping stood up.

Ms. Du Xiaoni: "OK. Now let's welcome Yang Jinping to explain it."

Student Yang Jinping walked up to the board and said, "This is our program for vertical cylinder to-and-fro movement, in order not to make contact point, we used a supplementary relay M0.0. When in initial state, the cylinder is at location position, the normally-open-contact I0.7 is connected. If we press down the button of I1.4, M0.0 gets electricity. Maintain it that way, and the cylinder Q0.4 could get to its location. Afterwards, location switch I1.0 gets connected, Q0.4 could reset. This is the to-and-fro movement of vertical cylinder. Press down the stop button I1.5, the cylinder would get back to its initial position."

Ms. Du Xiaoni: "In your program, is the movement of cylinder single pass or reciprocating?"

Student Yang Jinping: "Reciprocating."

Ms. Du Xiaoni: "Could it achieve cylinder reciprocating?"

Student Yang Jinping: "On platform H2 cylinder reciprocating could be achieved."

Ms. Du Xiaoni: "OK. Also on platform H2, also in the program designing for vertical cylinder, use Hall sensor. Please be seated, Yang

Jinping."

Student Yang Jinping went back to his seat.

Ms. Du Xiaoni: "Now everybody, the two programs are same in function and target, but the methods are different. The group of Song Peng employ start-maintain-stop electricity circuit; the group of Yang Jinping employ the output order of location and reset. In the program of Yang's group, they hope to get reciprocating motion. I have prepared this program. We will share and analyze it later. Now let's continue to watch other groups' program."

Each group of students preparing to answer.

Ms. Du Xiaoni: "Would Group 4 please give us an explanation?"

Student Ding Xuefei stood up and walked to the board.

Ms. Du Xiaoni: "OK. Let's welcome Ding Xuefei to make an explanation."

Student Ding Xuefei came to their board, pointing to the program and said, "We have designed small program on H2 Hall sensor." He pressed the start button of I1.4, "We use a supplementary relay M0.0, which gets electricity and maintains that way. In the second logical line M0.0 gets connected, reset button I0.7 gets electricity, which control the cylinder. When the switch I1.0 gets connected, cylinder gets reset. So this reciprocating motion repeats."

Ms. Du Xiaoni: "Keep repeating. When to stop?"

Student Ding Xuefei checked the program and said, "We didn't design its stop."

Ms. Du Xiaoni: "No design for its stop. Then the cylinder must keep going, on and off, on and off…"

Student Ding Xuefei began to modify.

Ms. Du Xiaoni: "I have noticed that Ding Xuefei is trying to stop the cylinder."

Student Ding Xuefei modified the program.

Student Ding Xuefei finished his modification and said, "I have changed it in a way that when we press down the I1.5 button to operate R order, reset to M0.0, then the second logic line's public control signal could be cut to cut the electricity, and then the cylinder could be stopped."

Ms. Du Xiaoni: "Is it OK? Have you got Xuefei's idea? His method is very simple. He also uses output form of reset order to achieve the control of supplementary relay M0.0, so as to control the connection and disconnect of Hall sensor, and make the vertical cylinder operate or stop. Very good, please be seated."

Student Ding Xuefei went back to his seat.

Ms. Du Xiaoni: "In the program of Yang Jinping and Ding Xuefei, we have learned how to start and stop cylinder, though the methods are different. Yang Jinping employed the disconnection of I1.5, to make M0.0 signal disconnected. While Ding Xuefei employed the connection of I1.5 to reset M0.0. All roads lead to Rome. Different methods could achieve cylinder's to-and-fro movement and make it stop."

Student Luo Shuai walked to the board.

Ms. Du Xiaoni: "OK. Now let's welcome Luo Shuai to give us an explanation."

Student Luo Shuai walked to the board and said, "our program is for H3 single-acting cylinder. After we press the start button I1.3, if I1.0 could be detected, Q0.6 is then connected, and the cylinder extends. When it reaches the target position, the normally closed contact switch I1.1 would disconnect, and Q0.6 would retract, back to reset position. This program could achieve to-and-fro movement."

Ms. Du Xiaoni: "Single acting cylinder's to-and-fro movement. When to stop?"

Student Luo Shuai checked the program and said, "We didn't add the control system as well."

Ms. Du Xiaoni: "Then what is I1.4 for?"

Student Luo Shuai: "I1.4?"

Ms. Du Xiaoni and other students said together, "I1.4 is the stop button, so there is stop signal already." "It is OK now, please be seated, Luo Shuai."

Student Luo Shuai went back to his seat.

Ms. Du Xiaoni: "As for H3 platform, their group used Hall sensor I1.0 and I1.1 to achieve the single-acting cylinder's target position and reset. The way is the same as H2 platform.

"Before we go to the training platform for program tuning and operating, please modify your program again to make sure it could work properly.

"Now, please see an example. (showed on the screen) This is the application program for platform H2, objecting to make Q0.4 vertical cylinder to-and-fro movement. In this example, by using supplementary relay M0.0 and start button I1.4 to achieve the start of Q0.4, I0.7 is reset switch. Then what is I0.2? (Student Yang Jinping stood up and answered, "It is H2 platform work piece detective sensor.") OK. What kind of sensor is it? (Some students answered, "photoelectric sensor.") Right, this is what we have learned in the last unit, photoelectric sensor, which you could chose to use it or not. There would also be a review and further study of it. So in this way, when the electric circuit gets through, making vertical cylinder stretch, I1.0 target switch gets through, then moves back. So that we could achieve the to-and-fro movement control of the cylinder."

Play video.

Ms. Du Xiaoni: "This is theoperational process of the program on H2 platform. As I have mentioned just now, when you design the program, the details including ladder diagram, statement list should be completed, and the function of program should be expressed by one single sentence, explaining its operating process clearly."

Ms. Du Xiaoni summarized video and Ding Xuefei group's program, pointing out the technological problem of Yang Jinping group's program, and suggested the solutions accordingly.

Summary

Ms. Du Xiaoni: "We have gotten acquaintance with Hall sensor initially, knowing its control principle, type and how Hall sensor works in practical through the discussion of your group assignment."

Each group of students sticked "Evaluation Form for Teamwork" on the display board.

Ms. Du Xiaoni: "In the next class we are supposed to do the following assignment: 1. operating and tuning the program; 2. studying Hall sensor's basic characteristics through the analysis of electric circuit; 3. knowing the application of Hall sensor in the practical production and life.

"Thanks for your attendance today!"

"The monitor: Stand up!"

The whole class: "See you later."

Ms. Du Xiaoni: "See you later, please be seated."

Thank you!

观摩课：卖场陈列技巧

李琴

老师：各位来宾，各位同学，大家上午好。

我是商学院的李琴，今天在这里我要讲授的课程是卖场陈列技巧。这门课程是我院市场营销专业开设的一门专业课。通过这门课程的学习，我们希望使我们的学生能够熟悉卖场陈列、商品陈列的基本知识，了解商品陈列的基本方法和常用的技巧，能够对卖场的布局、商品的配置、商品陈列的现状做出观察和分析，然后提出改进意见。在可能的情况下，能够在既定的条件下对特定的商品陈列设计一个陈列方案，并且将方案实施。在这门课程的教学过程当中，我们所使用的教学方法主要是项目教学法。

在这学期的授课中，我设计了三个典型的教学项目：项目一是卖场布局的观察和分析；项目二是商品陈列现状的观察和分析；项目三是特定商品陈列方案的设计与实施。其中，针对项目三商品陈列设计与实施，我们又设计了三个任务：任务一是特定商品陈列设计要点解析；任务二是对特定空间、特定商品陈列方案的展示与点评；任务三是对特定商品陈列方案的实施。我们这一堂课是40分钟，我们选取的是项目三当中任务二的前半部分。

今天的课是40分钟，我们在这里公开展示两个小组的陈列方案。

一会儿课程结束之后，我们有10分钟的休息时间，要开始下一门课程。非常感谢各位，我们课程即将开始。

各位同学，上次课的时候，我们通过一些食品类和服饰类商品陈列图片的解析，共同学习了这两大类商品在陈列过程中的一些要点和一些注意事项。在下课之前我给大家安排了实训任务，要求大家以小组为单位，选择某一类商品，这个某一类商品在上次课说的很清楚，可以是食品类的，可以是服饰类的，也可以是小家电、图书。五个小组都有自己的选择，都有一个给定的长8.5米、宽6.5米、高3.5米的空间。在给定的这样一个空间里，小组可以根据意愿自行选择某一个大类商品，设计一个陈列方案。这一次课我们是带着我们的方案过来做一个公开的展示。然后大家在一起互相点评，我们取长补短使我们的方案更加完善。

我目前看到了一组和二组的布局图和方案，我想问一下，剩下三个小组，方案你们都做完了吗？

学生：做完了。

老师：对我们现在已经做完的方案，大家自己感到满意吗？

学生：满意。

老师：我感觉有一点点底气不足。我想问的是，虽然我们很用心地去做了这个方案，而且我自己觉得很满意。但是，你觉得我们的方案还有需要改进的地方吗？

学生：有。

老师：如果你觉得需要改进的话，你有没有感觉这个改进自己搞不定，需要一定的帮助。

学生：需要。

老师：好了，接下来的时间我们就一起来看一下，我们存不存在问题？我们需不需要帮助？我们可以怎么样获得帮助？接下来的时间，我们就请一组和二组先后展示一下他们设计的方案。每个小组展示的时间是5分钟。展示完了以后，我们所有听的同学有5分钟的时间可以提问。在我们听的过程中，所有我们认为没听清楚、没听明白或者说我们觉得他这个地方设计的不合适，我认为他需要修改，都可以提出来，好不好？

学生：好。

老师：这样我们一组和二组同学汇报的时候，坐在下面听的同学一定要认真地听，然后我要求大家过来的时候要带纸带笔。所以说适当的地方该记录的要记录，把问题记清楚。一会儿完了之后，我们有5分钟的展示时间、5分钟的答辩时间。答辩完了我会邀请我们在座的一个同学来简单点评一下我们小组的展示成果，然后我也会做一个简单的点评，这样两个小组全部点评完之后我们大家再做一个集体意见，整合所有遗漏的意见，再把修改意见提出来，这门课程基本上就可以结束了。所以接下来的时间，请一组的同学先给大家汇报一下他们陈列的方案。

一组发言代表：大家好，下面由我代表一组向大家介绍我们的商品陈列方案。这是我们的目录，首先目录有五部分：一、商品陈列地点信息；二、所需展示柜；三、展示效果解析；四、所需陈列配件；五、平面展示图。

我们的设计地点是黄岛区的一个生鲜区，主要是火腿专柜，陈列空间就是 8.5×6.5×3.5（米）的一个空间，主通道预测为 1.5 米宽。

这是我们的展示柜，我们的展示柜分为两种，一种是背面柜，背面柜是一种全开放式冷鲜柜，我们预测的是七台。三、四、五号背面柜是 2×1×1.7（米），一、二、六、七号背面柜是 2.75×1×1.7（米）的一个规格。

促销台预计是六台，全部是 1×1×1（米）。这是六号背面柜，因为六号背面柜在我们的平面图上它是一个特殊的区域，它是一个混合的地方，它是卤味干熏区，所以它的黄金分割的地方也是我们消费者首先看到的地方。在这里放主要的产品风味卤味，然后上面两层放的是各种品牌的火腿肠。下面一层放的是卤蛋和松花蛋。

这是一、二、三、四、五、七号柜，它们的规格摆放的物品是一样的，在品牌上有所区别。类型一样，首先黄金分割的地方是它的主打产品香肠、火腿。上一层是培根、午餐肉。下面两层是烤肠和一些零散的小型的 QQ 肠。这是我们预计的一个效果大家看一下。

这是促销台，促销台就是促销各种产品、新产品、特价产品。我们预计六台的位置是在一块的，应该是在平面图的这一区域中间的中心区。这也是我们预计的一个图片。

我们还需要一些陈列的配件，像 QT 广告贴、爆炸花、品牌提示牌。QT 广告贴根据规格不同、尺寸不同，首先它对消费者有提示的作用，对产品有宣传、促销的作用。爆炸花会让消费者眼前一亮，它的形状就像鞭炮爆炸一样，首先吸引消费者眼球。品牌提示牌是提示消费者我们地区有什么品牌，是对消费者起码的一个解释。促销台广告架上面标明了我们促销品牌的今日价格，对消费者是一个提示也有一定的吸引作用。配件还有灯光、LED 等相互配合，使空间变得更加明亮，使消费者置身其中会更加舒服。同时配合舒缓的音乐，使消费者心情放松。舒缓音乐会使消费者在这空间滞留的时间比较长，会增加购物时间，有利于销量。

这是我们的平面展示图，首先我们的过道设计的是 1.5 米，足够两个消费者同时推购物车进入。促销区域展示柜摆放，我们设计的品牌是双汇、雨润、喜旺、王老太、得利斯、波尼亚、金锣。首先，金锣和双汇放在通道的两侧，因为这两个品牌是大众品牌，价格比较适中，消费者容易接受。用它们作为诱饵，把消费者吸引到该区域。消费者进入该区域以后，会进入里面，看到得利斯、喜旺、波尼亚等价位比较高一点的商品。消费者就会开始购物。促销区域在这个地方，前面可以放一排像礼品盒这一类的东西。我们组基本的情况就是这样，我的演讲完毕了，谢谢大家。

老师：我在刚刚听的过程当中，大家认为我们一组的方案有没有问题？

学生：有。

老师：那么接下来的时间，我们就要请我们的同学就你发现的一些问题或者说你认为不明白、不清楚、有疑惑的地方提两个问题。我们请一组的同学做一个现场的解答，然后看他的解答能不能够把我们的问题消除掉。谁有问题？女士优先吧！

女学生：听了一组同学的讲解，感觉一组同学讲得挺好的，一目了然，图文并茂，而且讲解很清晰，那么请问一组的同学，你们陈列的特点，或者说特色，或者说亮点在哪里？

一组成员：这个我可以代表我们组来解说一下，请翻到那个平面图。好，大家可以看一下，我们这个是有专门柜台的，并不是说所有的产品都是在一个柜台上逐一摆放的，而且每个品牌都有一个独立的柜台，这一点是我们的特色。而且我们这个柜面是分层的，上面每一层的产品都是一样的，不会出现那种非常杂乱的摆放。

学生：好，谢谢。

老师：还有吗？我们还可以邀请，刚刚是一位女士，你吧。

男学生：我想问一下你们这种商品陈列对你们的销售有什么作用？

一组成员：下面由我来回答这个问题，我觉得好的商品陈列首先可以使更多的产品品种摆放在货架上，可以照顾到单个品种的数量，照顾单个产品数量的话可以显示出产品的品牌形象。综合这两个，一个是产品的品种，一个是单个产品的数量，充分运用货架的节省空间，进行成品销售。再一个，我觉得简洁顺畅的商品陈列，方便顾客拿，方便顾客与其他产品的比较。顾客看起来会比较舒服，因为我觉得消费体验非常重要，谢谢。

老师：大家还有问题吗？还有没有问题？有好多同学说还有问题，但是对不起，我们没有时间了，如果还有问题的话，待会儿我们把它写在纸条上，好吧？因为时间关系，我们请一个同学就我们一组的方案做一个简短的评价，哪位？自告奋勇。我们女同学已经主动站起来了。

女学生：听了你们的介绍，我觉得你们组画的这个平面图简单明了，一目了然，展示柜的规格和商品陈列讲解得非常清楚，卖场所需的辅助工具也非常齐全。但是有一点不足，就是他们所选的那个图片下面的商品陈列有些混乱，可能是在选图片的时候有一些小疏忽。谢谢，我发现的就是这些。

老师：好的，谢谢。不好意思没有时间了，我简单说一下，我们一组同学的方案，设计的优点非常突出，但是问题也比较明显。首先，其实刚刚有的同学已经介绍到了，这个布局图我们可以看到，在这个布局图中过道的设计非常显眼，不足是，出入口没有标识。我知道这是一个主通道，但是应该在这个位置上把出入口显示出来，这是一个问题。另外一个问题呢，做的好的是，在我们布局图上包括我们同学讲解这个方案的时候，你在哪个点上用的是什么样的设备，并且是什么样的规格，你都说得很清楚，但是呢，比如说这个位置，我们三组柜是两米的规格，那么在我们这个空间，你的这个角上还剩 1 米的空间，你这个空间怎么样用？我反复地跟大家强调过，任何一寸空间都是要花钱的，你这就是资源浪费，你怎么样充分地把这个空间用起来？再就是，我们在考虑细节问题的时候，2 米的展示柜紧挨着的话也不可能刚好是 6 米，不可能刚好是 6 米，所以说这些细节问题大家还是要注意。此外呢，我们在营造氛围的时候，我们同学充分地用到了如 POP、灯光还有音乐这样一些元素，但这些元素在用的时候，在你的这个图上面你体现出来没有？比如说你这个中央促销区，你都说了促销台上我要放一个广告架，你的广告架在什么位置？你没有标志出来，这也是一个问题。最后谈的一个小问题是，各个品牌做了分区，但是你分区陈列的理由究竟是什么？在你这个整体布局当中，你最好的陈列位在哪里？你想要重点突出的品牌是哪一个？或者说你想要突出的那一种类的产品是哪一种？这个没有说清楚。我们接下来有请第二组同学，汇报一下他们设计的方案。

二组发言代表：大家上午好，我是二组的代表于欣，我们组给大家带来的方案展示，是餐具的陈列方案。我们给它起了一个很温暖的名字——致幸福。我们主要分五个部分来阐述这个陈列方案：第一是整体布局，二是中国风主题厨房，三是欧美风主题厨房，四是陈列柜的设计，最后是吧台的展示。

这个是我们整体的店面布局，店面设置有 2 个门口做出入口，其中入口为 1.5 米的宽度，出口是 1 米的宽度，主通道的宽度为 1.8 米宽，进入主通道之后，主通道的右侧是两个长方形的陈列柜，中间夹着一个圆柱状的、旋转的陈列柜，然后在正对出入口的一侧我们设计两个完全不同风格的主题厨房，分别是中国风和欧美风。

在接近出口的一侧，我们设置了两个长方形的陈列柜，中间夹着一个圆柱状的、旋转的陈列柜，和入口一侧是完全对称的，只是材质有所不同。入口一侧陈列柜的材质以玻璃为主，出口一侧陈列柜的材质以木制为主。出入口的中间是一个长达5米的吧台，它也有陈列展示的作用，同时也是收银台，这就是我们整体的布局。

接下来给大家展示的是我们中国风的主题厨房，大家现在看到的这个图片就是我们想要实现的风格，在中国风主题厨房里面，陈列柜以红木家具为主，在柜子的顶端还有把手部分会雕刻有龙和凤这种吉祥物。这个位置是我们的黄金陈列段，在这里我们会陈列一些典型的青花瓷的成套餐具，这张图片就是我说的计划摆放在黄金陈列段的餐具。在这个陈列柜的上段我们会陈列一些单品的盘型餐具，这个盘子的陈列方式采用立体摆放，不是许多盘子叠在一起的。在陈列柜的最上面顶端位置，会陈列一排以荷花、梅花、牡丹等花卉为主题的成套的盘子。

在环境营造方面我们注意了三点。第一点是灯光的设计，在不同的陈列位置我们会设计不同的灯光。其次是音乐，在两个主题厨房里面我们会放一些轻音乐，比如说在中国风主题厨房里我们会放古典民乐一类的音乐。其三在服饰方面，每一个主题厨房都会有专门的服务人员接待客户，他们的服饰都是适应现场氛围的。

接下来给大家介绍的是欧美风主题厨房，这张图片展示的就是典型的欧美风，陈列柜的材质一般是以玻璃和不锈钢为主。这个料理台的台面是欧美风主题厨房的黄金陈列段位，我们会陈列一些欧美风格的成套餐具，然后在这个位置，我们会陈列特殊型号的餐具，这张图片显示的餐具会放在料理台的其他位置上，在洗菜的池子里面我们会放一些品牌餐具的单品，还有抽屉里面我们会放一些刀叉，在料理台的这一端我们会展示成套的刀具。

然后说明一下陈列柜的设计。首先给大家展示的是木制的陈列柜，在靠近中国风主题厨房这一侧，这个陈列柜的黄金段在这个位置，大家水平视线最先看到的地方，主要展示一些精致的勺子和筷子。这个是陈列柜的上半部分和下半部分，比较大件的餐具会摆放在陈列柜的上部，在底层，考虑到顾客可能有孩子，会摆放一些可爱的儿童餐具。然后给大家展示的是玻璃制品的陈列柜，在靠近欧美风主题厨房的这一侧，和木质陈列柜的设计一致，中间黄金陈列段摆放一些精美的、小巧的西餐餐具，在上部摆放一些非常个性的不锈钢餐具和古朴的木制餐具。这是底层，摆放的是儿童餐具。在靠近出入口的陈列柜主要摆放礼品和礼盒，不管客人到店里来自己用还是把餐具送给家人朋友，都有精美的礼盒包装。两个陈列柜中间是半径为0.5米的圆柱状旋转陈列柜，主要摆放一些特别精致的、可用作礼品的餐具，客人可以根据自己的喜好来旋转着观看。

这是我们最后一部分，吧台的展示。这个吧台长5米，我们将其分成两个模块，一个模块是比较轻松明快，一个模块灯光相对来说比较昏暗，但也不是非常黑暗的那种，两种风格完全不同。然后，吧台后面、服务人员后面会有5米长的大陈列柜，这个陈列柜我们主要展示的就是杯具，这些是咖啡的杯具，这些是啤酒红酒一系列的杯具，这个是中国很经典的茶具的展示，然后还有适合儿童和青年人饮料的那些杯具的展示。没有了，谢谢大家。

老师：二组的同学选择的图片都非常精美，以至于我们都看呆了。那大家觉得他们的方案设计有没有你看不明白或者说你觉得不合适的地方呢，有吗？刚刚是这边的同学，现在我们请这边的小组提问。

男学生：我想问一下一组，咱们设计的两边陈列的是餐具，但是那个中间，主要是中国风和欧美风两个在里面，让我们进去以后误以为你们卖的是整套的那个橱柜啊。

二组成员：这个问题由我代表我们小组来回答。因为我们的主题是"致幸福"，通过一整套的组合的橱柜设计，会给大家一种家庭的感觉。你参考我们设计的这种情形，思考一下，在家里这个摆放是什么状态，可以刺激消费者的购买欲。

老师：还有吗？

男学生：首先，我非常喜欢你的这种风格，中国风和欧美风相互对应，创意独具特色。然后问一下，你们这种风格，在摆放过程中来展示家用品，会不会让消费者误认为主要销售的是包括你们厨房的全部家具，会不会有这种消费的歧义？

二组成员：不好意思，刚才这个问题跟刚才小杨同学问的那个问题比较类似。

男学生：我觉得不类似。我觉得我说的更具有针对性。

二组成员：首先，就你刚才所说的问题，就是说会让消费者误以为那个产品是和橱柜一起出售的。因为我们是营造的一种气氛，会提前告诉消费者那个橱柜是不一起出售的，我们卖的是餐具，餐具和那个橱柜并不都是一套的。我们只不过是为了切合我们的主题"致幸福"。让消费者有一种家的感觉，他看到我们这餐具，就会想到，在家庭里面也是这样的。我们的橱柜是为了烘托餐具的。

男学生：我还想问一下，如果消费者有意向说要购买你的那个橱柜，这样一来

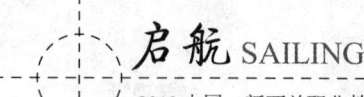

绝对有问题。

二组成员：比如说咱们买的这个东西很精小，可能赠送的那个东西会很大，有人看中那个比较闪目的、夺目的、大的赠送的东西，可能会有这种情况出现。这种情况的话，你想要那个比如说这个橱柜，可以给你联系，但比较少见。因为毕竟这个主题厨房是一个背景，里边陈列的餐具，不光我说的那个中国风的一套，它会有很多套在里边陈列的，不矛盾、不冲突，不会说就单一的一套。你不喜欢青花瓷就没有你可看的了。不是这个意思。

男学生：我觉得你的回答，有点脱离我的问题。我的问题是……

二组成员：我……

老师：不好意思，晓东，如果你觉得这个问题你还有疑问的话，或者说你觉得我们同学没给你解释清楚，我们欢迎课下继续交流，好不好？我们就二组的方案，请一个同学，就你认为最打动你的地方和你认为问题最大的地方，用两句话说明白了。刚刚我们是，不好意思，刚刚是你吧？都站了好几次了，我给你机会。

男学生：在点评之前我想问一下你那吧台有什么作用呢？是一个展台或者是……？

二组成员：这个问题我回答一下，首先我们吧台是个创新吧，与整体的格局相对应。其次，在我们吧台的一角有一个收银台，再有就是在我们吧台的后边有一个展架，在消费者休息或者是结账的时候，可以在那停驻一下，就是为了挽留住消费者要走的步伐。

男学生：好，谢谢！我认为二组的布局总体给我的感觉是非常新颖的，因为他们可以运用空间来做一个设计，非常有想象力，但是呢，我们给的空间是 8.5×6.5×3.5 米，宽度都是 6.5 米，中国风和欧美风加在一块，除去中间 1 米也就 5 米的空间。如果这样划分下来，一个板块也就 2 米多。空间我感觉有点窄，他们的那个设计有点多。

老师：嗯，还有吗？

男学生：还有就是，我认为他们那个有点杂，不如做得专，做一个风格的，可以是中国风，或者是欧美风，因为那空间有限嘛，可以做一些比较有专业性的。

老师：好的，谢谢！我知道有很多同学有想法，然后呢，请二组同学坐回去。如果我没记错的话，我们现在手头有一张红色的小纸条，有吧？至少是两张，对吧？

然后绿色的也有，至少是两张，把你所有想说的但是在现场没机会说的话写下来。我们在绿色的纸条上把你认为最好的地方写下来，一组二组，两个方案你觉得做得最好的，1、2、3把它写清楚。然后呢，在我们红色的纸条上，把你认为这两个方案当中做得最不好或者你觉得后期一定要改的地方，1、2、3把它写清楚。我们在课堂上大家提过的意见就不提了，不要屡次地打击，是吧？没有提到的，可能我们总结各方面没有提到的但是你想到了的，大家1、2、3写清楚，我们很诚恳地把这些意见写下来，一组的就贴在一组的图上去，二组的就贴在二组的图上。

  我们还是以表扬为主，我们把绿色的纸条贴上面，把红色的条贴下面。因为我们提批评意见是为了让我们大家更好地学习。同学写的时候会感觉时间有点紧张，我有太多的话想说，那么我们把手头的工作暂时一停，我们把想提的意见，可以利用这个机会，给我们两个小组提出来，也可以利用课下的机会互相在一起探讨一下，因为现在虽然我们只是展示了一组和二组的方案。但是实际上我们大家都在做方案，我们也可以邀请一组二组的同学来看一下我们的方案，包括在后续的课程当中，我们的其他三个小组同学展示方案的时候也会让一组二组给我们评一评。

  刚刚二组的这个方案我简单说一下，我认为它最大的一个亮点在于气氛的营造，从陈列方案的角度来讲，我个人认为，有一点点喧宾夺主。我们刚刚有两个同学先后提了两个问题，晓东反复说我问的不一样，但实际上我认为问的是一个问题。你的这个陈列方案，风格非常突出，也很吸引人，但是就陈列而言，亮点在哪里呢？为什么我们同学会疑问说你究竟是卖餐具呢？还是卖厨房的整套橱柜呀？为什么有这样一个疑问？其实我们在解答这个问题的时候，你很容易说，我是用橱柜来展示我的产品，配合价格标签，配合POP的宣传台，这个产品卖的究竟是什么？我可以把它做出来，但是咱们现在的汇报当中没有体现出这一点。所以我们汇报过程中大家有一个疑问。我觉得二组，相对一组来讲在设计的选择上更进一步。我们一组的同学做了规格的说明，二组连材质都说了。我要用什么样的材质，配合我的风格，这个是我们在选择设计的时候一定要考虑的一个因素。然后呢，二组相对来讲黄金段位的标识非常明确，我告诉你，哪个位置是黄金段位，我要陈列什么商品，我找图片给你看。我就是想做出这样的效果，这个讲解非常清楚，但是问题也很突出，就是我刚刚讲的，我们陈列的亮点究竟在哪里不够清楚。中国风也好，欧美风也好，

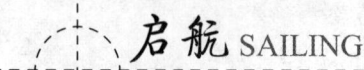

你突出要去主推的产品是什么？我们做陈列是为了促进销售，那么你主推的产品在哪儿，你主打在哪儿，你的产品的亮点在哪里？这个没有说清楚。两个问题，我觉得在后续的课程当中，我们进一步修改，把这个方案完善一下。当然还有我们同学提到的，比如说空间太窄小，我觉得要忍痛割爱，选择一种风格，就可以了。

这堂课程我们两个小组，一组和二组做的方案，我觉得都很棒，虽然我们仍然有很多问题，咱们大家第一次做，已经做到这个水平我觉得很好了，但是呢，在后续的方案改进的过程中，我们一定要牢牢记住，我们在设计陈列方案的时候，无论你选择的是什么样的商品，牢牢记住五个问题：第一个问题，从整体上来讲，我们的布局你究竟怎么样规划？你的动向怎么样设计？你这个动向一定是根据你这个店的经营规模。我们两个小组非常有特点，一个选择的是大卖场里面的某一个专区，一个选择的是要做一个专卖店，两种类型的卖场的设计。另外一个呢，就是我们这个店它的目标定位，我们的目标顾客它的消费习惯是怎么样的，根据这个来确定你的布局。第二个问题，我们设施设备的选择，设施设备的选择一定是和你这个卖场的面积，一定是和店的风格，一定是和产品的特点，密切结合的。第三个问题，辅助手段的应用，刚刚我们同学提到了，灯光色彩、POP等，这个手段应用的话，在方案里面能不能体现出来？不能光说"哎呦"，脑袋里面想得很清楚，一定要把它写出来，因为我们是做方案的，最终执行这个方案的人未必是我们，要把它写清楚。那么，第四个问题，我们的商品配置，您设备想得很好，什么都想得很好，具体到这个设备上，比如说给我一个展示台，我究竟要怎么样去陈列我的商品，我的黄金段位上放什么，我上层放什么，我下层放什么？我们是有规矩的。这个规矩你是怎么定的，不是说我在家里一拍脑门：行！就这么办吧。不是这样的。第五个问题就是细节，我们刚刚提到的，你的空间有多大，你怎么样充分利用你的空间。我们始终在讲购物感受，给消费者好的购物感受，太挤了不行，太宽了也不行。所以说呢，陈列说到底，首先是一个技术，然后在技术之上是一门艺术，是技术和艺术的结合。这需要大家在我们今后在不断的学习和实践中慢慢地摸索出来。

好，今天我关于这堂课程想说的话就这么多了，但是不等于我们这堂课就结束了，我刚说了，我们大家有很多话想说，把我们写的意见条展示一下，给大家看一看。尤其是给我们一组的同学二组的同学看一下，尤其是我们后面三个组，亮出来给大家看看。看看我们表扬的话有多少，看看我们批评的话有多少。然后课下我们的交流要继续，我们的改进工作也要继续。

本堂课就到这里，谢谢！

Skills for Setting Shopping Mall

Li Qin

Teacher: Good morning, ladies and gentlemen.

I'm Li Qin from business school. I'm here today to make a presentation about the display design of the marketplace. It is a course of marketing major. We hope that through the study, our students could be familiar with display design of the marketplace and the layout of goods. Then, the students can make an observation and analyze the current situation about the layout of the marketplace and the arrangement of the goods. If it is possible, we hope that our students can design a special marketplace layout project under a fixed condition, and moreover to carry it out. During the teaching of this course, we believe in teaching with practice.

During the teaching of this term, I designed three classical programs. The first project is about the observation and analysis of the layout of the marketplace. The second project is about the observation and analysis of the current situation of the layout of the marketplace. The third project is about the design and implement of the project of the layout of the fixed goods. As to the third project, we have three tasks. The first task is to make an explanation about the core of the project. The second task is to display and criticize the scheme of the special space and special goods. The third task is to carry out the project. Today's class will last for 40 minutes, and we will choose the first half of the second task of project three.

There are only 40 minutes for this class. In order to save time we will show the plan of the two teams.

After the class, we get 10 minutes for rest. Thanks for your attendance again, now let's start today's class.

Teacher: We have learned about the key point and attention of the layout of the food commodity and clothes commodity in marketplace through the pictures. Last time, I left the homework to you that is to choose a kind of commodity no matter it is food, clothes, small domestic appliances or books. Each of the 5 groups have the right to choose a kind of commodity, and also are given a fixed space which is 8.5 meters for length, 6.5 meters for width, 3.5 meters for height. Then the group can make their scheme for the display of the commodity. This time we make a presentation of our commodity layout. After the presentation, we will talk about the presentation and make advancement.

Now I see the layout pictures and plans of group 1 and group 2. How about the other three group, have you finished yet?

Students: Yes.

Teacher: Are you satisfied with your plan?

Students: Yes.

Teacher: I think you are kind of diffident. What I care about is whether you are serious about the plan and work hard on it. However, do you think there is also something to be improved?

Students: Yes.

Teacher: Do you think you need help?

Students: Yes.

Teacher: OK. I will join you to see if there is any problem. Do we need help or not? How can we get help? Next, we will see the plan of Group 1 and Group 2. Each group will have 5 minutes. After the presentation, the students present here can ask questions which will last for 5 minutes. We can pick up all the things which are not very clear or nor proper for the group, and the group have to think about how to improve those things. We can ask any kind of question, our aim is to keep them standing on the stage and struggling to answer our question.

Students: OK.

Teacher: I want you to listen carefully when group 1 and group 2 make the presentation. I also want you to take a pen and papers to take notes. You can also write down the questions you will ask them later. We have 5 minutes for both presentation and debate. After the debate, I will choose a student under stage to comment the presentation, and I will also make a simple comment. After the comment for the two group, we will make a conclusion and propose our opinion about modification. Then our class is nearly finished. So, let's welcome group 1 to make the presentation.

Presenter of Group 1: Good morning everyone. Here is the displaying plan I am presenting to you. This is the content including five parts: 1. the location; 2. displaying counters; 3. the displaying effect; 4. displaying accessories; 5. the whole view.

We chose a fresh market as our showing place in Huangdao district. We targeted on sausage counters with a 8.5m*6.5m*3.5m space and 1.5m width main lane.

Here are our showing cases including 2 kinds, with one of all opened refrigerator. We plan to have 7 in all with a category of 2m*1m*1.7m of No.3, 4, 5 and 2.75m*1m*1.7m of No.1, 2, 6, 7.

The other kind is the promotion counter. We plan to have 6 in 1m*1m*1m category. First let's look at number 6 fridge. The smoked and braised meat area actually is a special blending place. So we make full use of the Golden section as the specialty display in the most attractive area. And on the top 2 shelves we sell branded sausages and in the lower part we sell braised eggs and preserved duck eggs.

All the display of No.1, 2, 3, 4, 5, 7 are the same with the only differences in brands. As we usually do, branded sausages are put in Golden sections, with bacons and lunch meat on the top and the grilled assorted QQ ones on the lower two parts. The following is the anticipated effect I am going to share with you.

These are our promotion counters to promote all sorts of products including the new products and discounting ones. All the six are expected to lay out in the center one by one. Here is a picture.

Accessories like QT Ads stickers, explosion shaped stickers, and brand reminder cards are in need. QT Ads stickers will play as a reminder for customers upon different designs and sizes. Explosion shaped stickers will attract customers' eyes immediately by their unique appearance. Brand reminder cards will play as guidance. Besides the updating price marked on the shelf will also draw people's attention. We also adopt lights and LED in combination to make the space cozily brighter. Slow music is also applied to create an easy shopping atmosphere for a longer stay.

This is the whole view picture. We can see the 1.5m width lane is no problem for 2 shopping carts. In promotion area brands we considered to display are Shuanghui, Yurun, Xiwang, Wanglaotai, Delisi, Polonia, and Jinluo. Shuanghui and Jinluo as homeknown brands will be put at the head of the lane to draw people shopping further for the higher price goods such as Delisi, Polonia and Xiwang. Gifts boxes can also be considered to put on the first line. This is my presentation. Thanks!

Teacher: Any questions?

Students: Yes.

Teacher: To be honest. I also realized some problems about this presentation. So I would like you to propose two questions about your confusion on this. The presenter will reply. Lady first!

Girl: Personally it's a nice speech, clear, lively, and well ordered. My question is what do you think the feature of your displaying is.

Presenter of Group 1: Oh, if we look at the view picture we can see all the products are well classified. Each brand has its own counter rather than spread randomly. In addition, our racks are also divided into several levels. Same level with the same brand.

Student: Thanks.

Teacher: Any others? How about a boy this time?

Boy: What's the role of your design?

Presenter of Group 1: First, a good design of displaying will facilitate more kinds of goods on show, which will result in more items on show of the same brand. Further, more items displayed speaks for the good image of a brand. In all, 2 factors matter, the kind of goods and the quantities of the same kind. That's why we try our best to save space. Plus, clear organization of goods provides convenience to the customers to select and compare. We take into consideration customers' consuming experience. Thanks.

Teacher: I know there are still more questions but time is limited. You can write it down on slips. Now let's welcome one student to give a brief summary of this plan. Volunteers?

Girl: I like the graph of the plan, very clear and direct to show the category of the counter and the goods display, also the complete accessories. One minor defect is that I find the pictures of products you chose a little puzzling. Thanks.

Teacher: OK. Thanks. Now I will give a brief comment on this plan. Basically it is impressive but the weakness cannot be ignored.

Firstly, as you performed we can see the lane is very extinct on the plan but as a main lane without the mark of the entrance and exit it will be imperfect.

Secondly, you did a good job on the details. The problem is, however, how to use the extra 1m at the corner generated from your design. I repeated earlier that each inch of space costs money.

Thirdly, pay attention to details. When you put three 2m long fridges together you may not get 6. It's more than 6 considering the gaps between.

Fourthly, those factors you added to create shopping atmosphere such as POP, lights, music cannot be found on the plan.

For example, you did not mark out the Ads stand place on the plan as you said you would put it on the promotion counter.

Last but not the least, you did not illustrate clearly what is the exact reason to divide brands into sections, which is the golden place in light of the whole layout, and which brand is the one you want to promote most.

Time is limited. Now let's move on to the second group presentation.

Presenter of group 2: Good morning, everyone, I am Yu Xin, the representative of Group 2. What I bring to everyone is the layout of the cutlery display; we have given it a very gentle name—A Path to Happiness. The blue print of the display is mainly divided into five parts: the first is the layout of the display, the second is the theme kitchen of Chinese style, the third is the theme kitchen of European & American style, the fourth is the design of showcases and the fifth is the display of bar counters.

This is the overall layout of the shop front. It has two openings. One is the 1.5-meter wide entrance; the other is the 1-meter wide exit. The main channel is 1.8 in width. After entering the main channel, one will see a cylindrical rotating showcase between two rectangular ones on the right side of the main channel. Facing the main channel are two theme kitchens with completely different styles, respectively representing Chinese style and European & American style. Near the exit is a cylindrical, rotary showcase standing between the two rectangular showcases. All the showcases are completely symmetrical to the ones placed at the entrance. The only difference is they are made of different materials. The showcases near the entrance are chiefly made of glass, while the showcases near the exit are mainly made of wood. A five-meter long bar functions as a showcase and a check stand as well. This is the overall layout of ours.

Then, I will show you around our Chinese style theme kitchens. The picture you see is what we plan to achieve. In the Chinese style theme kitchen, most showcases are made of mahogany, with carved dragon and phoenix mascots on the top of the cabinet and the handle. In the gold display section, the table sets with the theme of blue and white porcelain will be exhibited. This picture illustrates the tableware we plan to display in this area. On the upper part of the showcase, there will be single-item plates exhibited in three-dimensional way, not stacked together. On the top of the showcase, a row of Chinese style plates with lotus, winter sweet, and peony on them will be exhibited.

In the environment construction, three key points are stressed. The first one is the design of light. Different light will be provided in a different display position. Then the music. Different light music will also be played in two different themes kitchens. For instance, we will play classical folk music in Chinese style theme kitchen. The last is the terms of clothing. There will be special service staff, wearing specially designed clothes to entertain customers. Normally, their clothes are specially designed to match the atmosphere of the theme kitchens.

Now, it is time to introduce the European and American style theme kitchen with the help of this picture. The material of the showcases of this style is mainly made of glass and stainless steel. The table board of this worktop is the golden display section of the European & American style theme kitchen.

A number of dinnerware of European & American style will be exhibited here. And in this section, a special type of tableware will be exhibited. As the picture shows, tableware will be placed on the other part of the cooking station. The sample single item of the famous brand tableware will be placed in the vegetable washing sink. Knives and forks will be placed in the drawers and sets of cutlery will be placed at the other end of the worktop.

Now, I will explain the design of the showcases. At first, I will show everyone the wooden showcases along the Chinese style theme kitchen. Some exquisite spoon and chopsticks are exhibited in the golden display section of the showcases which is the part that one can see first in the horizontal line of sight. This is the upper half and lower half of the showcase. The relatively large pieces of cutlery will be placed in the upper part of the showcase, while some lovely children's tableware will be placed at the bottom of it, taking into account the fact that some customers may visit with their children. Then I will show you the glass showcases along the European & American style theme. The layout of the glass showcases are similar to the blueprint of the wooden showcases. Some exquisite compact western style tableware are placed in the golden display section. Some very personalized stainless steel cutlery and quaint wooden utensils are placed in the upper parts. At the bottom of them are the places for children's tableware. There are some gifts and gift package on the top of the showcases close to the exit. No matter how the tableware is used by the customers themselves or prepared as gifts to their family members or friends, all the gifts are exquisitely wrapped. There is a 0.5 meter cylindrical rotating showcase lying between the two showcases. It is specially designed to place the extremely exquisite tableware used as gifts. Customers can rotate the showcase according to their own preferences.

Here is the last part, the bar show. This bar is 5-meter long, and can be divided into two modules: one module is more relaxed and lively; the other module is dim but not very dark, with completely different styles. There will be a 5-meter long and big showcase behind bar show, the bar and service personnel. This showcase we mainly use to show our glass display. These are the cups of coffee; these are a series of beer or wine cups, and this is a very classical Chinese tea show. Furthermore, there is some suitable glass display for children and young people. That's all. Thank you.

Teacher: We are all amazed that the pictures chosen by the second team are so beautiful. Now, what do you think of their design? Is there something you don't understand or feel suitable? Yes or no? Let's ask the team over there.

Boy: I want to ask the first team, tableware is what is displayed by the two-side module we designed, right? But the Chinese and European-American tableware displayed in the middle led us to believe that you are selling the whole set, rather than tableware alone.

Presenter of Group 2: I will answer this question on behalf of our team. Our subject is to be happy. Thus, the combination of a complete set of the cabinet will give you a sense of family. So we thought while designing what kind of state it is at home inorder to stimulate the desire of consumers.

Teacher: And?

Boy: At first, I really like this kind of style. Chinese style and European-American style are corresponding to each other, creative and unique. Then I want to ask by showing the product in home supplies, will consumers mistake that your selling include your kitchen furniture?

Presenter of Group 2: Sorry, this question is really similar to Xiao Yang's.

Boy: I don't think so. I think what I said is more targeted.

Presenter of Group 2: We are creating a kind of atmosphere. We will let consumers know that the cabinet is not for sale. The tableware and the cabinet is not a set. That is to say, what we project is relevant to our subject, to our happiness. We want consumers to have a feeling of home. Cabinet is to showcase the tableware, not for sale.

Boy: I still want to ask, if consumers are interested in buying your cabinet, you definitely have a problem.

Presenter of Group 2: As to this problem, for example, what we bought is very small; maybe what he presented is large. And what the ordinary people saw is big and highlighted. Generally speaking, if the customer want the cabinet, we can help contact. But it would rarely happpen, because the theme of the kitchen is only a background. It displays the tableware, not only Chinese style ones, but a lot more. If you don't like blue and white porcelain, you can find others.

Boy: I don't think you answered my question. My question is ...

Presenter of Group 2: I ...

Teacher: Sorry, I have to interrupt you. Xiao Dong, if you think you still have some questions, or feel that our classmates didn't explain it clearly , welcome to discuss it after class, OK? As far as the second team's program is concerned, do we have another classmate to say what impressed you most and what you think the biggest problems is? Say it clearly in two sentences. I' m sorry, is it you? Stood up several times. I'll give you a chance.

Boy: I stood up several times, feeling I have a lot to say. I want to ask you how useful the bar is?

Presenter of Group 2: Let me answer this question on behalf of my team. Firstly, our bar is an innovation. The whole pattern is corresponding. Secondly, there is a cash register in one corner of our bar, then there is a solo exhibition at the back of the bar. When consumers rest or have a check-out, they will stop at that spot for a moment. The purpose is to keep consumers from leaving.

Boy: Thanks. I think on the whole the layout of group 2 is original. They are very imaginative in designing the space. However, the space offered is 8.5*6.5*3.5 and hence the width is 6.5m. There is only 5 meters left if the design combines the Chinese style and European style. If so, one plate is only over 2m. And I think it is a bit narrow and the design look a bit complicated.

Teacher: OK. Anything else?

Boy: Besides, I believe their design is a bit mixed and from my point of view, it will be more professional if the design can be of only one style, Chinese or European, since space is limited. It could be better if it was more specialized.

Teacher: Good. Thank you. I know you have many different ideas about it. OK Let's welcome Group 2 back to their seats. If I am not mistaken, you have some pieces of red paper at hand, at least 2, yes? And you have some pieces of green paper, also at least 2, right? Now please write down on the small piece what you don't have a chance to express in class. Write down the best parts of the designs of Group 1 and Group 2 and then put down the parts of the two designs you think that are not good enough or need to be changed in the future. But please remember you don't have to write out the weaknesses of the designs already mentioned in class. Don't give them a second blow, OK? And please write down your opinions clearly that have not been mentioned and then please stick the small piece of paper with your opinions to different groups.

Of course, we focus more on praise. Please put the green paper on the top and the red paper at the bottom. The purpose we express our different comments is to help the whole class to learn better. Maybe when you start writing your opinions, you'll feel nervous or maybe because you have too much to say, you don't know where to start. Never mind. You can just stop for a while and think over your opinions. You can put forward your opinions now or you can do that after class, when you can exchange opinions with your classmates since there are only two proposals that have been represented today. In fact, you are all doing a proposal and you can invite members of Group 1 and Group 2 to give you some comments. Of course, the other 3 groups can ask the two groups to give their opinions when they represent their proposals in the follow-up classes.

I believe you have learned a lot today. I'd like to say something about the proposal of group 2 briefly. Its greatest advantage lies in the atmosphere construction. However, the displaying, I think, is distracting. And just now two students have already raised two questions about the display. Xiao Dong, just now you said repeatedly the question you had asked was different, but in reality it wasn't. The style of your displaying proposal is outstanding and very attractive. But as far as displaying itself is concerned, what's your highlight? Why did some students ask you whether you were selling tableware or a complete set of cabinet cupboards? Why is there such a question? It's easy to say "the purpose for using the cupboards is to display the selling product". However, you can do more to show what you are selling, for example, by using price tags and POP table-boards. But it's a pity you didn't do that. And that's why some students have raised that question. I think Group 2 did better than Group 1 in designing. Besides specifications showed by Group 1, Group 2 tell the audience the material of the product. What's more, Group 2 the marking of the golden section more clearly. We know easily from their statements which position is the golden section and what product they are displaying. But the problem of the design of Group 2 is serious: what the highlight is, as mentioned just now. No matter what style you are using, Chinese or European, you must tell people what's the main product you want to promote. The purpose of displaying the product is for sale. It's essential to state the highlight of your product very clearly. Pity you failed to do that.

Two issues, I suggest, should be further revised in the following course, of course as well as those which have been mentioned among class, limited space for example. In my opinion, only one style prevails in your design.

In this class, Group 1 and Group 2 presented their designs, both of which were highly appreciated, even though some problems existed. And in the further revision five points should be taken into our consideration, firstly, how will you lay your goods in outlets, which depends on the size of outlets. Both groups were assigned with two locations, separately exclusive store and a special area in a shopping mall which are typically different in their size and market positioning. What kind of customers should be our first choice and how they choose their products when shopping? Secondly, the facilities we choose are supposed to be equipped with the characteristics of products, size of outlet as well as its style. Thirdly, as to the application of aid means which was just mentioned by our classmate such as lights, POP etc., how do you plan to employ these factors should be also presented in our designs instead of in our minds, because we are just plan-makers, not executioners. Fourthly, commodity allocation. Now you have figured out facilities, but how do you lay your goods on the facilities? Take a showcase as an example, how will you lay your goods on it, what kind of goods are supposed to be laid on golden section, what on upper layer, what are on lower layer? To solve the above problems, some principles should be given accordingly in your design. Lastly, details as we have mentioned in class, such as space, shopping atmosphere. In a word, commodity display is a kind of technology in its nature, and also an art. How we combine them needs exploration and practice in the future.

OK. My comments end here, but our design does not end. Many classmates did not have chance to talk on class, so I suggest we might as well put them in words after class, and then show them to our designers (Group 1, Group 2). No matter how much our design works are appreciated, how much are criticized, further revision and study continues.

So much about our class today. Thanks.

观摩课：挑战性受教者的教学过程参与

Julia Bruce

Julia 老师：

很高兴与大家见面。我一直期盼有这样一个机会。下面我要先简单做一下自我介绍，并且简单介绍一下今天这节课我们要做什么，还有我们要完成的授课目标是什么。

我的名字是朱莉亚·布鲁斯。你可以在屏幕上看到我的名字。我过去是在新西兰教美发的，我现在教职业培训师，也就是说我在学院里培训老师。我们主要讨论如何学习。昨天我的同事 Selena Chan 在她的演讲中讨论过这个话题。人们有不同的学习方式，在这方面有许多理论，并且其中一部分是学习风格。我们喜欢学习的方式和我们喜欢老师如何授课的方式，这就是今天上午我们将要学习的内容。

首先，像我刚才说的，我要进行一下自我介绍，比如我是从哪里来的。这是我在新西兰居住的地方。这是从我家往外看的风景，我是住在郊区，但是离我工作的地点很近。这个小镇居民很少。这是我养的狗和猫。这是我的四个孩子。关于这四个孩子，我有很重要的内容要谈论。在这个视频中，他们正在唱圣诞歌曲。现在介绍一下这些孩子。这是我儿子，这两个是我侄女，这是我侄子。他们在同一个家庭成长，但是关于如何学习，他们却有不同的观点，并且他们的行为也是不同的。他们上同一所学校，所以他们拥有同样的老师。这两个孩子在同一个班级，但是他们的学习方式却不同。这个小孩总是爱说话，她从来不停止说话，这是她的学习方式。要确保在给她上课时有很多的讨论活动，让她有机会讨论她是如何学习的。当她在做家庭作业时，我们也要和她讨论她的作业。这是她的学习方式。这个孩子喜欢实践。他总是闲不住。如果让他一天都坐在教室里听课，他会非常淘气。所以他的老师要确保给他事情去做。这个孩子喜欢视觉学习方式，所以她喜欢画画。她的老师确保j讲课时使用很多颜色，并且让她有机会绘图。这个孩子是幸运的，因为她喜欢以不同的方式来学习，所以她的学习能力很全面。她喜欢看、听、说，并且喜欢动手做事情。所以她的老师需要确保上课时有一系列活动来满足她的学习风格。这节课，我们要来比较这些不同的学习风格。这是我们今天学习的目的。

下面我来展示一下这节课的学习目标。在这节课结束时，在座的每一位需要确定你们每一个人的学习风格，并且列举出至少三个能够满足你的学习需求的学习方法。为什么这么重要？因为学习者需要知道如何面对学习，上课如何做笔记，用哪种学习方式对我们更有效，并且作为老师，我们需要知道现在教室里我们都有哪些学习风格，如何满足所有的学习风格。在我们继续学习之前，我想了解一下大家并且知道大家的姓名，还有教什么专业的。好，从 Jo 开始。

Jo：
我的名字是 Jo。我是位英语老师。

Kathy：
我是 Kathy。我的专业是英语，并且和你一样，我是培训老师的，这是我现在的主业。

参与教师的自我介绍。

Julia：
好的，在这个教室里有许多有趣的专业。我们有许多不同的学习风格。这是我们要开始讨论的话题。在我们做练习之前，我们将先来找出你们自己的学习风格是什么。听觉型学习法，适合这种学习方法的人，喜欢听并且喜欢讨论。视觉型学习法，帮助你以看的方式来学习。运动型学习法，适合这种学习法的人喜欢动手做事情，并且触摸，所以在他们学习的时候，喜欢用上他们的所有感觉。可能你拥有多种的学习方式，但是通常你会有强烈的倾向，就像视频中的那个女孩一样，喜欢所有的学习方式。所以下面我们要进行一个活动。我要向大家展示一下如何进行这个活动，来发掘一下你是哪种学习风格。首先我可以问一下在你的小组中，谁听说过 VAK 学习风格吗？请举手。谢谢。听说过此学习风格的同学们可以与你小组成员分享你们的答案。这将对大家很有帮助。所以，你可以帮助你身边的组员。好，首先我们要做的是，请老师们帮忙，发下去活动的内容。我马上告诉大家如何去做。在这个练习中，答案没有对错之分，但是对于每一个问题，你只能圈出一个答案。看，第一个问题说，当我放松时，我喜欢读书和看电视；听收音机或音乐；做运动。你可能这些事情都喜欢做，但是你需要选出你最喜欢的一项。好，下面进行小组互相讨论，并且可以互相帮助。我可以与大家一起看一下每一个问题。第一题,你需要选择 A、B 或 C。大家做得都很好!在这个练习之后,我会给大家一张纸,上面有关于你的学习风格的详述。你不需要签名,在这个活动之后,将再发给大家一张白纸,你可以把你的学习风格写在这张纸上。你所需要做的是回答这些问题。如果你在第一个问题中的回答是 A,那么你需要填对应的 V。好,比如说,对这个问题,我的答案是 A,所以最后,我们可以数一下有多少个 A、多少个 V 和多少个 K。在表格中,第二个问题,我的答案是 C。如果你对比一下表格,应选择 V,所以我写下答案。我会帮助大家,每个人的答案是不同的。好,下面我要大家做的是,一旦你得出你是哪种学习方式,我想让你们移动到不同的桌子上去。现在,如果你的答案为 K,请与 Jo 坐一起。如果你的答案大部分为 A,与 Keren 坐一起。如果你的答案为 B,你是视觉型学习者,所以你过来与艾登坐一起。所以请大家站起来移动位置。

小组讨论。

Julia:

现在,谢谢!你们都在新组中,我将给大家一个新任务。好,在你们组中,你需要做的是看一看这些招贴。每个组都有一张招贴。这是听觉型组的招贴。在这张招贴上有一些教学和学习方法。这张是视觉型的,这张是运动型的。这些只是一部分,还有更多的学习方法。这些只是帮助你们思考。我希望大家互相讨论一下你们所喜欢的学习方式,并且选出三种不同的学习方法。所以每个人将列举出三种不同的学习方法。在这张人纸上,比如,听觉型学习者通常喜欢讨论。他们常常以小组形式讨论。如果你是听觉型学习者,我会再找一位同样的学习者,我们要讨论问题的答案,并且互相提问。对听觉型学习者这是适合的。他们喜欢通过听来学习,所以他们喜欢录下课程,并且事后去听,并且边听边做记录。他们可以不断去听,因为这是他们的学习方式。他们可能喜欢回家向家人描述,这就是听觉型学习者喜欢的学习方式。在这边,运动型学习者,喜欢去做。他们反应很快,通常,他们喜欢野餐。他们喜欢在实验室工作,他们喜欢尝试,角色扮演,解决问题,并且边做边学,这是运动型学习者喜欢的学习方式。这边,是视觉型学习者。作为视觉型学习者,如果我要学习,我会使用图片,用荧光笔标示出重点单词,并且回去后看一看幻灯片中做的笔记。我会使用招贴。我会这么做,因为我擅长记忆图片,并且我喜欢老师以这样的方式授课。在你们组中,在大纸上写上你们的姓名和最适合你们的三种学习方式。

好的,在写之前,请讨论一下。我们只有五分钟时间。

小组讨论。

Julia:

好的,我们现在只有一分钟来完成这个练习。好的,现在停止。如果你还未完成,你可以事后回家写。我非常希望坐下来想想你们最喜欢的授课和学习方式是什么,并且帮助你们学习。虽然我把大家分成不同的组,我们仍然是独立的个体,我们仍然喜欢不同的学习方式来学习。所以对学习者和老师来说,这意味着什么呢?这意味着,对学习者来说,他们应意识到自己的学习方式,并且使用适合自己学习风格的学习方式。所以我对学生的教学方式是,在我帮助他们总结出他们的学习方式后,我首先让他们课上课下互相帮助,但是作为老师,这提醒我,我应该使用多种多样的授课方式,来满足不同的需求。对我来说,了解学生喜欢的学习方式很重要,所以,如果教室里全是运动型学习者,我要确保他们有事可做,如果是视觉型学习者,我要确保使用色彩、视频和可以看到的东西。虽然我们使用了三种教学方式,但是我们不可能满足每个人的需求。所以很重要的是常询问,这是我们需要做的。在每个桌子上,有一张招贴。请每位拿一张并且写下你对这节课的意见,你最喜欢这节课的什么内容,有什么需要改进,比如我需要更彻底解释的内容。还有你要问的问题。请不要写下名字,只需要写下意见、评价。如果我再上这节课,我可以怎样不同的方式去上。如果完成了,请交给每组的组长。好,下面对本节内容进行总结。下课会留一些时间让大家继续做!很好!我们已经完成了我们的教学目标。每个人已经总结出各自的学习方法,并且大部分人已经列举了三种学习方法最适合你。如果没有完成,可以课后继续。最后非常感谢积极参加这节课的同学们。大家表现非常好!同时,也要感谢今天来参加授课的老师们。通过观摩,我学到了很多!再次感谢!

课程结束!

Engaging Challenging Learners

Julia Bruce

Julia:

I am glad to meet you all today. I am looking forward to it. But to start with, I am going to just tell you a little bit about myself, and a little bit about what we are going to do this morning in this session, what we are going to achieve this morning.

My name is Julia Bruce, as you can see. And I used to teach hairdressing students in New Zealand. I am now teaching vocational trainers. So I teach teachers in the Waikato College. With all my students, whether they are hairdressers or teachers, we talk about how they learn. We talk about learning to learn. My colleague Selena Chan talked about it in her presentation yesterday. There are a lot of terms how people learn and how people learn differently. And small part of it is learning style—the way we like to study and the way we like our teachers to teach. These are what we are going to look at this morning.

And first, as I said, I tell you a little bit about myself in New Zealand, where I come from. This is where I live, and this is the view from my house here. So you can see there is lots of space, and I live in the country, but I live very close to where I work. But these are tiny little villages with not many people. And this is my dog and my cat. And these are four children in my life. These goanna be something quite important that I tell you about these children. And they are singing Christmas song. Now, these children, this one is my son, and these are my nieces, and my nephew. They are growing up in the same family, but they got similar ideas about how we should learn, and how we should act and behave. They go to the same school. So they have got the same teachers. These two are in the same class. But they all learn very differently. They all learn in different ways. This little one talks, talks and talks, and does not stop talking. That's how she learns. So here teacher needs to make sure in her classes, there are lots of discussions. So she has got time to talk about how she learns when she does her homework. We talk to her about her homework. That's how she learns. This one likes to do. He's always got to be doing something. If he has to sit in class that he has to listen all day, he would be very naughty. So his teachers make sure he's got lots of activities to do. This one learns by seeing. So he likes to draw pictures. His teachers make sure there are lots of colors in the presentation and he gets to draw. And this one is lucky because she likes to learn in all those different ways. So she's the one that we called a maximum mold learner. She likes to see, she likes to hear, and speak, and she likes to do things. So her teacher needs to make sure there are a range of activities going on to meet all these learning styles. Because in this class, we'll compare all these learning styles, so that's what we are going to do today.

I'll show you the learning outcomes for this session. So by the end of this session, what we are aiming to do is for you each to identify your own learning style and to list minimum at least 3 different learning strategies that meet your learning needs. Why is this important? Because as learners, we need to know how to face study, how to take notes in class, how this learning might work for us. And as teachers, we need to know what learning styles we have now in this classroom, and how to cater all these learning styles. And before we go, you know me now. I just want to go around and find out what your names are and what major that you teach. OK, why don't we start with Jo.

Students introduced themselves.

Jo:

My name is Jo, and I am an English language teacher. Thank you.

Kathy:

I am Kathy. My major is English. So I am an English teacher. And the same as you, I also train teachers. That's my main task.

The rest of students' voice was clearly recorded, and it was too small to hear.

Julia:

Right! It's very interesting in this room. We have got a range of experiences. I am sure you all have a range of different learning styles as well. OK, that's where we are going to start. As we are going to look and we got an activity that is going to help you work out what learning style you are, whether you are Aural, which you like to listen and talk most, or visual—you like to see things for meanings or Kinesthetic—they like to use all their senses while they are learning. Maybe you will have all these styles but usually you'll have stronger preference, and like the girl in the video to like to learn things in all those ways. So what we are going to do—we are going to give you an activity and we are going to work through it. I will show you how to do it. So you can work out what learning style you are. Can I ask you first in your group who hears VAK learning styles before? Put up your hands. Cool, thank you. Those of you who had heard VAK learning styles that can share the answers of your styles of learning with the group that you are working with. That would be very helpful for your peers while you are learning. So you can help the group that you are sitting with. OK, what we are going to do first, the teacher could hand out the activity. I will show you how to do it. You know in this activity, there is no wrong answer. You can't get it wrong. The trick is that you can only circle one letter on each question. See, the first one says when I relax; I like to read and watch TV. Listen to the radio or music. Play sport. You might like to do all those things. But you need to choose one that you like most. OK, talk to each other in your groups that you have people there to help you. And I can go through each question with you. So question No. 1 is this one. You need to circle A, B or C. You are all doing very well. At the end of the practice, I'll give you a piece of sheet. It will tell you out what your learning styles are. You don't need to sign your name. Right, we knew at the end of the activity, there is another sheet. This sheet will help you work out what learning style you are. What you need to do is to go down and see what questions you answered. If you answer A for question A, that's a V. So for example, for this question, I answered A. So at the end, we'll have how many As, Vs, and Ks in the column. The second question, No. 2, I answered C. So if you look down C column for question 2, that's a V. So this is what I wrote for this column down here. I'll come around and help you. So everybody is different on the table. OK, what I am goanna ask you to do, once you worked out your learning preferences, I would you like to move to a different table. Now all the Ks of your answers are going to sit here with Jo. If you are mostly As, you are going to sit here with Karen. If you got mostly Bs, you are a visual learner, so you can come over here to sit with Aiden. So could you just stand up and move to the table you need to go to now.

Discussions in groups.

Julia:

Now, thank you. You are in your new group. I am going to give you a task. So in your groups, what you need to do is to look at the posters. Each group has got a poster. This is the aural poster. And it's got some teaching and learning strategies. This suits aural learning base. So this is the visual one, and this is the kinesthetic one. These are just some. There are more learning strategies. These might help you think about. In your group, I want you to talk to the other aural learners, and the other visual learners, and the other kinesthetic learners about different ways you like to learn, and choose 3 different learning strategies. So each person is going to list 3 learning strategies on the big piece of paper. There is an example: aural learners usually like discussions. So they like to discuss in groups. So if I was aural learner, to study, I would find another aural learner, and we would talk about the words, talk about the questions. And maybe ask each other question.

That would be good for an aural learner. They will learn by listening. So they might like to record the classes, and listen to it later on. And talk to a recorder about the notes, so that they can keep listening to it, because that's how they learn. They might like to go home and describe things to people. So this, in some ways, that might aural learners like to learn. Over there, kinesthetic learners, who like to do. They respond quite well. Usually, they like field trips. They like work in laboratories. They like experiments, case studies, problem-solving, all those sorts of things with busy doing and learning. So these are some ways in which kinesthetic learners like to learn. And over here, we got visual learners. I was going to study and I was a visual learner. I would give my notes. I would use pictures, and I would highlight keywords. I would go back and take a look at my PPT slides. I would make posters. I would do all those things, because I remember pictures in my head. And I would like a teacher who gives all those materials to me. And so in your groups, with the big piece of paper, write your names on it, and list three learning strategies that would suit your needs. Good, before you write, discuss. Unfortunately, we got limited time to do this task, so I am going to ask you to do it in five minutes.

Discussions in groups.

Julia:

OK, we have just one minute to finish off. OK, I have to stop you here. If you haven't written down your three, this is a task you can finish off later on at home. I really eager you to sit down and think about what learning and teaching strategies you like in your classrooms, and to help you study. So even though we put people into different categories, they are still individuals, and they still like to learn in all different ways. So what does it mean for use as learners and teachers? It means, for learners, they are aware of their learning styles, and they can study using the methods that suit their learning styles. So what I do with my students is that after I ask them to form support groups so that they can support each other in class and also after class. But as a teacher, it reminds us I think to ways use a range of teaching strategies, to suit all the different learning needs. It is important for me to find out how my students like to learn. So if the classroom is full of kinesthetic learners, I will make sure there are lots of doings. If I got visual learners, I will make sure I use lots of colors, lots of videos, and lots of things I can see. Though we use lots of teaching strategies, but we can't meet everybody's needs. So it is important to ask. So that's what I am going to do. On each table, you got some poster notes. Each people, please, just take one and write down something you enjoyed about this session—something you liked about what we did today. And something that could be bitters—something I could explain more thoroughly. And any questions you still have. You don't need to put your name, and just write your comments, so I know from my teaching, if I would do this session again, how to do it differently. When you finish, just give those to your group leaders at your table. So I am going to sum up now. I will leave you time to do it afterwards. Well-done! We meet your learning outcomes. Everybody has identified their own learning styles. And most of you have listed three learning strategies that suit you best. And if you haven't quite finished, you can finish after this session. So thank you very much for all my students who participated so willingly in this activity. It was really good. And I just like to also say the teachers who taught this morning to their opening classes. I have learned so much from watching those. So thank you!

The End of This Session!

五、教学点评
Class Comments

课堂点评

新西兰怀卡托理工学院博士 John Clayton:

首先非常感谢在座的各位,今天来的无论是参与的还是旁听的,感谢你们。今天听的课,对我来说非常新奇。昨天我做的演讲中就提到我们非常希望我们的课程是非常积极的,能够有更多的活动。我现在想提醒一下大家,怎样拿一盒各式各样的铅笔,带到你的这些孩子们面前。你要送他们铅笔的话,彩色的铅笔画笔你要买什么样的,你希望他们怎么去画。首先你们要想想你要送他们多少送他们几支。送给你的儿女,有人想送五支的,想送五支铅笔的举一下手。因为我们知道所有的颜色都是来自五种基色,对我来说不一定非要具体地去讲哪一种,但是我想让你们知道最基本的要素,这也是我们做教学最应该考虑的。

第一,研究发现从高层次的学习上来说,创造环境非常重要,就是说你一开始给学生提供的环境,给学生做的介绍。我们这三堂课的开始,每一位老师都把教学目的、要学习的内容讲得非常清晰,课堂要安排参与的活动、教学过程、方式都给学生介绍得非常清楚。第二就是反馈,对学生的反馈就是评价,你对学生负面的评价会影响学生的学习,对学生正面的评价就会更加调动学生的积极性。在过程中发现三位老师都对学生有积极的评价。那么刚才也看到说他们不单是有老师的评价,这些老师非常注重学生之间评价,因为学生之间的评价会让学生更多地参与,对他们会有很好的学习效果。第三就是教学的评价,我们要采用的教学的方式、过程要实现怎样的目标,好的教学的评价方式不仅仅是能够评价学生的学习效果,而且还要能够评价教师你的教学的效果。我感觉,这三堂课,从学生所学习的内容到教学的内容,能够和我们的现实非常接近。学生知道老师要让他们做什么,也能够完成老师给他们布置的任务，这非常公平也非常合适，而且，给学生布置的这些任务也都非常好，这些任务与学生整个的专业相关，而且与他们专业所涉及的领域也相关，这个相关性非常重要。在这里呢，要祝贺我们的三位老师，也祝贺今天参与我们教学的学员们，谢谢你们。

The Class Comments

Dr. John Clayton, Waikato Institute of Technology:

  Firstly, thanks for everyone's attending. Whether you are participating in or just sitting in on, thank you very much. It is very curious for me to listen to today's class. As I mentioned in the speech I delivered yesterday, we hoped our class was active and had more activities. Now I want to remind all of you how to bring a box of varieties of pencils to these children in front of you. If you want to give pencils as present to them, what kind of color pencils do you want to buy, how do you think they can paint? First, you have to think about how many pencils you will give to them? For your sons and daughters, someone wants to sent five pencils, if yes, please raise your hands. Because we know that all the colors are made of primary five colors, for me, it is uncertain to say what kind specifically, but I hope you know the basic factor, that is what we should consider when teaching.

  Firstly, after research, from the study of high level, the environment of creativity is very important, that is to say, the environment you provide for your students at the beginning and introduction. At the beginning of these three classes, every teacher said the teaching purpose and contents to learn clearly, as well as the activities arranged during the class, teaching process and method. Secondly, feedback. The feedback for students is evaluation, the negative evaluation of students will affect their study, but positive evaluation will arouse the enthusiasm of students. During the process, we notice that all the three teachers made positive evaluation of the students. But there is not only the evaluation from teachers, but the evaluation between students, because this kind of evaluation will make students participate more, which will have good effect on their study. Thirdly, teaching evaluation. What kind of goals and standards will be achieved during the process of teaching method should be clear. Good method of teaching evaluation is not only able to evaluate study effect of student, but teaching effect of teachers as well. About my opinion, these three classes are accessible to the reality from the contents students learned and taught by the teachers. Students know what they are asked to do by the teacher, and finish the task arranged by the teachers. It's fair and proper. Also, the task is pretty good, which is related to the major of the students, and the field their majors referred to. This relevance is pretty important. We felicitate these three teachers and the students participating in our teaching. Thank you very much.

课堂点评

新西兰惠灵顿理工学院 Malcolm Doidge：

Kia ora tatou 大家好！（这里是毛利语，向大家致以问候）

我们都希望我们的学生不仅能够进行团队协作，而且能够独当一面。自立的同时，也必须要意识到我们也要依赖他人。学生们通过不同的方式来认识自己的能力，我们作为老师在教学过程中也应当帮助学生来发掘他们的能力和潜力。

作为高职学院的老师我们都希望自己的学生能找到一份满意的工作，能够在世界上立足。我教育我的学生要有创新意识，同时他们必须在世界上创造属于自己的一片天地。

新西兰和中国两种文化的共同点之一是强调领导能力，即通过实例来实行和展示。一个成功的领导表现在人们愿意追随他。我相信，当我们在一起讨论我们的需要时，这种信任越发重要和强烈。

我听到刘女士在讨论性别，为此我很受鼓舞，意识到这是一个很重要的议题。我们每个人都是不同的，我们有各自的学习方式，比如性别以及其他的不同方面。但是我们都是同类，因此，我们需要建立一个共同的指导方针，来指导我们的协作。

在新西兰，我们有一种理念叫作"turangawaewae（这里是毛利语）"，意思是我们站的地方，我们来自哪里。

作为远道而来的客人，我很感激青岛职业技术学院对我的欢迎和款待。

在这里得到的尊重和关爱同时也是一种文化的共享。

我们的经历也反映了我们的文化。新西兰的文明是一个基于两种文化融合的文明。作为一个国家来说我们还很新，很年轻。

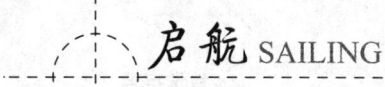

新西兰作为一个有着二元文化的社会，文化体现着多样性，即多元文化。我们是一个拥有较短历史的国家，喜欢尝试新事物、尝试挑战。

中国作为一个拥有悠久历史的国家，有许多值得我们学习的地方，并且中国也在寻求在世界发展的新方向。

我们很荣幸能够受邀参与此次访问研究，"Ka kite ano"（这里是毛利语：希望能够很快再次见到你们！）下次再见。

The Class Comments

Malcolm Doidge, Wellington Institute of Technology:

Kia ora tatou (greetings to you all).

We all wish for our students to work together and stand tall as individuals. To become independent, we need to recognise we also depend on others. Students understand their abilities in different ways and as teachers we need to work with our students to share this understanding.

As vocational teachers we also wish for our students to find a place in the world. I teach students about being creative and sometimes, they have to make their own creative place in the world.

One idea that both our cultures share is that, leadership is about doing and showing by example. A leader is successful when people wish to follow. I believe this trust is stronger when we also discuss our needs, together.

I was heartened to hear Madam Liu discuss gender and recognise it as an important issue. Again, we are all different. We all have individual learning styles. We are different gender, and many other things beside. But we are all human so we need patience to develop guidelines, ones that we agree on to work together.

In NZ, we have an idea called turangawaewae which means a place to stand. Where we come from.

教学点评
CLASS COMMENTS

As a guest, I am grateful for the care and welcome showed to us by Qingdao Technical College.

The respect and care being afforded to us is something that we also share as cultures.

Our experiences are also reflective of where we come from. NZ is a culture based on the partnership of two cultures. We are very new as a nation.

New Zealand has diversity as a bicultural society, one that is also multicultural. We are very new and we like to try new things because our culture is young.

China is a very old culture and we have much to learn from the depth of Chinese history and nationhood. China is also seeking a new direction in the world.

We are honoured to be considered part of that journey. Ka kite ano.(We hope to see you all again soon).

课堂点评

青岛开发区职业中专校长崔秀光:

　　这一次是来学习的，收获很大，感触很深。谈两个问题，一是收获，二是感触。收获有三点：第一个，不管哪节课，分组合作教学这样一种形式是符合现代教学发展规律的，并且把课堂放手给学生，这是我们教育教学过程当中必须要做到的。第二，所有教学手段的运用确实使得我们的教学进行得更加顺畅，使得我们的课堂更加丰富多彩。第三，我们所有老师的素质和教学的基本功是值得在座各位学习的。这也是我们三个课的优点，但是有句话，没有最好，只有更好！

　　谈点感触，第一，我们要努力把"教室"变成"学室"，把"课堂"变成"学堂"。杜晓妮老师的课堂我们一看就是传统意义的教学，老师跟学生有很多互动，但始终看上去还是"教学的课堂"。试想：如果先让学生在机器上做这个东西，如果做的不对我们再去告诉他错在什么地方、怎么样做才能做得对，然后再让学生去做对，这就是学堂。第二，就是希望我们的"教师"变成"导师"，希望我们的"教学"变成"学做"。职业院校培养人的最终目的要让学生有动手的能力和思考问题的一种方法，所以我们的教学应该是在做的基础上，倡导老师指导学生去探索。所以我们课堂上不必有统一的答案，也不一定老师说的就是最终的答案，让学生表达好自己的观点，自圆其说就行了。第三，通过观摩中新两个国家的老师的教学，我们感到：教学应该是一种交流。而我们中方的老师可能在交流这一方面做的还是有所欠缺，教师应该放弃身前的讲桌，迈下脚下的讲台，走到学生中间去，看着是形式的改变，但应体现的是一种民主，民主的课堂和平等的师生关系。离开讲台走进学生，别站到学生的对立面，这样的一种方式应该是一种更好的方式。最后一点，我们也共勉，

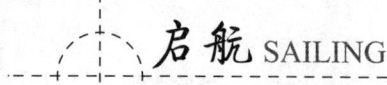

希望颠覆自我传统的那种教学方式，将教学的改革进行到底。我们老师总是囿于"小学怎么上的，高中怎么上的，大学怎么上的"，我当了老师还是这么上，这种潜移默化的东西已经内化为我们自己到了课堂上必须表现的一种风格，师道尊严的那种感觉。解决这个问题的方法就是让我们走出去，更多地到国外去，走进西方的课堂多看一看，借鉴一下，甚至拿来主义，希望所有的领导为我们的老师提供这样一种机会。班门弄斧，胆大妄言，希望各位谅解。谢谢各位，也希望各位到我们中专学校去参观指导，谢谢。

The Class Comments

Cui Xiuguang, President of Technical Secondary School of Qingdao Economic and Technical Development Zone:

I come for learning and have big achievement. I have two comments, one is achievement, the other is thoughts. Firstly, no matter in which lesson, group work teaching is a model fitting for modern teaching development orderliness. Students becoming master of lessons is what we must do during our teaching process. Secondly, the utilization of teaching methods let our class run smoothly and more colorful. Thirdly, the teaching skills and quality of all teachers are worth to learn. These are three advantages, and we can say there is no best but better.

My thoughts, firstly, we should change classroom to learning room and change teaching lesson to learning lesson. Teacher Du Xiaoni had a traditional class. There is improvement but still a teaching lesson. If we ask students to practice in the machine, teacher correct them only after the students did wrong, telling them what is wrong and how to amend it, which will be a learning lesson. Secondly, I hope our teachers change to be tutors, and change teaching and learning as learning and doing. The final aim of vocational institutes is to train practice ability and thinking methods, so our teaching should tell students to explore basing on practice. Our class does not need unified answer. What teachers say do not means final answer. Encouraging students to find themselves is a better way. Thirdly, we can feel through the teachers from China and New Zealand that teaching is a kind of communication. Chinese teachers may lack this skill. We should walk into students. Giving up the teacher desk is not only a changing of teaching style but also an expression of democracy. Democratic class reflects an equal relationship between teacher and student. Leaving the teacher desk, instead of standing at the opposite side of students, is a better way. At last, we should try together to change our traditional teaching way and push the teaching reformation. Our teachers always say how they spent time in primary school, high school and university, which has become a potential and integrant style of our class, a style of respecting teachers. How to solve this problem? We should go overseas and walk into western class to experience. Hope all the leaders could offer this chance to our teachers. These are all my own opinions, thanks you for your understanding. I hope you could visit my technical secondary school in your convenience. Thank you.

教学点评
CLASS COMMENTS

课堂点评

教育部职业教育中心研究所比较教育研究室主任刘育锋：

今天上午用了整整一上午的时间听了三堂课。两堂是由青岛职院的两位老师授课，一堂是来自新西兰的教师授课。通过这三堂课的观摩，我相信在座的各位参与者一定有很多感受。根据会议的安排，两位中方专家、两位新西兰专家，将要进行点评。

我先简单把我的一些感受与大家分享一下。总的来说我觉得这三堂课都上得非常好，各有特色。我觉得杜晓妮老师的那堂课传感器与过程控制上得非常不错。整个教学过程比较完整，包括回顾以前的教学、课程的引入、学生的自主性的引发以及学生能力的培养。教学注重多种教学方法的使用，教学过程使用了演讲、小组作业、还有学生演示等方法，并使用了多媒体。但既然是点评，目的是使她做得更好。所以，在这里提出如下几个需要改进的方面。

第一，虽然老师们做了很多努力，但我感觉学生的参与度还不是很高。比如说提问的时候，应该给学生一点时间反馈，然后说"你们谁想发言？""谁有问题？"但是我觉得这个过程好像没有。往往是"你来回答""你来回答"，这没有给更多的学生机会，应该给学生更多的思考时间，给更多的时间以提问的机会。另外一个要征求学生的意见，当学生回答完了之后，就很简单没有太多地问其他学生的意见，比如说这个学生回答完了，没有问其他学生你们对他的回答感觉怎么样，我觉着这是一个弱项。

第二，我发现所有的发言同学几乎都是男同学，可能跟理工科有关系，但是即便如此，我们要更多地激励女生参与发言。这是对杜晓宁老师这堂课的一些看法。

总的建议是今后还是要更多地给学生思考问题的时间，给更多的学生以参与课

331

堂教学的机会，这是总的感觉。当然，由于实际情况可能会面临许多问题，但是对这些问题要一一补足。有不足不对就要去克服。这是对杜老师的点评。

李琴老师的课与杜晓妮老师的课比较，在内容上会更活跃一些，给我一个比较深的印象就是，学生之间的提问和学生之间的对话很有意思，甚至还有辩论，不是单向的。李琴老师的课比较活跃，目标清晰，方法综合，过程比较完整，使用了很多现代的教学手段，我感觉比较不错。但李琴老师的课有这几个方面需要注意。

第一，讨论的时候，学生提出的所有问题都是有价值的。在这里面李琴老师有一句话当时给我印象很深，比如说当时有一个同学提问题辩论的时候，李琴老师说"你这个问题有点鸡蛋里头挑骨头"。这句话确实不应该说。这一点应该向新西兰教师学习。Julia给学生填表的时候说了一句话，"所有学生的问题都没有对错"，这应该是鼓励，尤其是在我们中国职业院校的课堂里这一点是很重要的。

第二，要求学生提问之前老师自己不能先给出一个评论。比如当一个小组展示完之后，李老师问"你们发现什么问题没有，反正我已经发现了一些问题"。这样的话应该是留着后边评论的时候说的，此前应该先问学生的意见。

第三，课堂结束时候，不应是老师一个人在总结。最好是带着学生一块回顾，"同学们你们还记得上节课我们主要学了什么？"让学生来讲，或者课堂结束之前我们可以带着同学们一块回顾，"今后我们一定要注意什么方面了？"让学生来提，然后"有什么不足的我们一块来总结"，这个可能是咱们两堂课都要关注的。这当然仅是个人对两位老师的一些观点和看法。

Julia这位新西兰老师的上课我觉得很有意思。她的课首先很有趣味性，很生活化。刚开始时，她给大家看的画面就是她家住的地方，几条狗和几个小孩子，然后引入教学。这种引入使人耳目一新，我觉得很有趣味。另外一个就是在课堂里面真正体现"课堂以学生为中心"的概念，绝大部分的时间是学生在那做，按照老师的要求在做。那么老师在做什么呢？就在那转来转去，一直问"你有什么问题"，然后给予指导。我觉得在这期间老师的作用就发挥在这里，这是一个很重要的方面。还有一个给我印象很深，全员参与。每个人回答的时候经常会用到两个字一个是"谢谢"，一个是"好的"。我们国内的老师应该要多关注这一点，要多鼓励我们的学生。另外像项目教学等大家都比较关注，这也是值得学习的一些方面。这种教学方法是好，同时也是一个问题，这也是可以接下来跟新西兰的朋友们一块讨论的问题，即时间的局限性问题，最后我们这个新西兰老师也说了"时间不够了，那我们就这样吧"，就是当时间有限的时候，如何更有效地教学。所以，我们中国课堂差不多四五十个学生，在西方很多发达国家课堂十几个学生，二十几个学生甚至三十个，那么面对这种问题如何来使用不同的教学方法，如何控制教学时间，这也是今后我们之间需要继续探讨的问题。

The Class Comments

LiuYufeng, Director of Comparative Education Research, CIVTE:

Today, I spent the whole morning to listen to three classes. Two classes were taught by two teachers from QTC, and one class was taught by the teacher from New Zealand. Through the three classes, I believe that all the participants must have a lot of thoughts. Based on the meeting arrangement, two Chinese experts and two New Zealand's experts will present some comments.

In general, I think these three classes are very good, and very special. In my opinion, the teacher Du Xiaoni's "Sensor and process control" is very good. Her teaching process is complete, and she reviews the contents at the beginning of this class. She focuses on the student autonomy and pay attention to adopting many kinds of teaching method, including presentations, group work, and student presentations, and multimedia applications, which I think is very good. However, there are some aspects to improve for Tutor Du.

Firstly, although the teachers did a lot of efforts, but I feel the students' participation level is not very high. The teachers should ask any volunteers to answer the questions rather than pointing specific students to do. It doesn't give students the opportunity, nor encourage the brainstorm of students. I think Du Xiaoni should arrange more time for students to think about the contents. This is a weakness of hers.

Another aspect suggested that teacher should solicit the opinions of the other students, after the student finished the Q&A. Now all the students who answer the question are almost male, which may be related to the nature of the major of science and engineering, but even so, we should inspire girls' participation. These are some views for Du Xiaoni's class.

The general advice is to arrange more time for students to think about the contents of the class, in order to increase the level of student participation. Of course, there may be some problems during operation but these questions should be overcome. All of these comment for Tutor Du.

Compared with Du Xiaoni's class, Li Qin's is more active. The Q&A between students is very interesting. Even the debate is very impressive. The class of Li Qin is active and the objectives are very clear and the teaching methods are very comprehensive. All of these are prefect and fantastic. But there are some aspects that should be paid attention to.

Firstly, when the students discussed the questions, we should value the nature of question. For instance, Li Qing could not say "It is too critical a question". It is not appropriate. And then, Julia suggested that there is no absolutely right or wrong for the questions of students. All of the questioning should be encouraged, which is important in the vocational schools like us.

Secondly, the teachers could not prejudge before the questioning of the students. For instance, when a team finished their presentation, Tutor Li asked whether they found some problems. It is not appropriate. The students' opinions should be firstly asked.

Thirdly, it is one common question that when we review what we have learned, all of the candidates should participate in the activities of review before or in the end. Of course, these are my personal views and opinions.

Julia's class is very interesting. Firstly, the class is very entertaining, and very active. For instance, at the beginning, she shared the picture of where she lived and then introduced herself the whole class. This kind of introduction is very creative. Moreover, her class is really students centered. Students dominated the class and during the student discussion, the teacher usually monitored the whole process. I believe that is the responsibility of the teachers. The teacher should ask "what is your question", "oh, you did this". And another aspect impressed me is the level of participation and appropriation. The teacher always says "wonderful and thank you" all the time. Therefore, the Chinese teacher should pay more attention to the encouragement. Also, we should focus on the project teaching. Project teaching is good, but sometimes when the time is limited, how to effectively organize the learning process is essential. There are more than 40 students in the Chinese classes while there are about 20 students in the foreign classes. Therefore, different teaching approaches should be adopted.

课堂点评

青岛职业技术学院院长覃川：

我们用一天半的时间，开展了三个版块的活动，基本上达到了预期的目的和效果。在此，感谢各位支持和参与这项活动的专家和各位同仁，当然也包括我们青职学院的团队。

当时我们创意这个活动的时候，主要考虑在当下全球化竞争的情况下职业教育该如何聚焦，从高到低，从大到小，尽可能地让学校的教学工作从"空谈"转到"实在"。这个题目，其实也是最难做、最纠结的。

总体来看，这三个版块都体现了"学教做合一"，突出了学习、学生这两个最关注的问题。在此，提几个题目与大家分享：

第一，高职院校人才培养要关注的定位。有三个关键词，一个是可持续、一个是终身化、一个是有效性。进一步说，就是我们作为教育工作者，如何在培养学生基本生存和工作能力的基础上，进一步培养其领导力。以前我们在这方面有些忽视。

第二，教师即课程，教师即教材。比方说刚才李琴老师那堂课，下课后我和她交流，如果说产品是你要强调的东西的话，那你就要考虑环境、思维、产品的推销介绍与服务，还要引导学生进行哲学思考，分清主次。如果你想推销你的产品的话，还要考虑促销的方式，包括产品的服务措施、使用功能等。你可以做一个推荐，消费者来参观的时候作为一种纪念品赠送给他们，这就涉及到营销学方面的知识。当然考虑消费者的心理，还有消费心理学的一些元素，只有营造家一般的感觉，让他们参观的时候感觉到一种温暖，他才会对你这个产品、对你这个商店产生共鸣。我们青职院正在推出一个"1+N"的教学体系，就是在主讲一门课的同时，使用到其他课程的元素，比如说哲学、消费学，经济学等等，这就是为什么强调"教师即课程"。

当然，这对教师是个挑战，我们课程改革的培训就是要帮助教师有意识地去寻找这种课程资源。

第三，工具的使用在教学当中体现出来。比方说我们在小结的过程中、在回顾的过程中强调这节课的主题的时候，可以更加强化使用板书。板书这个停顿对加强记忆很重要，多媒体事先准备的一些提要都可以在最后这个过程中呈现出来，帮助学生记笔记，实际上也就是怎么善于运用工具的问题。一些课堂上承载不了的东西，可以第二课堂、第三课堂延伸。

第四，课程的取舍问题。我们现在正在思考，如何组合成模块化的微课程。一堂课要注意节奏，就像刚才刘主任说的，有张有弛，这个节奏的把握就是我们作为教师需要掌握的东西。作为一名优秀的教师应该善于讲故事，刚才刘主任的点评我也很认同，讲自己的故事，这是一种生活化的教学。刚才Julia那堂课我刚开始打了很多问号，后来翻译出来之后一整合顿时有一种解谜之感，感觉她这种方式就是多元智能理论的表达。她的分类、分组方式我觉着很有创意，我边听边在思考，对过二本线的学生、对高职单招学生、对对口录取学生应该怎么分类对待，这是一种方式方法，也给我们一个启示，那就是如何在教学的过程中、在教学的设计过程中尽可能照顾到每一个学生的情况，包括作业、课堂，要有意识地针对不同的学生进行不同的教学设计和要求。这种方式不仅能够帮助老师了解学生，而且还可以帮助学生进行自我认知。从另一个角度讲，这也是学生职业生涯规划当中的一种表达方式。

最后一个，就是要让课堂动起来，是主动的"动"，而不是那种应付式的"动"。Julia的这堂课，她在动，学生在动，呈现出各种各样的动，每个人都参与讨论发现问题并积极进行回应。当然，要做到这些，首先要求教师必须有良知，否则一切都是空谈。

这两天我们度过了轻松愉悦、充满智慧、引发思考、和谐友好、互动交流的一段时光，感觉时间过得太快了。作为承办方，我们在此次会务组织中难免有这样或那样做得不足的地方，也感谢大家的理解、支持和参与。今天下午我们就要各奔东西，希望有缘再相会，一回生，二回熟，朋友伴我一生行。

谢谢！

The Class Comments

Qin Chuan, President of Qingdao Technical College:

Our activities of these three sectors took us a day and a half to basically reach our intended purpose. During this process, we would like to extend our sincere gratitude to the specialists, every colleague and the team of QTC that supported and took part in this activity.

At that time, we took the focus into our consideration under the circumstance of global competition when we designed this activity. Our focus should shift from generalization to focus, from high to low, from big to small and on this occasion. We should try our best to change our teaching jobs from empty talk to reality. This aspect puzzled us most to discuss. I think we have highlighted these two remarkable problems—study and student.

I would like to share some topics with you. Firstly, there are three key words about the talents training in vocational college. They are sustainability, deepening and effectiveness. Moreover, we, as educators, must take the cultivation of students' leaderships based on the cultivation of the abilities on students' basic survival and working, sometimes we always ignore it.

Secondly, the teacher is the curriculum, the teacher is the subject. For example, I communicated with teacher Li after class, I have learned that if you want to emphasize your products you must take the environment, thought, inducing of the products, service into consideration, you had better put some philosophical thinking into your class to guide your students, such as which is the primary and which is the secondary. If you peddle your products you must consider the strategy of peddling, you must tell the consumer the service, foundation of your products and you could prepare some souvenirs for the consumers. All of this, it is relevant with marketing. Of course, you must think about the minds of consumers, and other elements of consumer psychology—how to give them the feeling of being home, sweet, then they would resonate with your products and your shop. We, Qingdao Technical College, put forward a teaching system of "1+N", that is to say, when you teach one subject, it may be related with other subjects, such as philosophy, consuming, economics, or other elements. That is why we emphasize that the teacher is the subject, which is also a challenge for teachers, but curriculum reform would help teachers to find the resources of such kind subjects.

Thirdly, the use of tools plays an important role in daily teaching. For example, in the course of summary, we emphasize the topic of this class, and we use blackboard-writing and multimedia which are good tools to help students to memorize. All these factors do well in strengthening the topic of this class, which is the problem about how to use tools well to make class more successful. For example, knowledge we can't learn well in the class could be learned after class, such as in the second class and the third class.

Fourthly, nowadays, our many classes, especially some vocational school classes can be cut off and reserved. The reserved can change the long classes into the short ones, like micro lecture, that is the micro lecture in modular model. We are thinking about how to create it well. A period should pay attention to teaching rhythm, like what Director Liu said just now—tensed and relaxed alternatively, which our teachers should have at their fingers' ends.

An excellent teacher should be good at telling stories and I can't agree more with how Director Liu evaluated Julia's class. Telling their own stories is a life-related teaching style. At first I didn't quite understand her teaching purpose, but later when the class was translated, I had a feeling of solving a riddle, feeling that her teaching style is really an expression of Multiple Intelligence Theory.

Julia's class is very creative. I was thinking carefully when seeing Julia classifying all the students into small groups. What can we do to those who can be admitted to ordinary college, those who will only be admitted by vocational school, can be solved by the measures similar to Julia's teaching style.

We can get a revelation from Julia's teaching style. When we set up a new class, we can adopt Julia's classification or other ways, dividing the whole large class into several small groups. Only in this way can we give individual attention to children in class. Even the homework and class can be different in different groups. Julia's teaching style is not only a teacher knowing students but also students' self-realization. In fact, from another angle, it is also an expression of students' career planning.

What's more, a teacher must activate his class for real. You can see Julia is activating her class with every kind of activities. Students really discussed, found out and answered the questions. First of all, a teacher must have a conscience, otherwise it would be empty talk merely.

At last, I want to say we had a time full of pleasure, wisdom, harmony and exchanges. And time was flying. As a Co-Organizer, we had some shortcomings in this activity and thanks for your understanding, support and participation. We will part this afternoon. Hope to meet again next time, and then we will be more familiar with each other. You, my friends, are my life companions. That's all. Thank you.